DYNAMIC LOGO

DOPRESS BOOKS

Dynamic Logo

Author: Dopress Books
Commissioning Editors: Guo Guang, Mang Yu, Yvonne Zhao, Grace Feng
English Editors: Jenny Qiu, Dora Ding
Copy Editor: Frances Moxley Zinder
Book Designer: Peng Tao
Special thanks to Gtn9 Inc. (www.gtn9.com) for the provision of some of the design works in the book.

First published in the United Kingdom in 2013 by CYPI PRESS

Add: 79 College Road, Harrow Middlesex, HA1 1BD, UK
Tel: +44 (0) 20 3178 7279
E-mail: sales@cypi.net editor@cypi.net
Website: www.cypi.co.uk
ISBN: 978-1-908175-19-9
Printed in China

CONTENTS

PREFACE

As the concept of company branding expands and more complicated concepts appear, it's difficult to express multi-layer brand concepts with a single logo. Dynamic logos and identity designs including various forms are the best solution to this problem. Based on a logical and systematic design structure, dynamic identity design changes according to different environments. Although dynamic logos are difficult to design, the effect is more vivid, infectious and impressive. It has become a new trend, and a new kind of brand design.

This book is a collection of this kind of dynamic brand logo designs. Including different trades, it displays the newest outstanding dynamic logo designs around the world. In addition to displaying the logos, also introduced here are the design backgrounds, which helps readers fully understand the designs. This book is a new brand design resource for readers and will advance their design knowledge to the next level.

COMMERCE

RETAIL

SERVICE

Client_STEP Group
Design Firm_ Logoped
Designer_ Denis Ulyanov
Country_ Russia

STEP Group encompasses over a dozen different business lines. The key businesses center on the design and construction of cold-storage terminals, mall storage units, and equipment. Its corporate identity is based on two main colors — white and blue. The contrast of a strict grid and a light orientation of the image defines the company's character as both stable and active. Based on the idea of integration of component parts, all the lines of the company's activity form a single group, allowing promoting projects of any complexity.

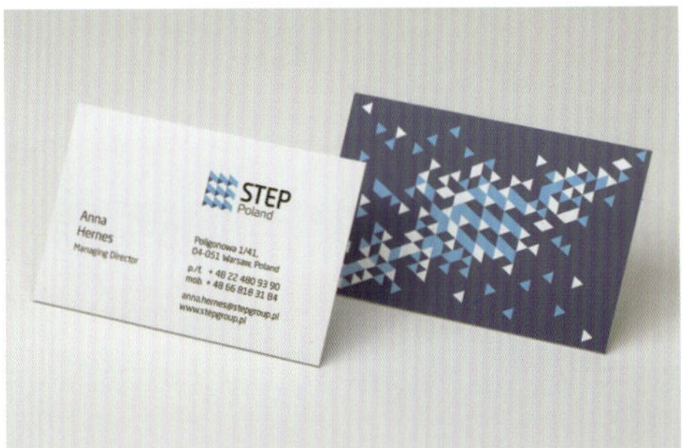

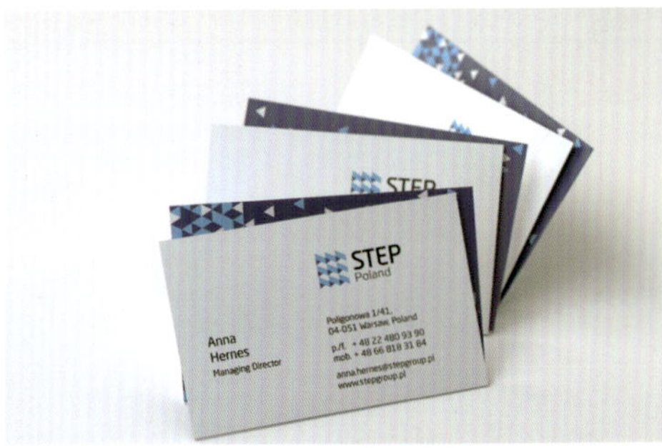

STEP
building

STEP
service

STEP

OVG REAL ESTATE

Client_OVG Real Estate
Design Firm_ Studio Dumbar
Country_ Netherlands

This project was created for OVG Real Estate, the leading European re/developer in zero-carbon sustainable buildings. Studio Dumbar reinvigorated the brand by creating a new visual identity. It sought to communicate the unique combination of values that distinguish OVG from its competitors. In its simplest form, the new logo suggests notions of strength and rigor; projecting the logo onto a variety of shapes transformed it into a "living" identity. The studio also created a descriptor, "re/developers," to identify the company's activities and its pioneering spirit.

OVG
OVG

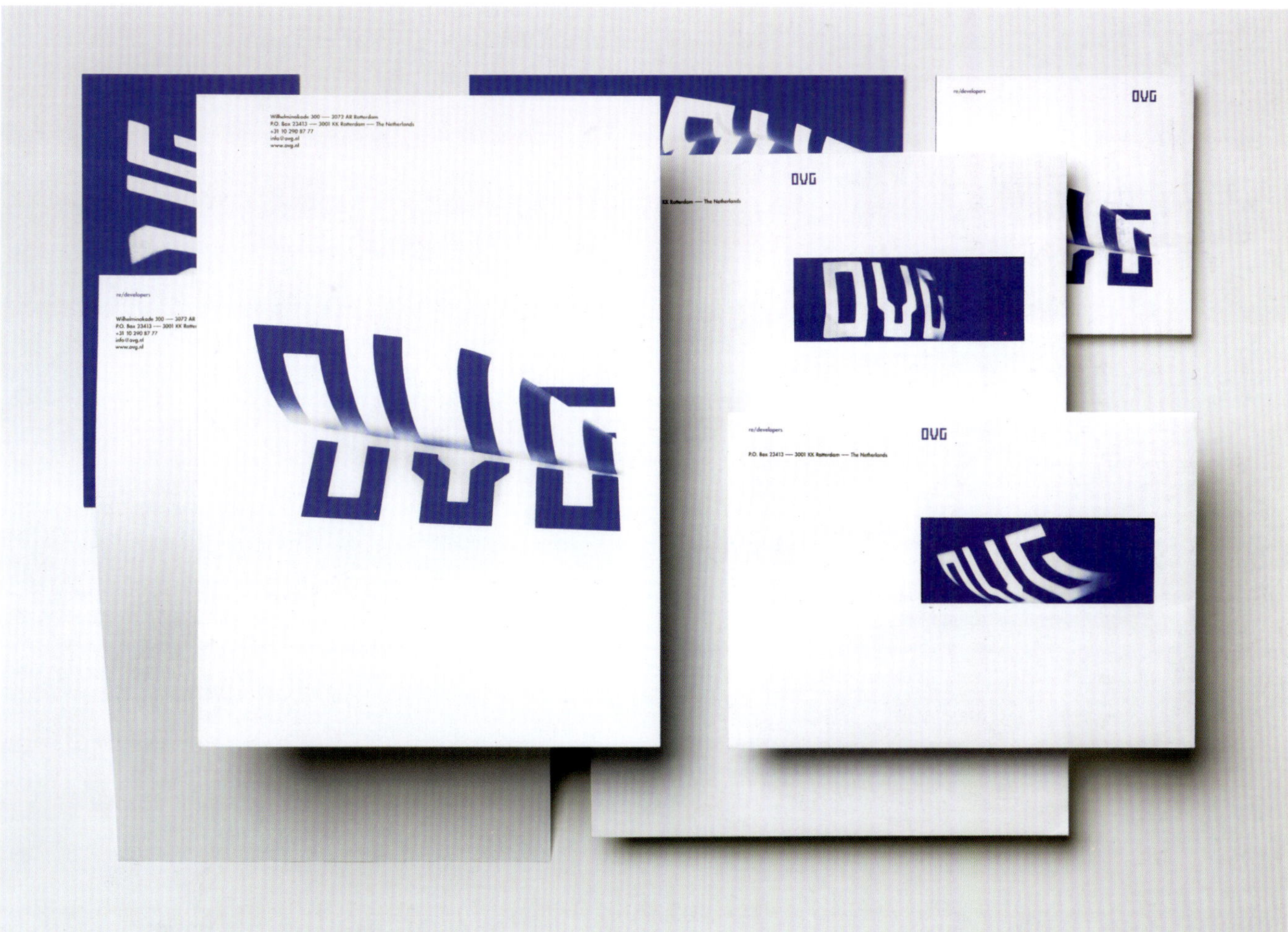
OVG
OVG
OVG

re/developers
Ahead of the Curve
Annual Report 2011
OVG

PROJECT OVERVIEW AND STORIES
A VISUAL TOUR THROUGH OUR PROJECT PORTFOLIO
HIGH LIGHTS

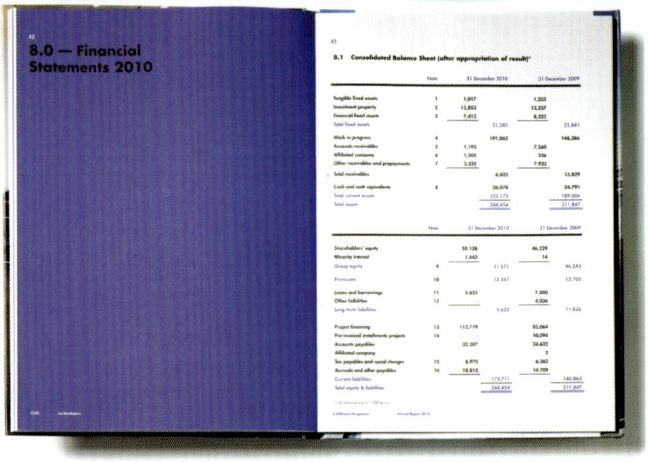
8.0 — Financial Statements 2010
8.1 Consolidated Balance Sheet (after appropriation of result)

re/developers
OVG

OVG

Las Palmas
"Las Palmas nominated for the
Rotterdam Architecture Award 2010!"

Maastoren —
Winner FGH Real Estate Award 2010
"On completion the Maastoren was
already far ahead of its time."
FGH jury —

SYNGROUP

Client_ Syngroup Management Consulting GmbH
Design Firm_ Moodley Brand Identity
Creative Director_ Mike Fuisz
Designer_ Josef Heigl
Country_ Austria

Special refinements characterize the new corporate image of Syngroup, Austria's biggest industrial consultant company. The mix of the three colors and two typefaces, as well as the high-quality print materials, show as much versatility and attention to details as the work done by Moodley's 60 staff members.

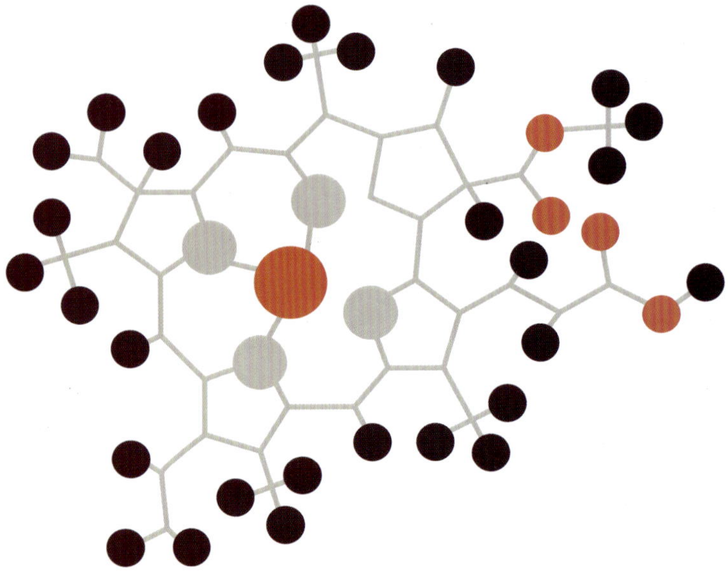

EFFICIENCY IS
RUNNING UP THE RIGHT MOUNTAIN

syn

syn
EFFICIENCY IS
LIVED STRATEGY

THE EFFICIENCY CONSULTANTS
syngroup

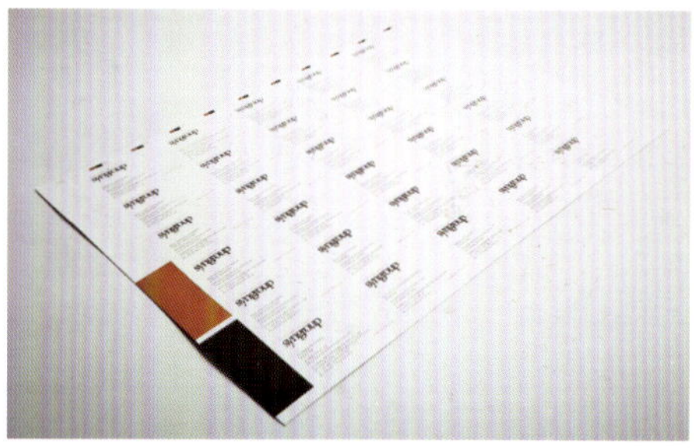

syngroup

syn

MIKHAILOV & PARTNERS

Client_ Mikhailov & Partners
Design Firm_ BTS
Creative Director_ Dimitar Gavanski
Designers_ Daniil Malkin, Alexey Shtof, Kirill Novikov, Olga Gorbatykh
Country_ Russia

This is the new corporate symbol of Mikhailov & Partners. It combines the basic archetypal images, which shimmer in a hexagon, creating a direct metaphor for the new brand idea — "Synthesis of Images." The bright graphic patterns are set as a contrast to the black-and-white imagery style used for all communication materials.

MIKHAILOV
& PARTNERS
COMMUNICATIONS
ADVISORS

MIKHAILOV
& PARTNERS
COMMUNICATIONS
ADVISORS

MIKHAILOV
& PARTNERS
COMMUNICATIONS
ADVISORS

MIKHAILOV
& PARTNERS
COMMUNICATIONS
ADVISORS

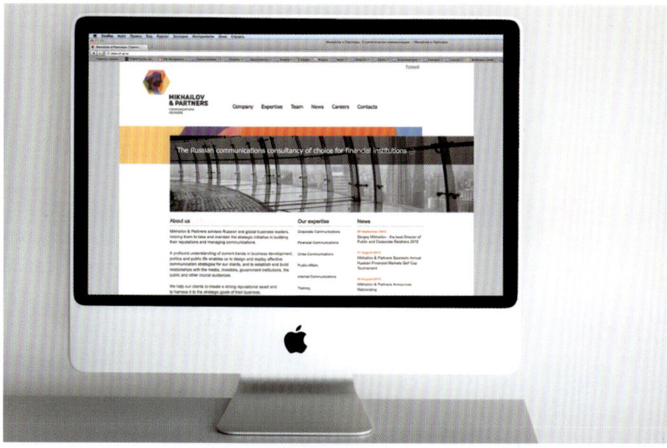
MIKHAILOV & PARTNERS
Company Expertise Team News Careers Contacts
The Russian communications consultancy of choice for financial institutions
About us
Our expertise
News

MIKHAILOV & PARTNERS
COMMUNICATIONS ADVISORS
10 Paternoster Square

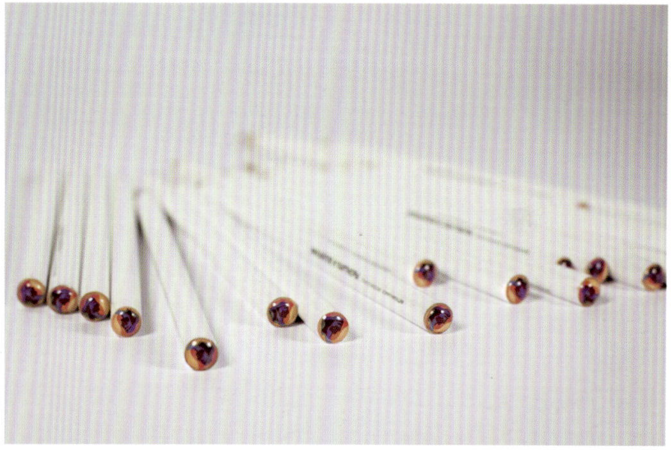

МИХАЙЛОВ
И ПАРТНЕРЫ
СТРАТЕГИЧЕСКИЕ
КОММУНИКАЦИИ

Client_ AgilOne Inc.
Designer_ Gaston Yagmourian
Country_USA

This is an identity for a leader in predictive customer intelligence that allows companies to turn their raw data into effective marketing programs. With a logotype that's part text and part code, as well as coupling the dynamic technological-looking pattern with high-contrast silhouetted imagery, the identity embodies AgilOne's perfect blend between human intellect and machine intelligence to provide solutions.

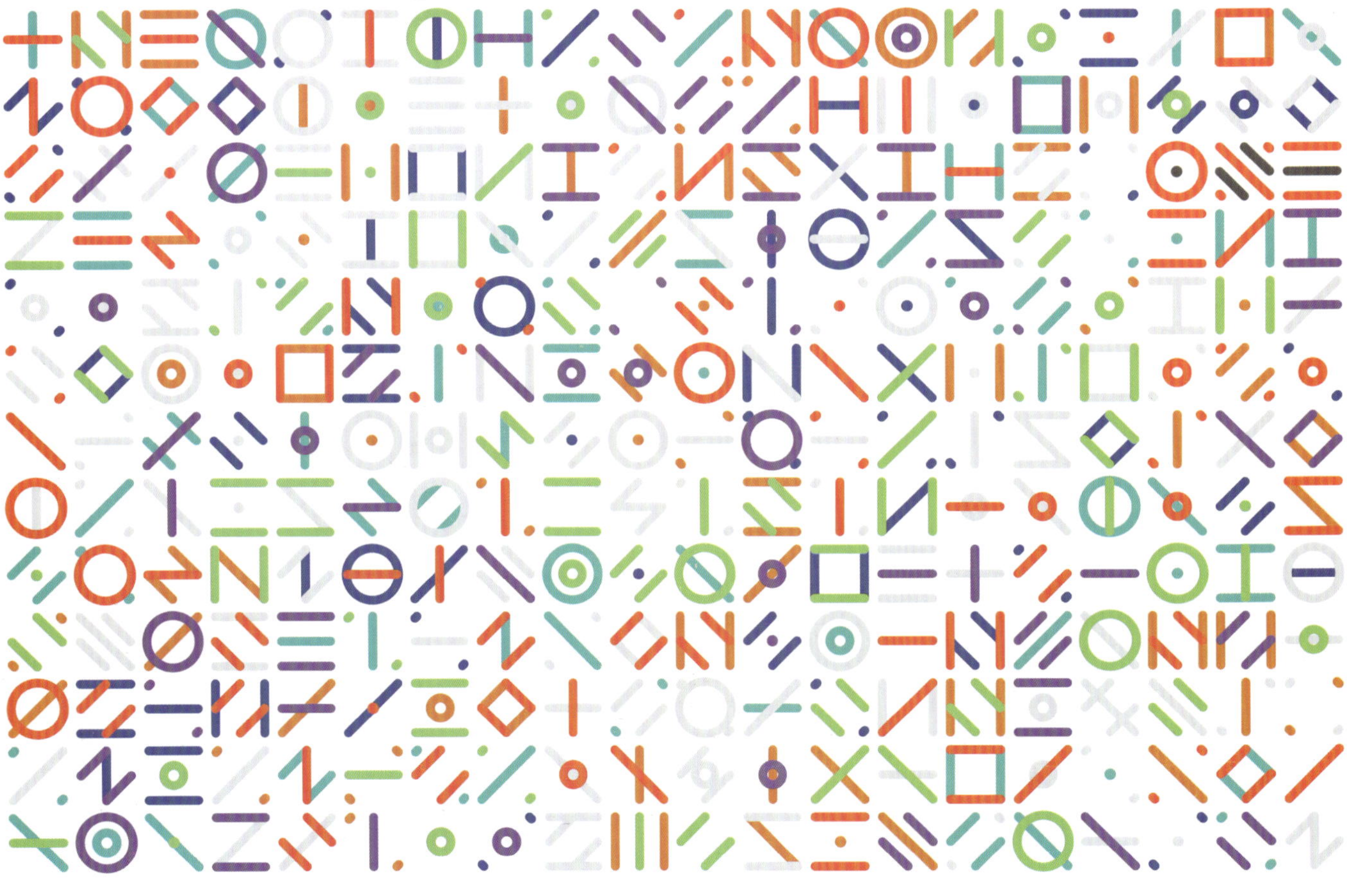

AGILONE
Predictive Marketing in Fashion Retail

AGILONE
Smart Data, Superior Math
Our Approach

AGILONE
Integrating, cleansing and analyzing data to grow your strategy

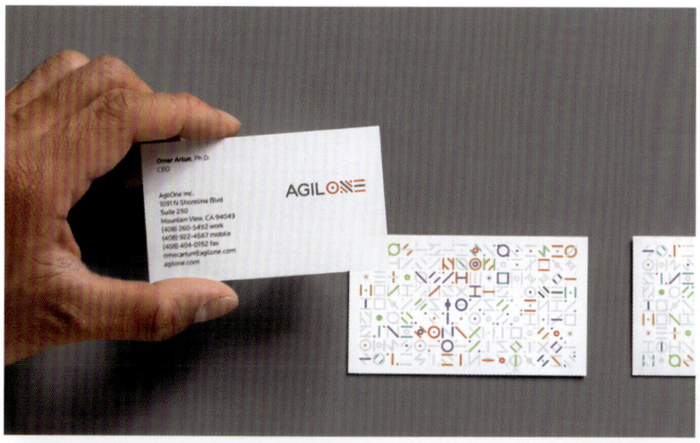
AGILONE

agiloneSketch9_PDF | Processing 2.0b6
agiloneSketch9_PDF
agiloneSketch9_PDF
agiloneSketch9_PDF

Client_ AhnLab
Design Firm_ Plus X
Designers_ Kyungdong Kim, Myungsup Shin, Seungwon Huh, Sabum Byun, Jiyoung Yoon, Junhyuk Chun, Dongwoo Lee, Jihoon Kim, Chunwoong Park, Junggun Park, Siwan Noh
Country_ South Korea

The board of directors realized that they needed a long-term solution for a new image. Plus X created the new identity for AhnLab, the oldest and largest security solution provider in Korea. After analyzing the company's strengths and its management plan, designers drew a brand concept of "Flexible Security Solution" as a tag line for various security actions and set "tangram" as a design concept to articulate it. "Tangram" represents AhnLab's total security solution to creatively respond to unexpected security offences. Through the flexible combination of "tangram," designers made the image of a huge wind wave for the main graphic element, representing this leading security system's innovative flow.

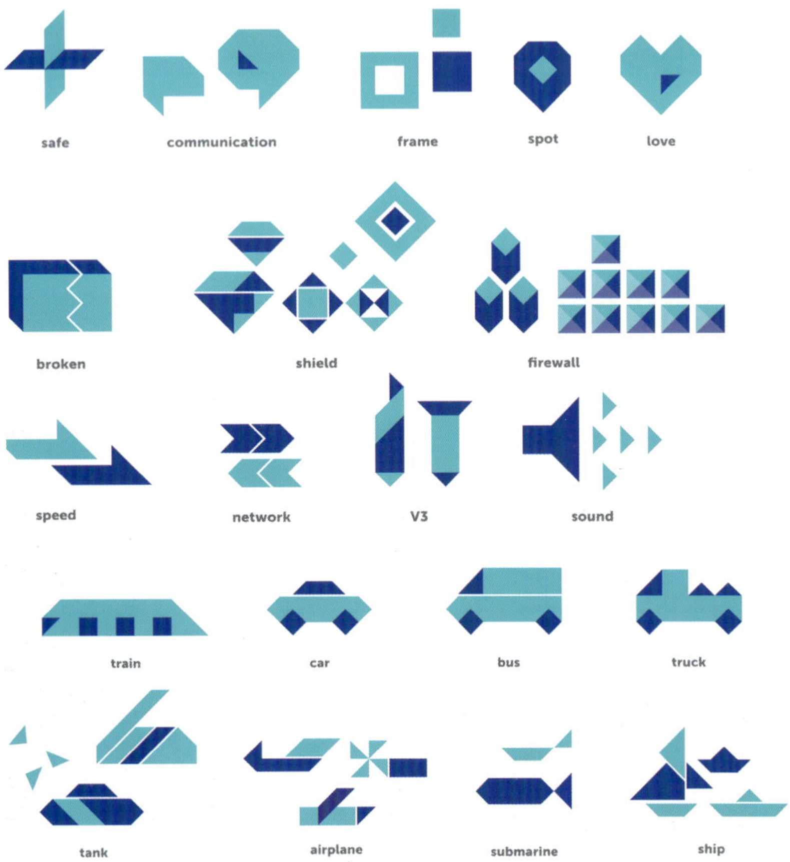

AhnLab
ISF 2011

**AhnLab
INTEGRATED
SECURITY FAIR
2011**

AG2R LA MONDIALE

Client_AG2R LA MONDIALE
Design Firm_ Studio Dumbar
Designer_ Rejane Dal Bello
Country_ France

The differentiating strength of this corporate identity lies in the iconic strength and simplicity of the logo, the expressive use of typography, the clear photography design, and the versatile use of color. This concept was further utilized in surprising yet consistent designs for all the company's other public communications, including a Tour de France team and the "Transat" sailing race, of which AG2R LA MONDIALE is the main sponsor. The retail design was done in collaboration with Unit-Design. Brochure photos by Gerrit Schreurs.

AG2R LA MONDIALE

PIERRE
DE LUNE
TERRE
DE VIE

ENSEIGNES
MARKETING DIRECT
PICTOGRAMMES / SIGNALÉTIQUE
PUBLICATIONS
SPONSORING / LA TRANSAT
TRANSAT
TRANSAT
AGENCE COMMERCIALE
ÉDITIONS
RAP-
PORT
FINAN-
CIER 09
OBJETS DÉRIVÉS
DÉ-
COU-
VRIR
MOTIVER
ET FIDÉLI-
SER VOS
SALARIÉS
SPONSORING / ÉQUIPE CYCLISTE
ÉCONOMISEUR D'ÉCRAN
PIERRE
DE LUNE

NEZAVISIMOST INSURANCE COMPANY

Client_ Nezavisimost Insurance Company
Design Firm_ Aero
Creative Director_ Vladimir Sinelnikov
Designers_ Sergey Melnikov, Denis Olenik
Country_ Russia

This is the new brand identity for Nezavisimost Insurance Company. Nezavisimost (meaning "indepen-dence") is presented through three key values, shown in the mix of three colors in the logo: independence of circumstances, new technologies, and modernity. The blend of the three shows the high quality of the insurance company and the comfort level of its clients. The dynamic structure of the logo describes the high level of technology of the business.

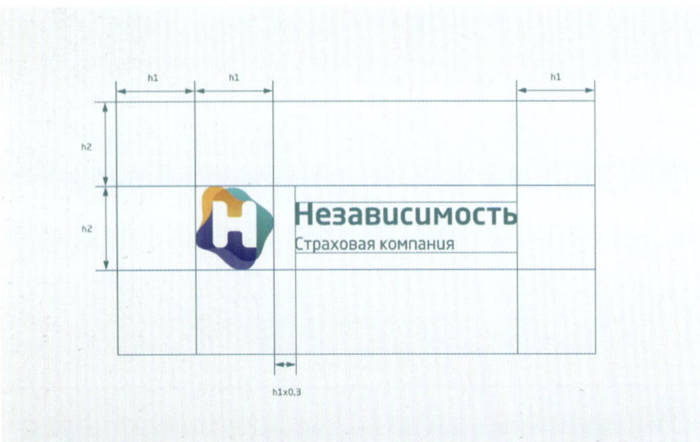

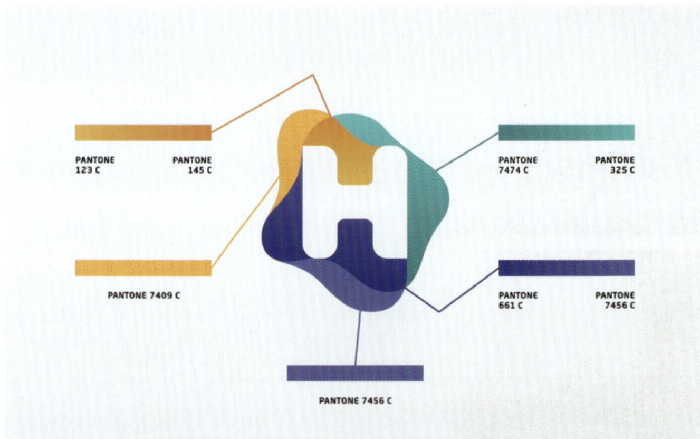

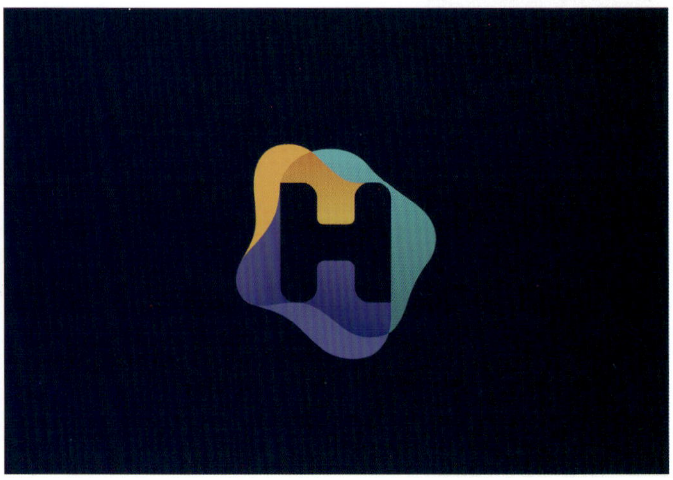

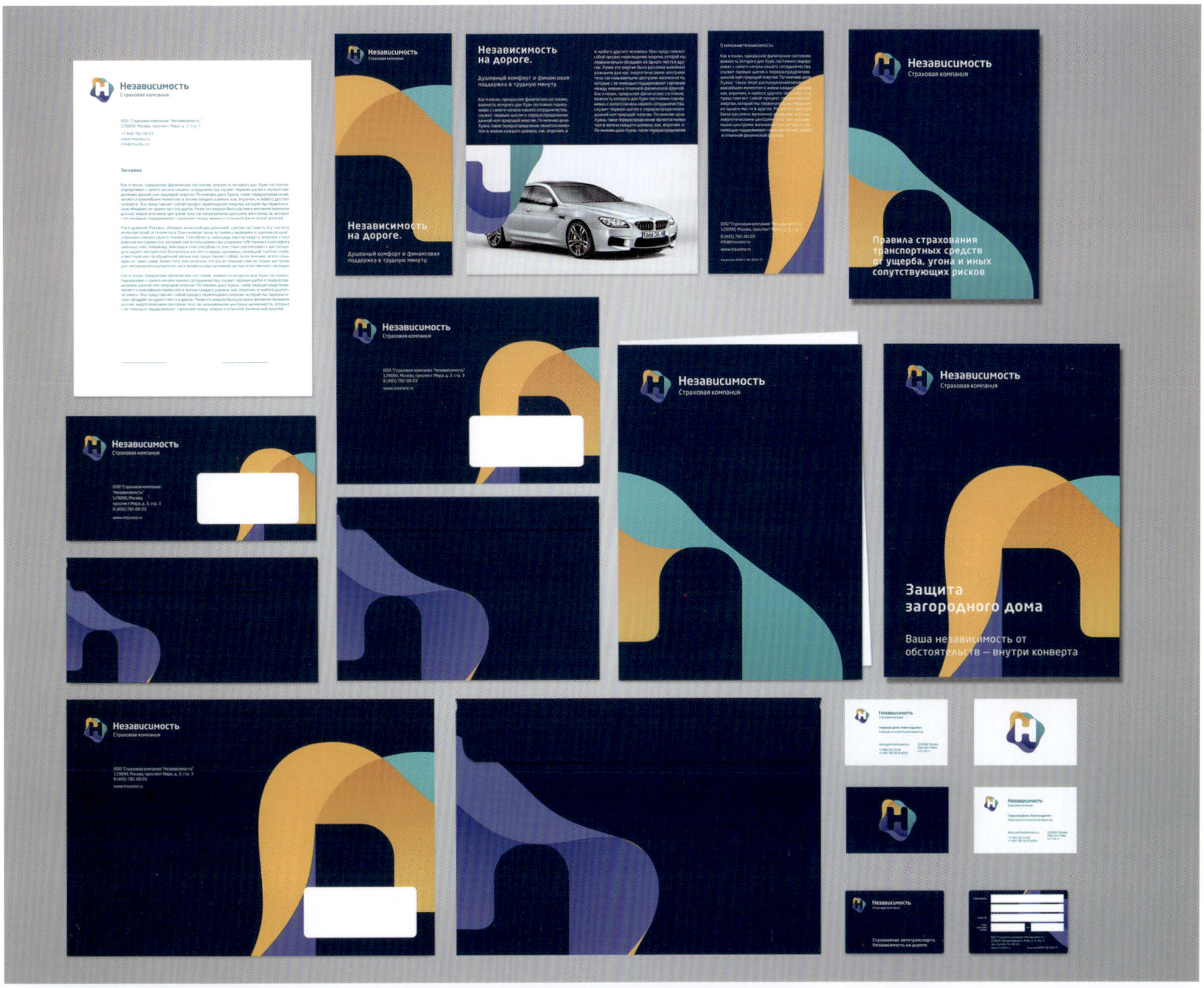
Независимость
Страховая компания
Независимость на дороге.
Душевный комфорт и финансовая поддержка в трудную минуту.
Правила страхования транспортных средств от ущерба, угона и иных сопутствующих рисков
Защита загородного дома
Ваша независимость от обстоятельств — внутри конверта

TRIVALENT

Client_ Trivalent
Creative Director_ Nina Georgieva
Designer_ Nina Georgieva
Country_ Austria

This corporate identity's look and feel gives an impression that it is modern, digital and geometric, yet warm and friendly at the same time. The color palette is very atypical, but also quite harmonious. The designer wanted to soften the harsh industrial numbering with inviting colors, and create something that looks both very artificial and organic at the same time. Trivalent started as a geometric exploration, and incidentally, it became the first trademarked identity the designer has created.

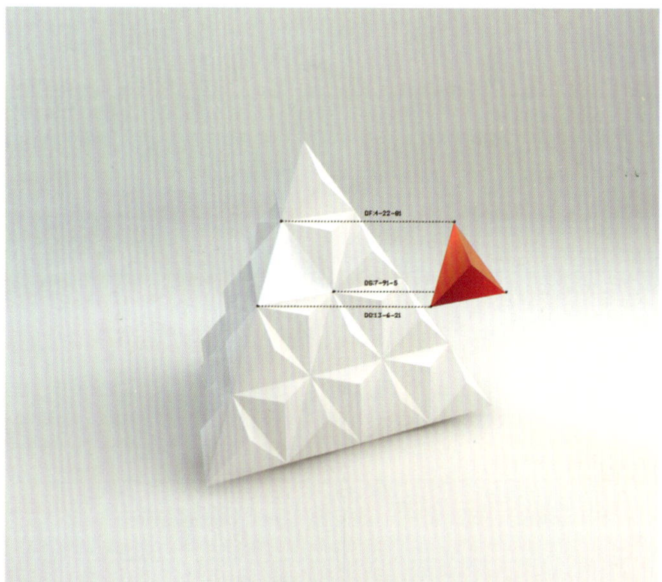

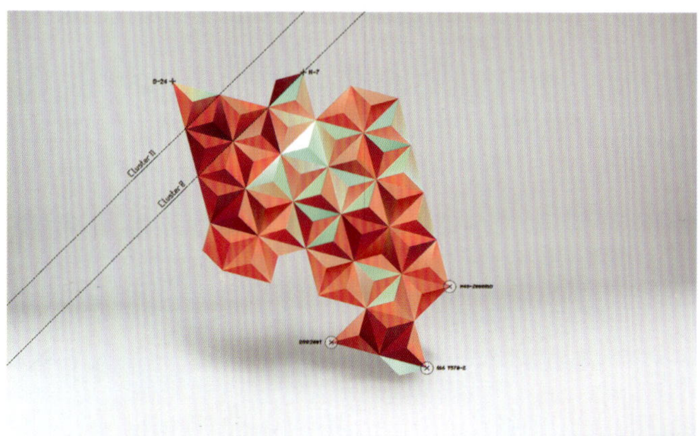

TRI
VAL
ENT

TRI
VAL
ENT

COLOR
PALETTE

1.5
TIMES
BETTER
THAN
BIVALENT

TRI
VAL
ENT

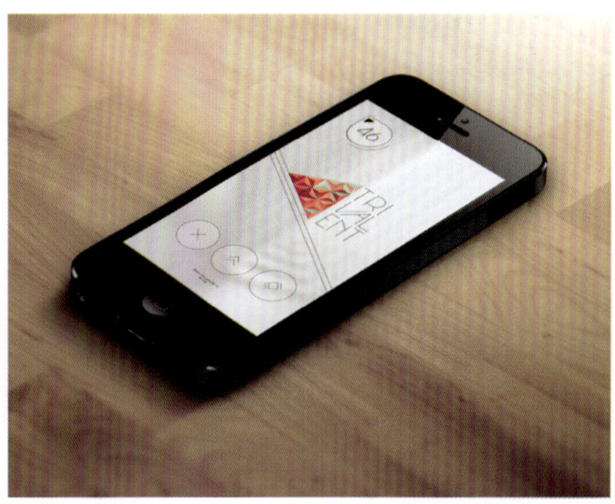

KAMNIN

Client_ Kamnin
Design Firm_ b2s6
Creative Director_ Alexander Pomidor
Designer_ Alexander Pomidor
Country_ Russia

Kamnin is an innovative bank. The layered forms shown below create a feeling of dynamic motion and have become the graphic language of the brand. The logo becomes the center of the communication; it works on different types of media, improving the communication flexibility and consumer awareness of all advertising messages.

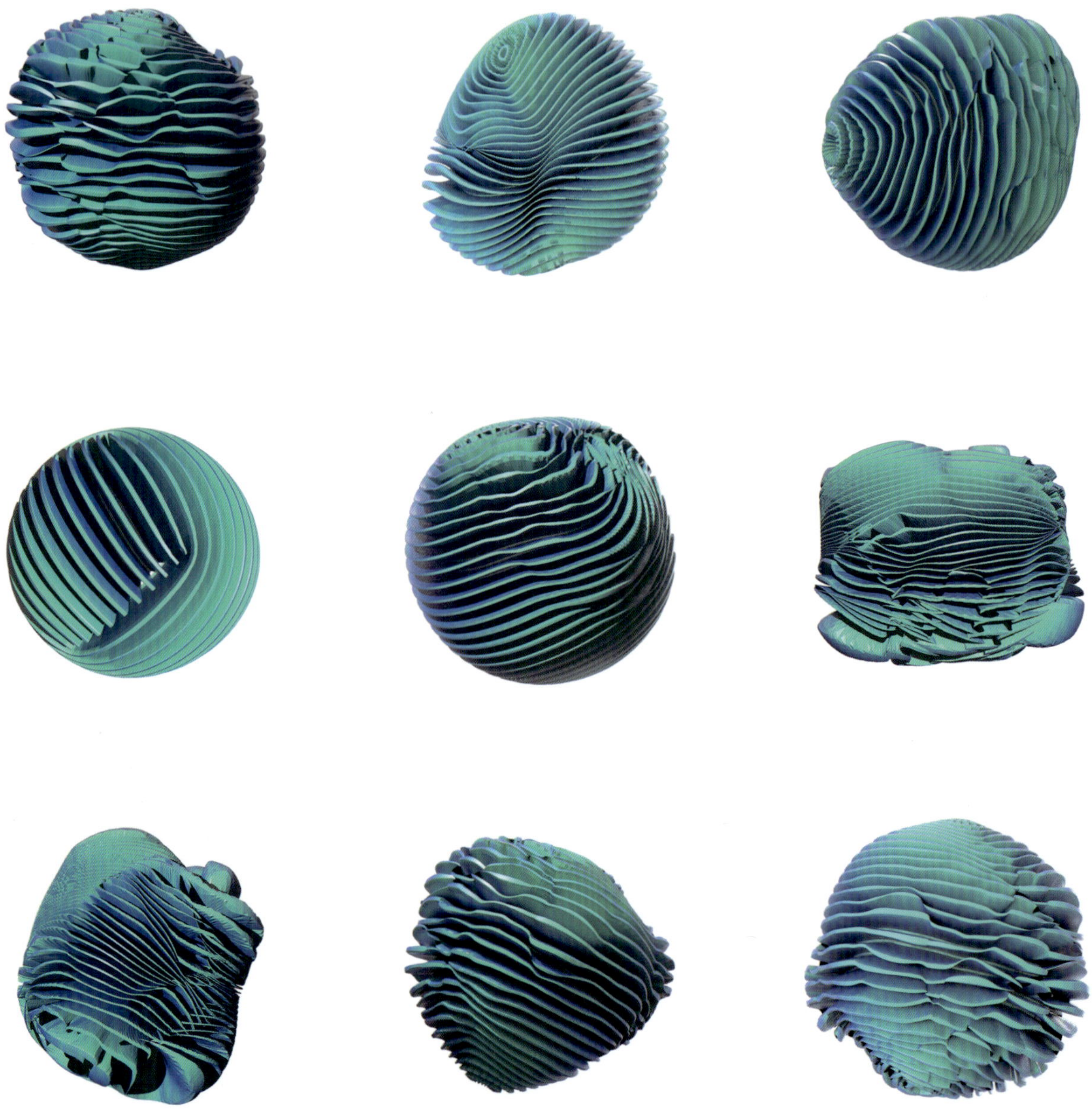

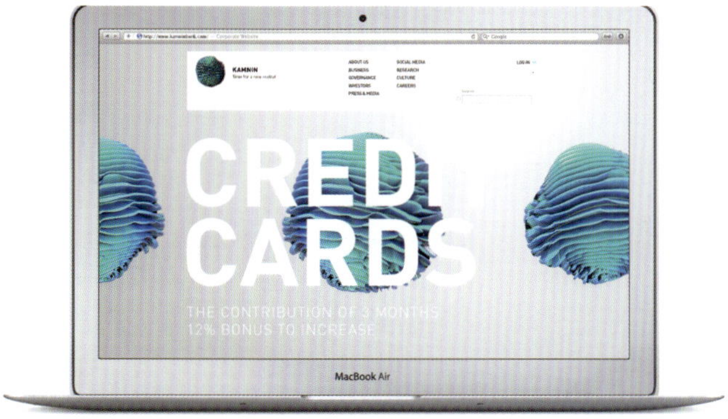
CREDIT
CARDS
THE CONTRIBUTION OF 3 MONTHS
12% BONUS TO INCREASE
MacBook Air

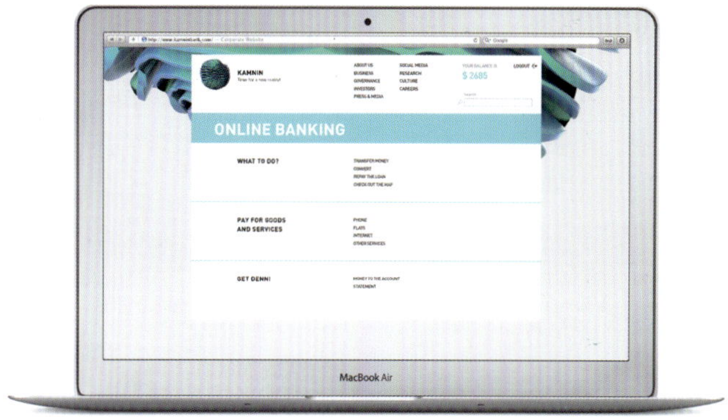
ONLINE BANKING
MacBook Air

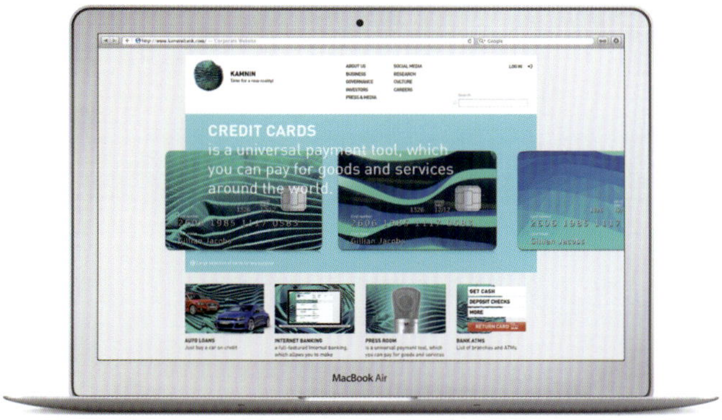
CREDIT CARDS
is a universal payment tool, which
you can pay for goods and services
around the world.
MacBook Air

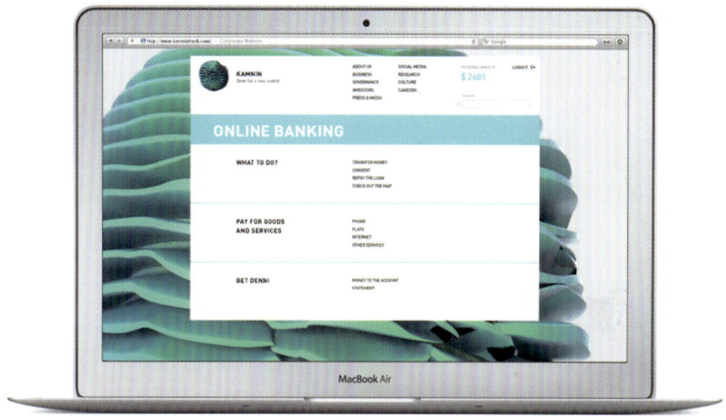
ONLINE BANKING
MacBook Air

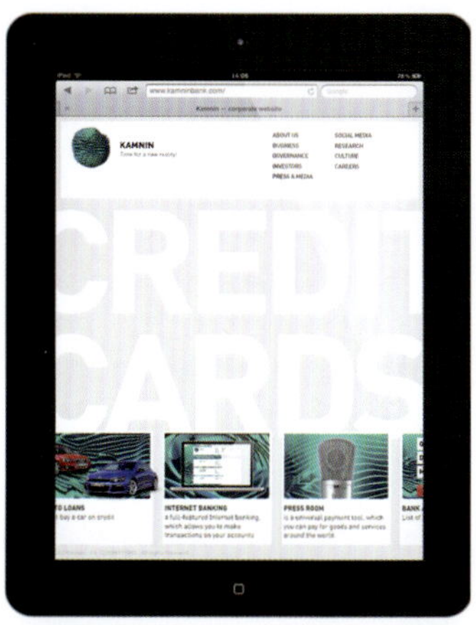

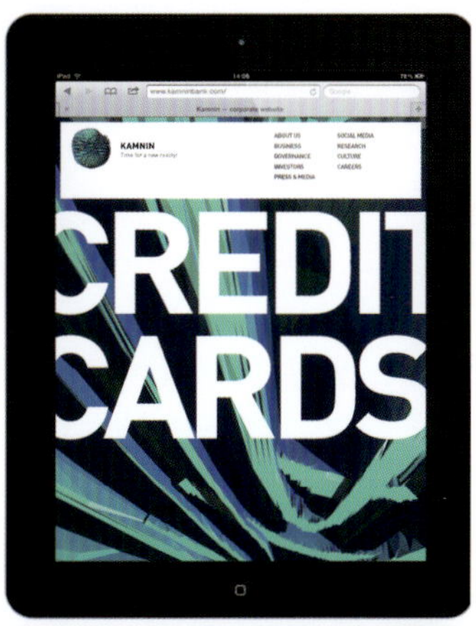

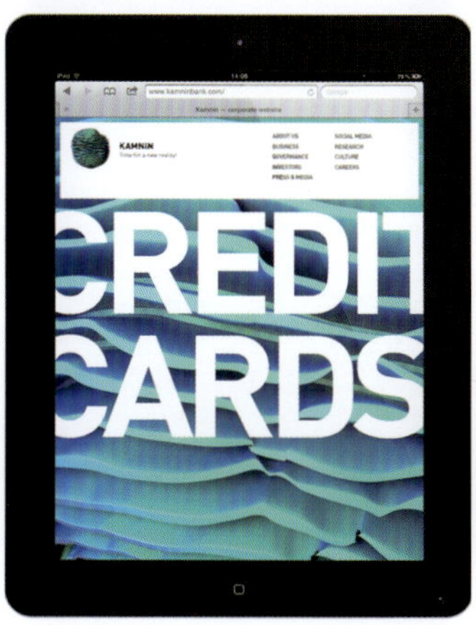

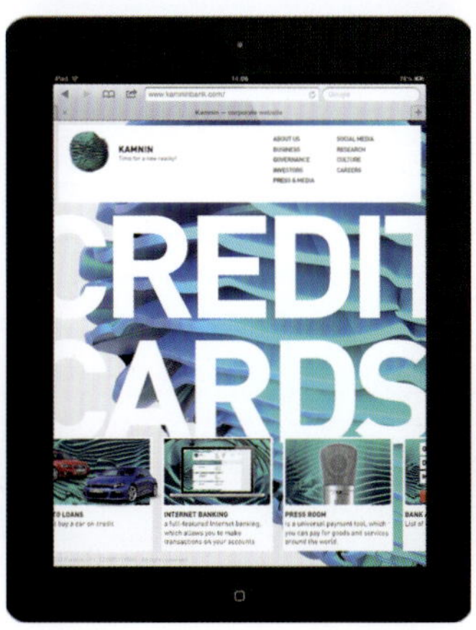

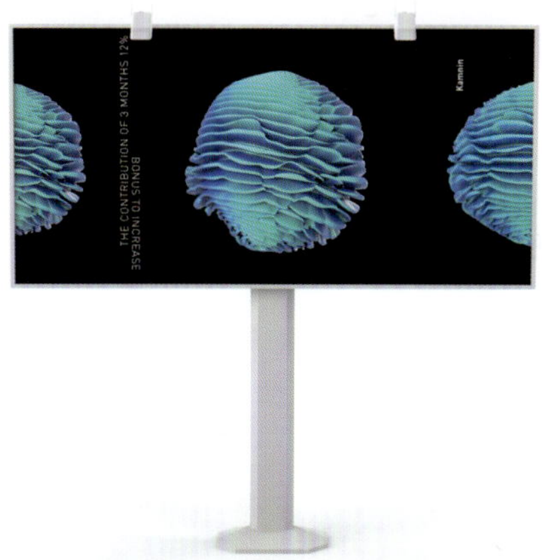
THE CONTRIBUTION OF 3 MONTHS 12% BONUS TO INCREASE
Kamnin

Time for a new reality!
Kamnin
www.kamninbank.com

Client_ Choco
Graphic Designer_ Elvire Delanote
Creative Programmer_ Nuno Diniz
Country_ Belgium

This is the corporate identity of Choco, a communication agency. Its inspiration came from the relationship matrix of the agency. Each dot and each letter is located on one of the positions of the matrix, which represents the values of daily life relationships. These values are not fixed, but always evolving. The logo is moving accordingly in a unique and creative way. Additionally, the aesthetic of the rounded sans-serif typeface softens the impact of the rigid grid structure.

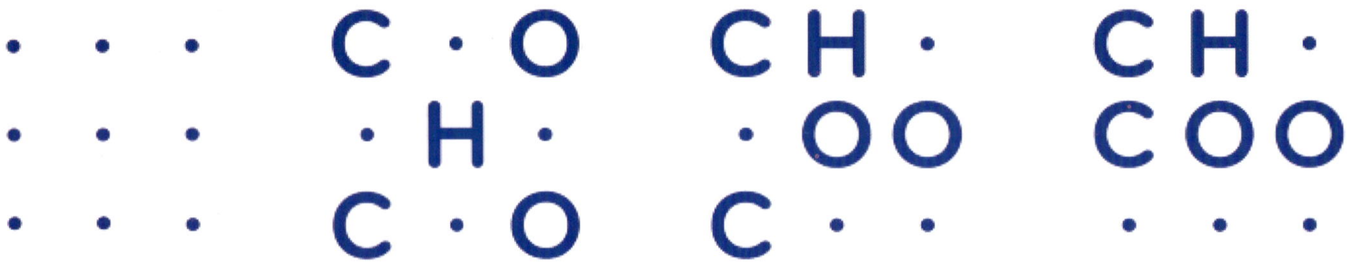

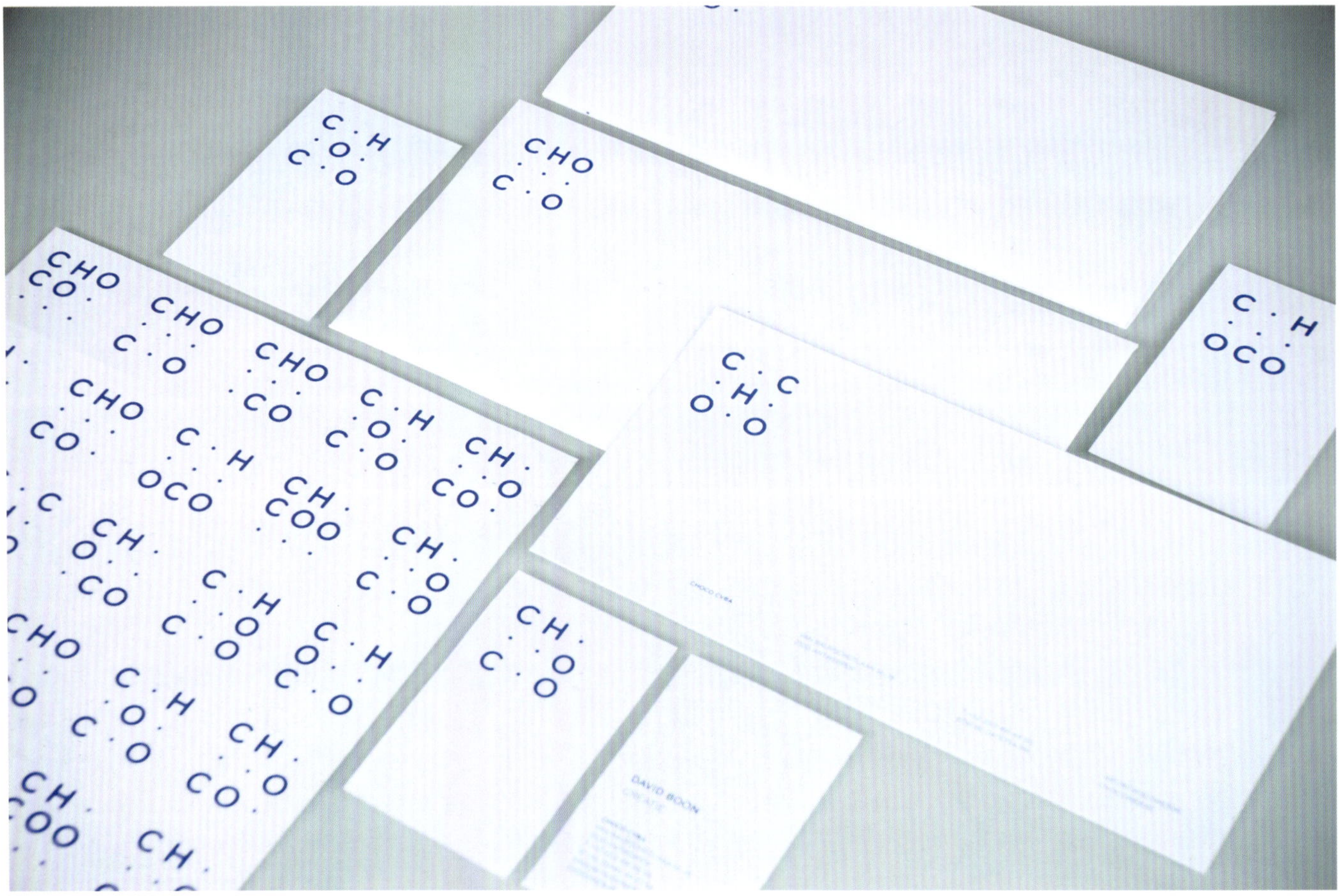

CO ·
F · ·
FEE
S · A
· U ·
G · R

KO ·
F · ·
FIE
· T ·
HE ·
· · E

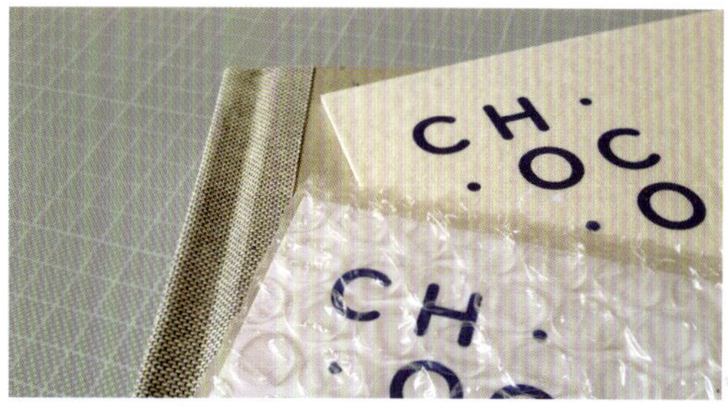

SRC
· · ·
LOL

CH ·
· · C
O · O

Client_Lovesac Alternative Furniture Co.
Design Firm_Pompei A.D.
Creative Director_Bart Higgins
Designers_Michael Tyznik, Alyce Waxman
Country_USA

Best known for their line of beanbag-esque chairs, Lovesac recently introduced a line of innovative modular sofas. The team worked to evolve their previously youth-oriented brand to help them to be taken seriously in the furniture market, without losing their core fan base or quirky sense of humor. With their slogan, "Life changes, so should your furniture," a dynamic logo system was the perfect solution. The logotype can be contained in any black shape, adapting to new campaigns each season.

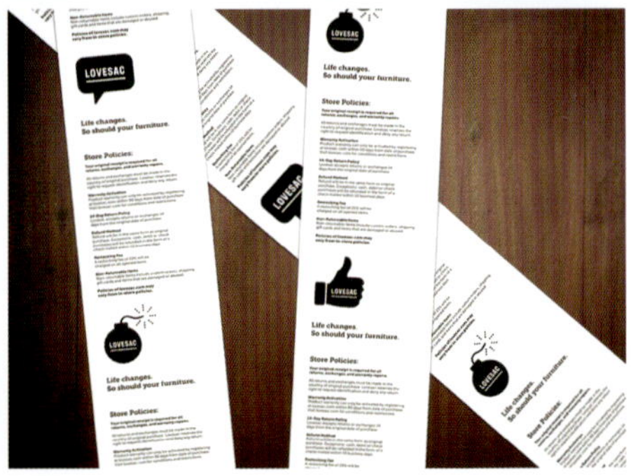

It's not a damn beanbag.
Sac Pricing
Gamersac
Citysac
Pillowsac
Moviesac
Supersac
The Big One
Khaki
Herringsuede
Rhinoplush
Standard Phur
Premium Phur

Two-Lifetime Guarantee
The secret is Durafoam.
Durafoam
Accessorize your Sac
Sodasac
Tubesac
Footsac
Throw Pillow
Squattoman
Buy now. Pay later.
Make your purchase with the Lovesac Credit Card
LOVESAC
The Rocker $99
Body Pillow $149
STORE INFO
LOVESAC
Sac Guide

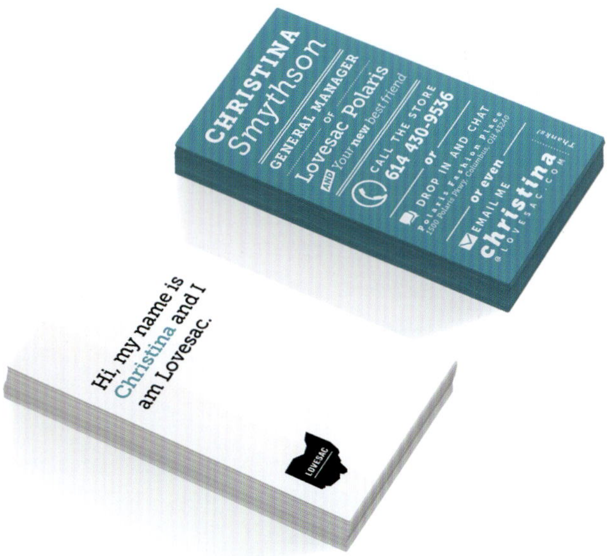
CHRISTINA Smythson
GENERAL MANAGER
OF
Lovesac Polaris
AND Your new best friend
CALL THE STORE
614 430-9536
or
DROP IN AND CHAT
or even
EMAIL ME
christina
@LOVESAC.COM
Thanks!
Hi, my name is Christina and I am Lovesac.
LOVESAC

Hi, my name is Nancy and I am Lovesac.
LOVESAC
even
ancy
@LOVESAC.COM
Thanks!

Hi, my name is Shawn and I am Lovesac.
LOVESAC
Shawn D.
NELSON
Founder, Chairman,
AND
CHIEF SAC
CALL MY CELL
801 243-8880
or
MAIL LOVESAC HQ
700 Canal Street, Stamford, CT 06902
or even
EMAIL ME
shawnd
@LOVESAC.COM
Thanks!

Sac
Cover
LOVESAC
Moviesac
Machine-washable.
Tailor-fit.
Durability-tested.

Sac
Cover
LOVESAC
Gamersac
Machine-washable.
Tailor-fit.
Durability-tested.

Sac
Cover
LOVESAC
The Big One
Machine-washable.
Tailor-fit.
Durability-tested.

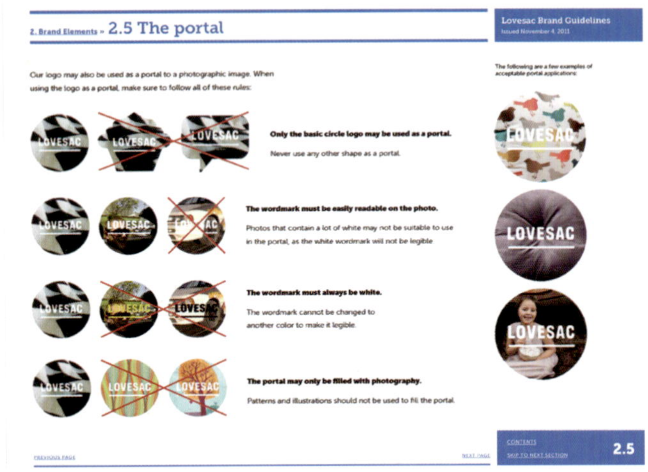
2. Brand Elements » 2.5 The portal
Lovesac Brand Guidelines
Issued November 4, 2011
Our logo may also be used as a portal to a photographic image. When using the logo as a portal, make sure to follow all of these rules:
Only the basic circle logo may be used as a portal.
Never use any other shape as a portal.
The wordmark must be easily readable on the photo.
Photos that contain a lot of white may not be suitable to use in the portal, as the white wordmark will not be legible.
The wordmark must always be white.
The wordmark cannot be changed to another color to make it legible.
The portal may only be filled with photography.
Patterns and illustrations should not be used to fill the portal.
The following are a few examples of acceptable portal applications:
LOVESAC
CONTENTS
SKIP TO NEXT SECTION
2.5

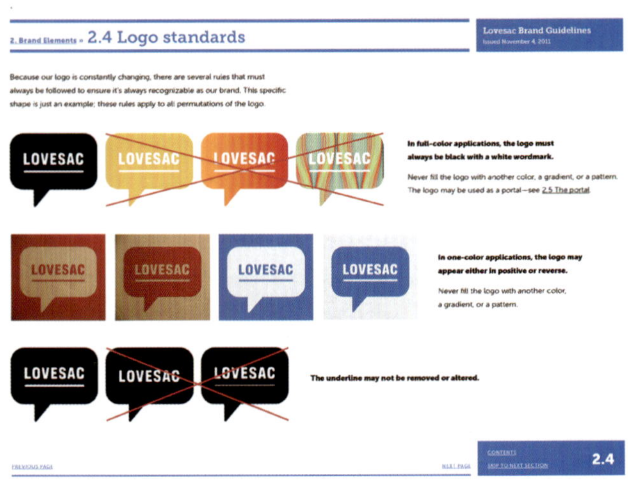
2. Brand Elements » 2.4 Logo standards
Lovesac Brand Guidelines
Issued November 4, 2011
Because our logo is constantly changing, there are several rules that must always be followed to ensure it's always recognizable as our brand. This specific shape is just an example; these rules apply to all permutations of the logo.
LOVESAC
In full-color applications, the logo must always be black with a white wordmark.
Never fill the logo with another color, a gradient, or a pattern. The logo may be used as a portal—see 2.5 The portal
In one-color applications, the logo may appear either in positive or reverse.
Never fill the logo with another color, a gradient, or a pattern.
The underline may not be removed or altered.
CONTENTS
SKIP TO NEXT SECTION
2.4

Sale
SALE
SALE ƎlVS SALE
Sale?
Sale!
Selected items.
While supplies last.
LOVESAC

Sale
25% OFF
Sale? Sale!
Selected items.
While supplies last.
LOVESAC

Sale
20% OFF
Sale? Sale!
Selected items.
While supplies last.
LOVESAC

Sale
75% OFF
Sale? Sale!
Selected items.
While supplies last.
LOVESAC

THIS JUST IN
the latest news
FROM
Lovesac Polaris
LOVESAC
BACK IN
5 MINUTES
WE'RE
OUT
Delivering a
Sac to a happy
customer.
LOVESAC

THIS JUST IN
the latest news
FROM
Lovesac Polaris
LOVESAC
MERRY
Christmas
WE'LL BE BACK TOMORROW.
(After we get tired of all our shiny new toys.)
LOVESAC

THIS JUST IN
the latest news
FROM
Lovesac Polaris
No
FOOD
LOVESAC
No
DRINK
Kindly wolf it down
BEFORE YOU COME INSIDE.
LOVESAC

THIS JUST IN
the latest news
FROM
Lovesac Polaris
Now
LOVESAC
Hiring
LOVESAC

Sac
Cover
LOVESAC
Moviesac
Machine-washable.
Tailor-fit.
Durability-tested.

Happy
Valentine's Day.
LOVESAC
CONGRATS
Felicitations
GOOD WORK
PRO PS.
Kudos
LOVESAC
LOVESAC

Good call.
LOVESAC
Sactionals
6 Series

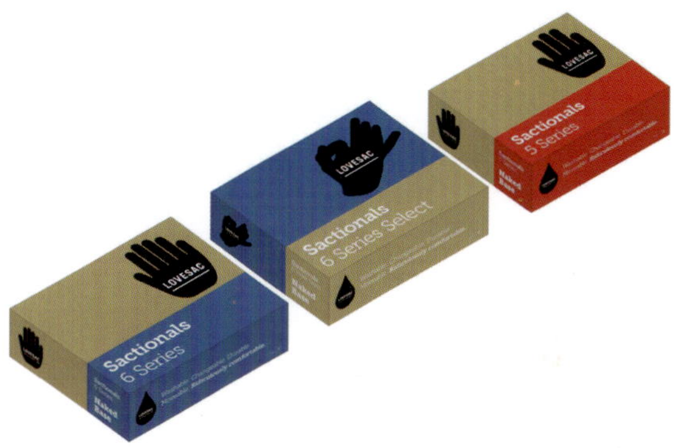
Sactionals
5 Series
Sactionals
6 Series Select
Sactionals
6 Series

LOVESAC
Limited
Editions
LOVESAC
Accessories
LOVESAC
50% Off
LOVESAC
Must-
Haves
Buddha Bowl $24
Noodle Bowl $29
Sactionals Blocks $49
D.I.Y. Deerhead $49
Papier-Mâché Birds $39

NEOLAB

Client_ Neolab d.o.o.
Design Firm_ IlovarStritar
Creative Director_ Robert Ilovar
Designer_ Robert Ilovar
Country_ Slovenia

Neolab is an IT company specializing in building and connecting business information systems, web applications and websites. The fusion of various old elements creates a fresh, new identity; conceptually, this is related to various merging technologies and business systems. Every element is transforming in pixels from left to right, relating to their online operations. Motifs were selected based on their meaning, such as images of a pigeon and a cheetah for the envelope (postal service + speed).

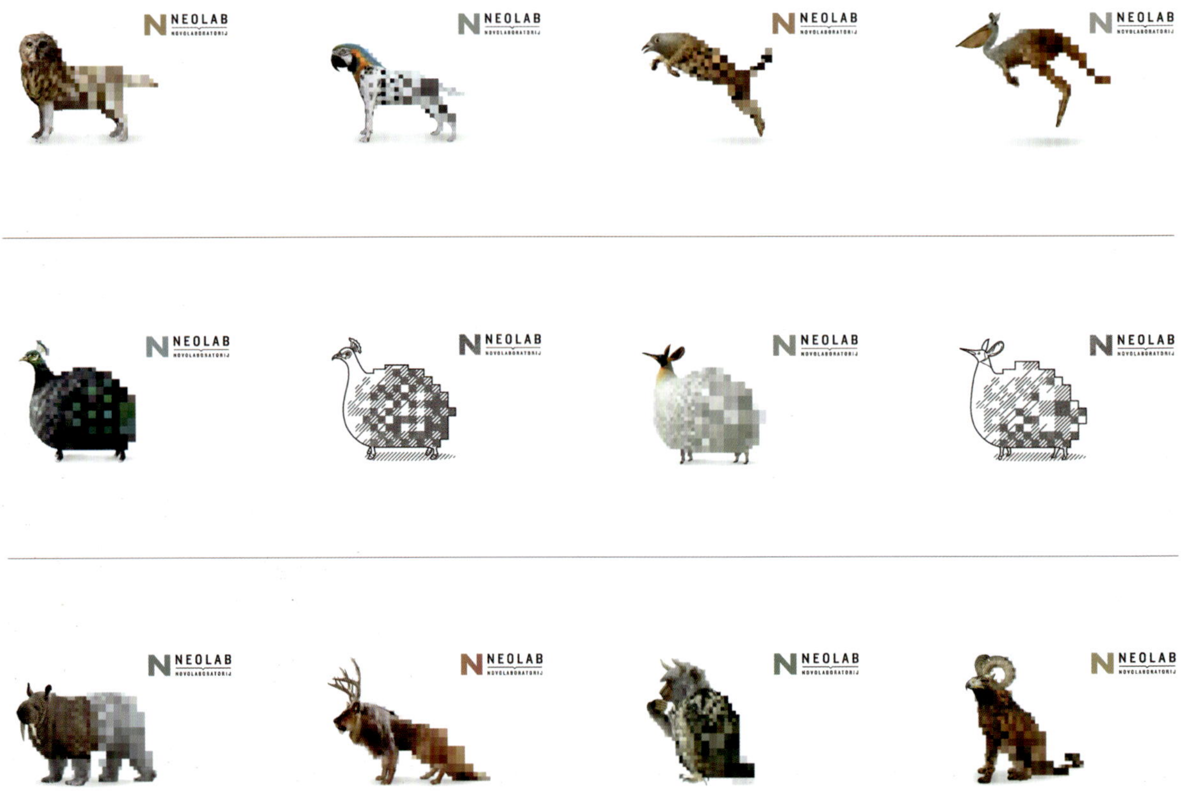

1

2

3

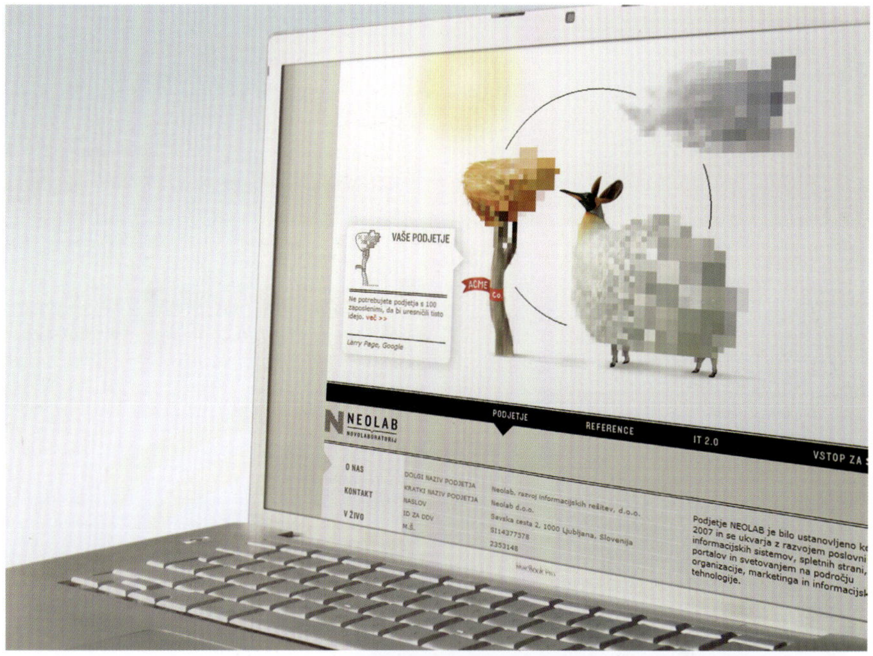
VAŠE PODJETJE
NEOLAB
PODJETJE
REFERENCE
IT 2.0
O NAS
KONTAKT
V ŽIVO

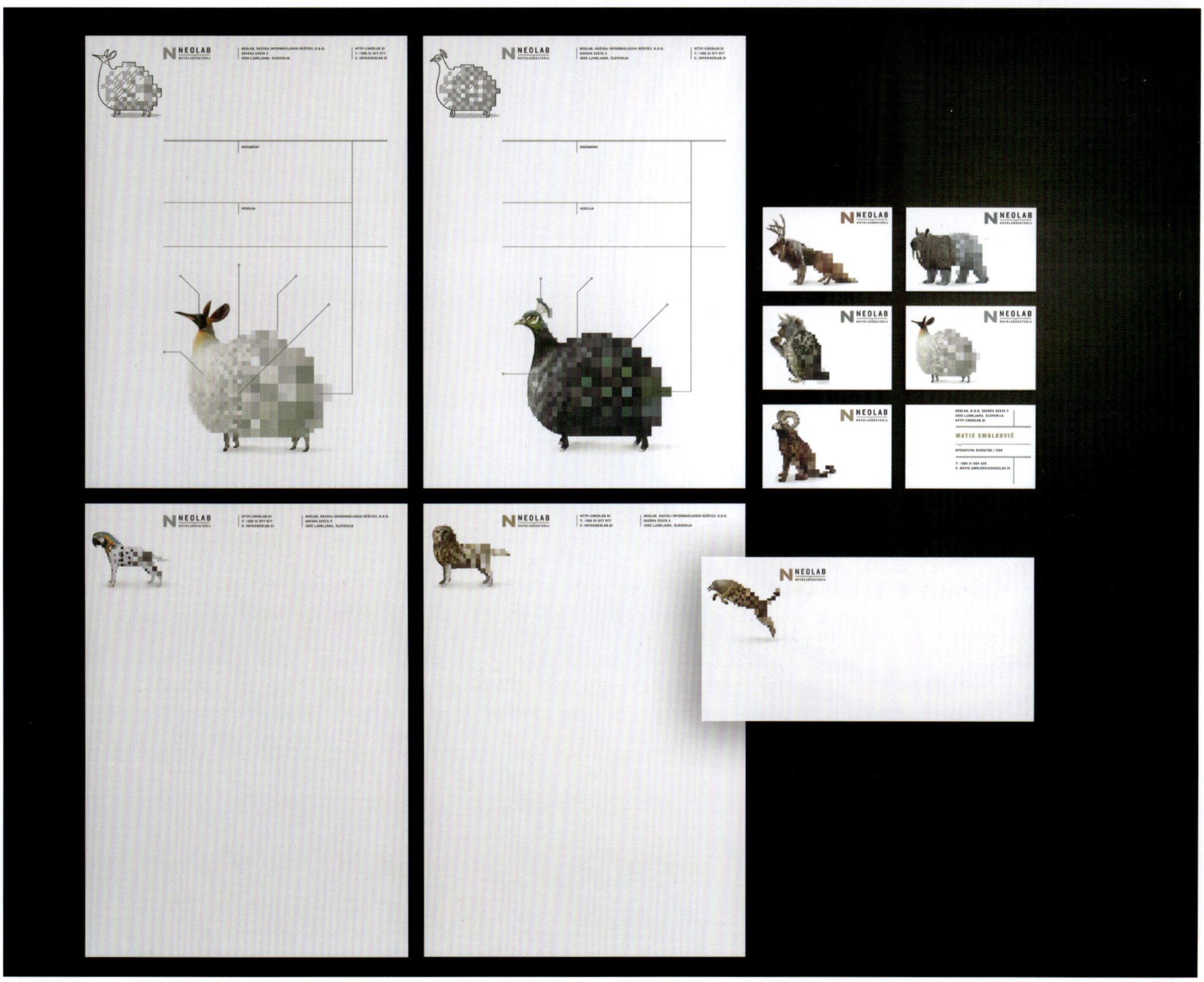
NEOLAB

BEM

Client_ Yandex
Design Firm_ Flëve Design Consultancy
Creative Director_ Vit Abramov
Designer_ Olya Balina
Country_ Russia

BEM, a toolkit devised and used at Yandex, stands for "Block," "Element" and "Modifier." Flëve was to create a flexible brand identity that is easily adaptable to different contexts. Additionally, the client specified that the identity should not be logocentric or create a corporate feel. Designers took "b_" from the code "b_e_m" and made it the main style-forming element. Creating the "b_" in different styles makes it not only easily adaptable to different contexts but also appealing to different target audiences.

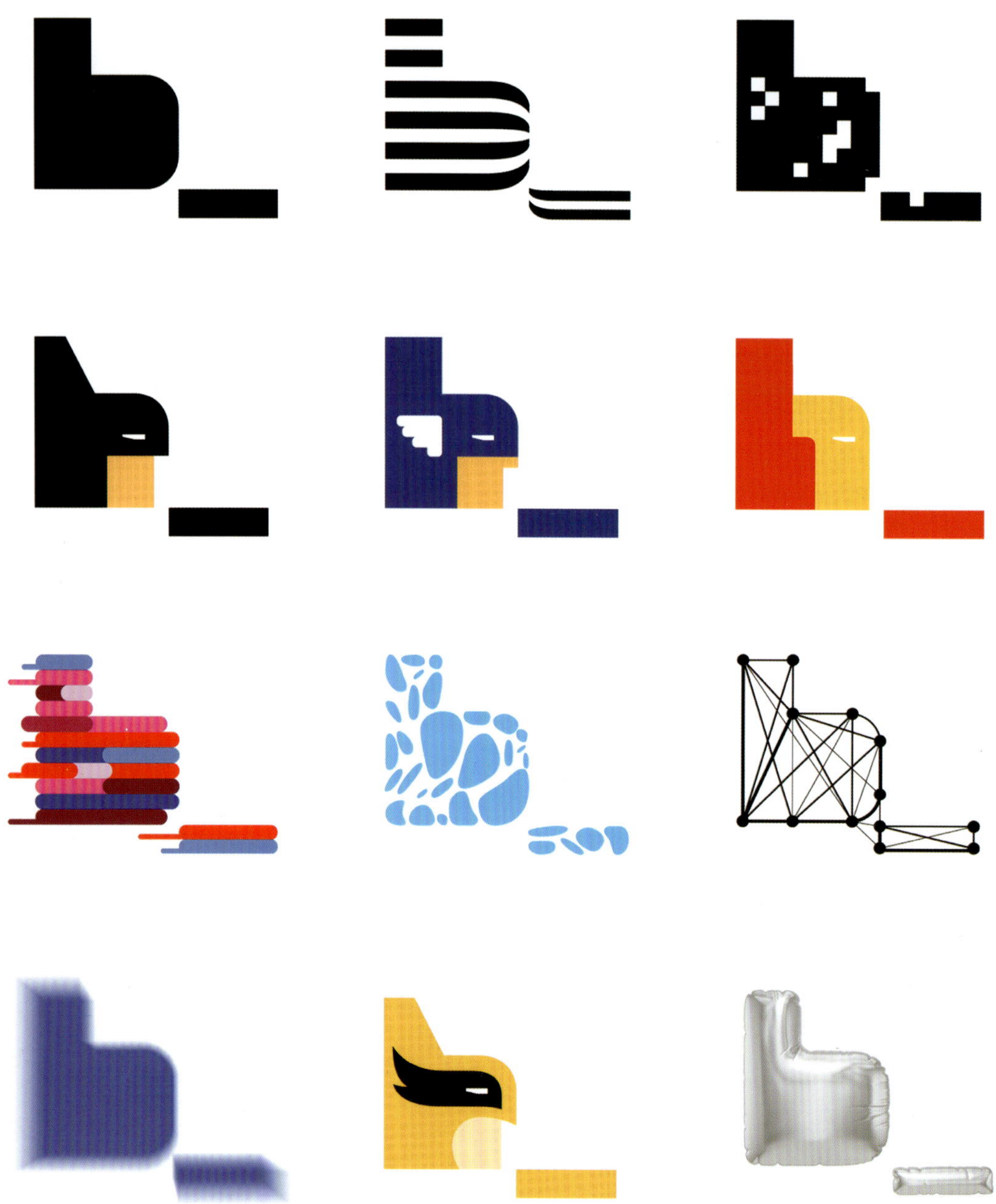

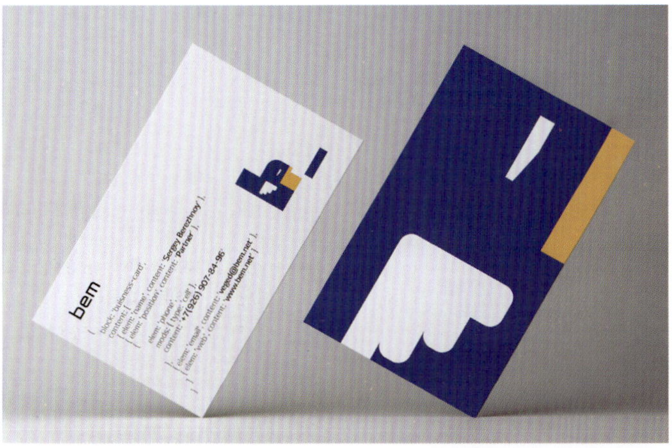
bem

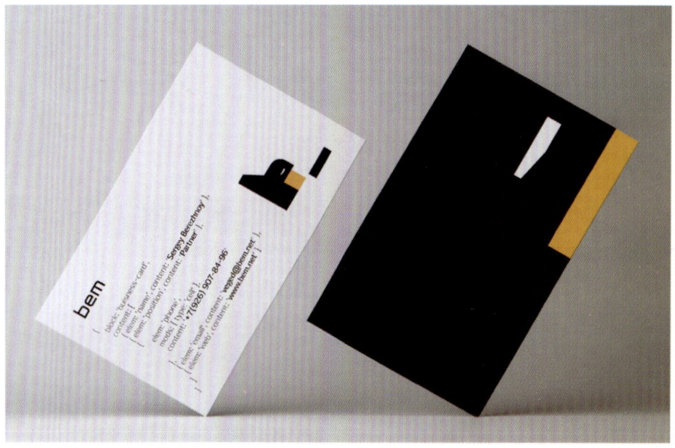
bem

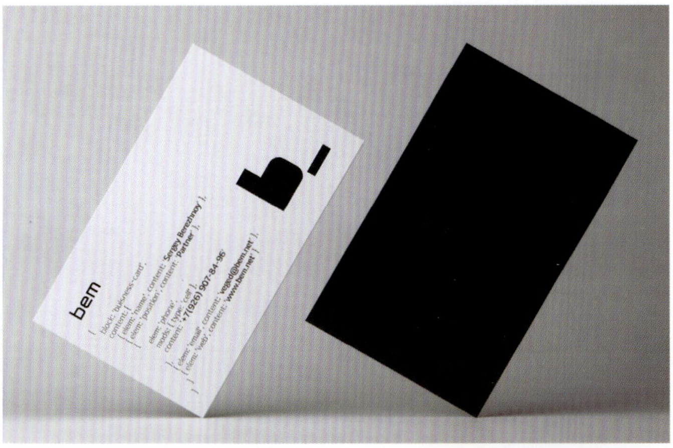
bem

bem

Client_ Kid-O
Design Firm_ 2x4
Creative Director_ Susan Sellers
Country_ USA

The 2x4 studio was asked to develop a design system for Kid-O, a line of children's toys founded on the principles of modernist toy design and progressive education. The approach was built upon the open-ended nature of play by using illustrations that emphasized the creative possibilities inherent in abstract forms — blocks become buildings, and puzzle pieces become flowers. Embracing Bauhaus ideals of simplicity and honesty in materials, the print and packaging design followed a clean, clear and systematic visual system.

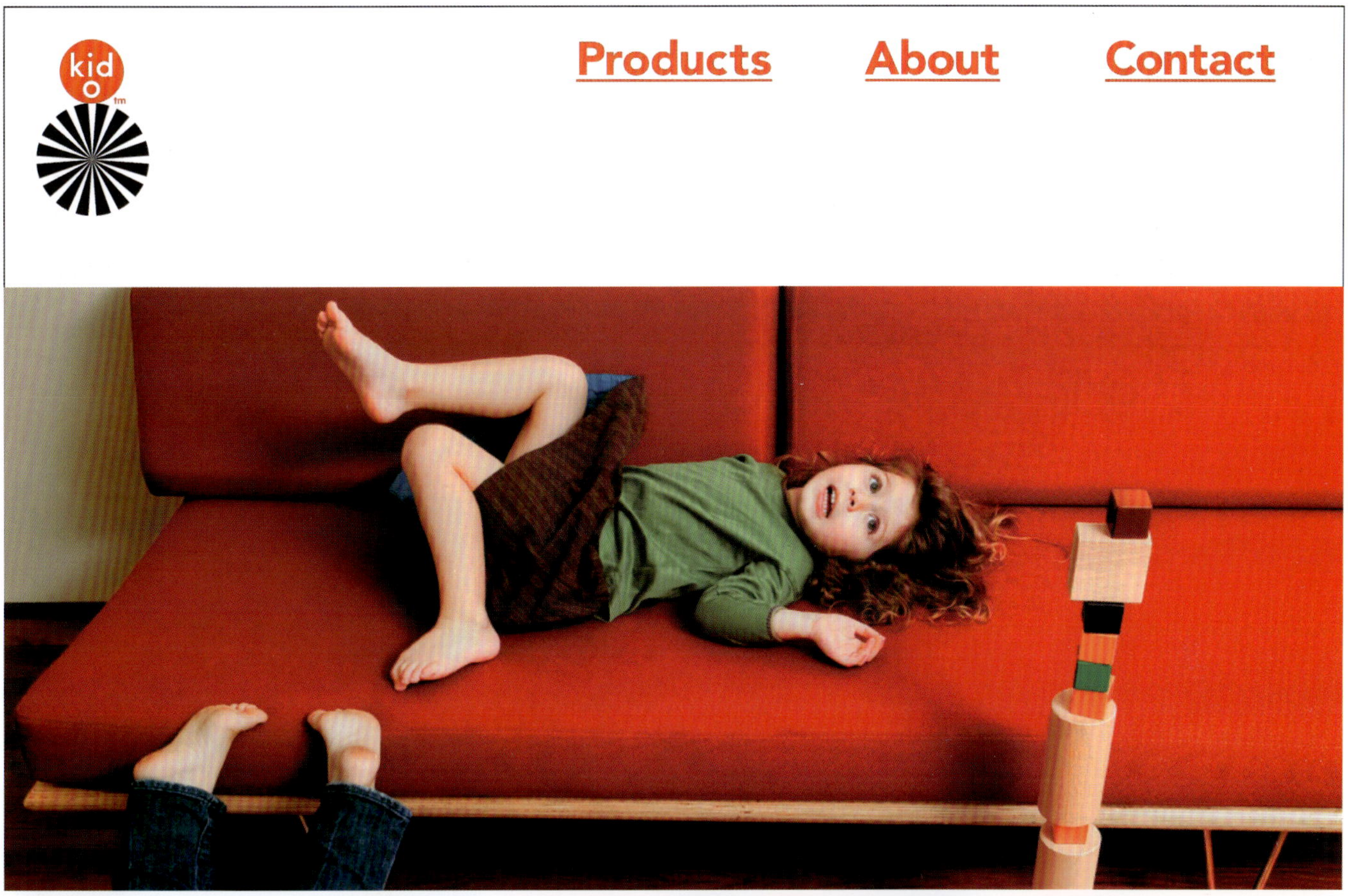
kid o
Products
About
Contact

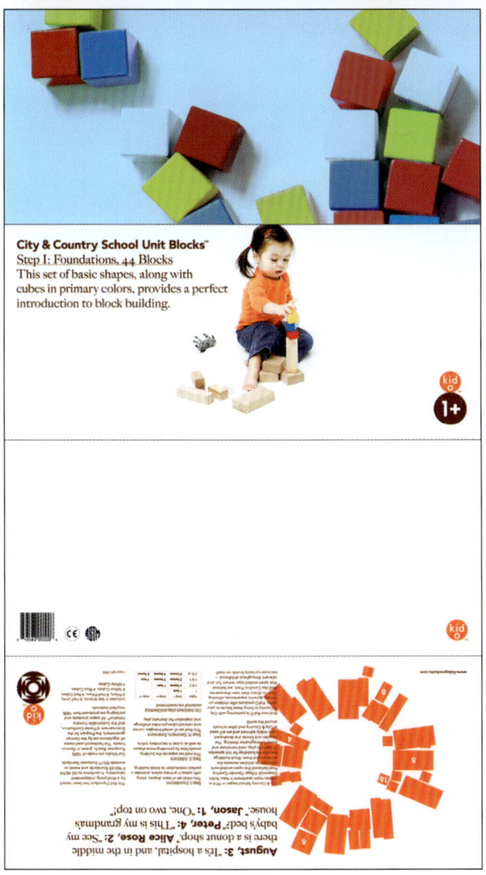
City & Country School Unit Blocks™
Step I: Foundations, 44 Blocks
This set of basic shapes, along with cubes in primary colors, provides a perfect introduction to block building.
1+

City & Country School Unit Blocks™
Step II: Additions, 24 Blocks
This set expands the building possibilities by providing more shapes as well as cubes in secondary colors.
2+

City & Country School Unit Blocks™
Step III: Extensions, 36 Blocks
This set of varied triangles, curves and colored cubes provides challenge and inspiration for dramatic play.
4+

Client_ALAND
Design Firm_ Studio Fnt
Country_ South Korea

This is an identity design for the new fashion brand 3.3 Field Trip, including brand naming, logotype and various application designs. From the explanatory notes of maps and weather forecast, a set of graphic elements was designed and utilized as building blocks of the logotype and pattern design.

3.3 FIELD TRIP

3.3 FIELD TRIP

3.3 FIELD TRIP
1234…

3.3 FIELD TRIP

3.3 FIELD TRIP
1234…

Client_ Natasha Trayan
Design Firm_ Evan Dorlot
Creative Director_ Evan Dorlot
Designer_ Evan Dorlot
Country_ Czech Republic

NAAA TAA is a unisex clothing brand created by young fashion designer Natasha Trayan, based in Prague. She creates one-off clothes, and needed a convincing brand image to accompany the collection without competing with it. Evan's solution was to interpret all the sides of each of the clothes she designs by a "same mind" identity: unique, minimalistic, edgy and structural.

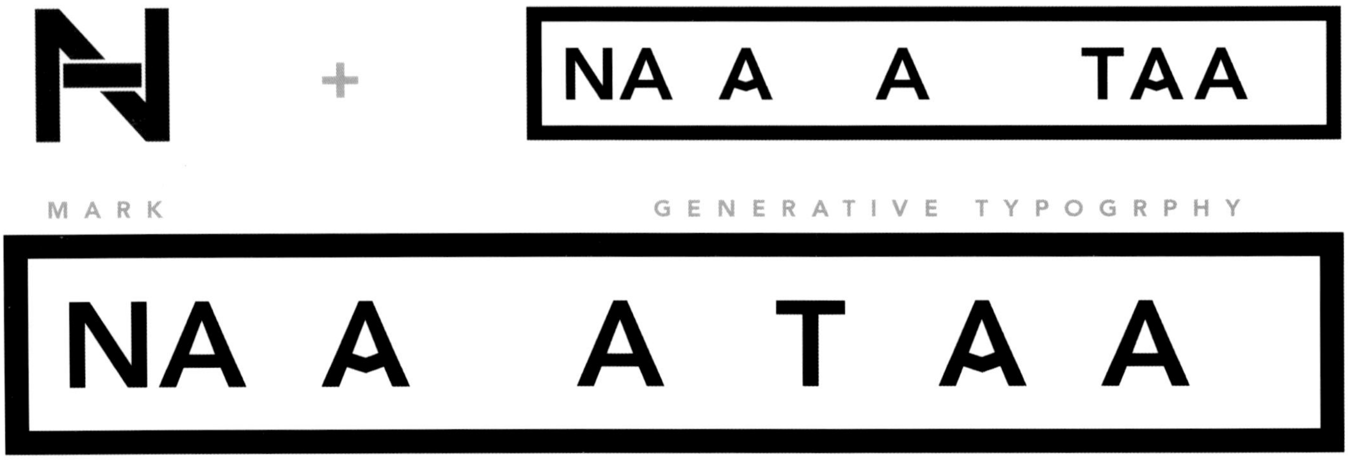

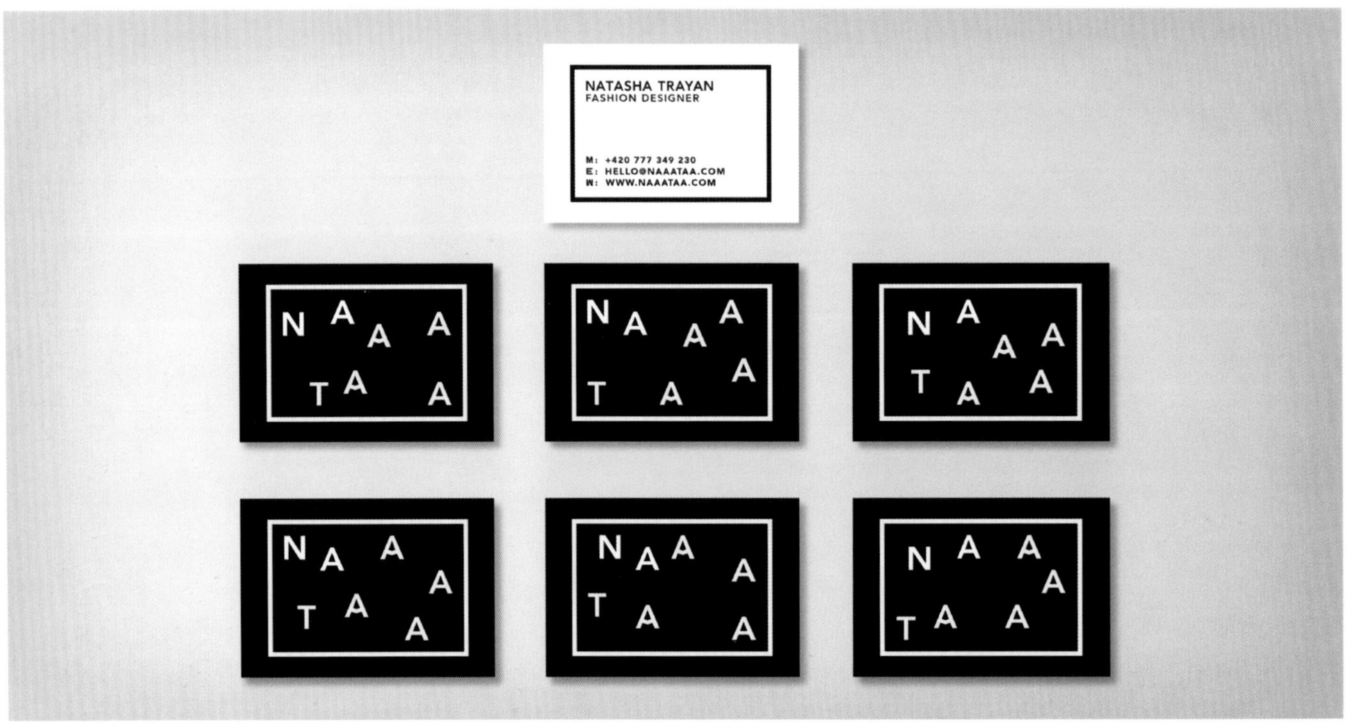

NATASHA TRAYAN
FASHION DESIGNER
M: +420 777 349 230
E: HELLO@NAAATAA.COM
W: WWW.NAAATAA.COM
LAW OF ATTRACTION
A/W 2014

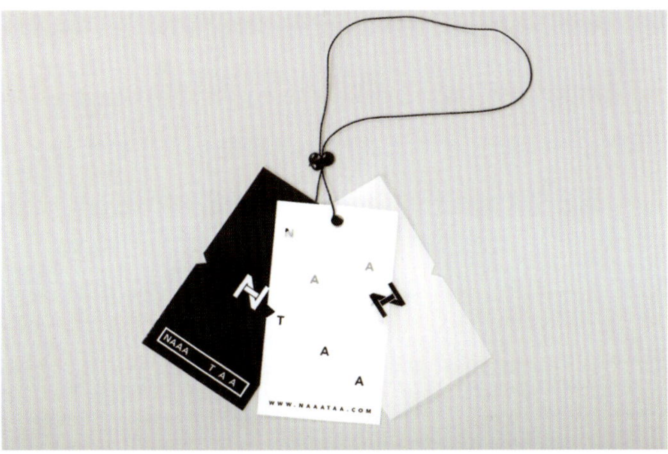
WWW.NAAATAA.COM

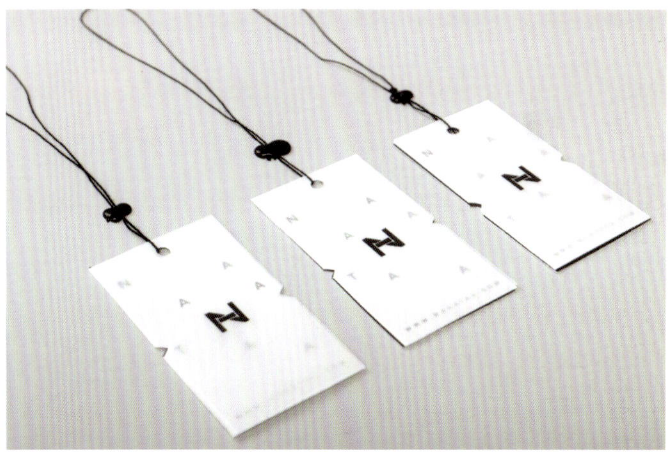

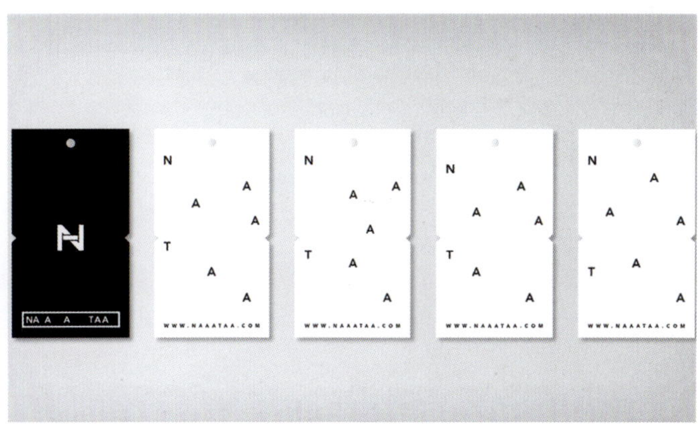
WWW.NAAATAA.COM

THANGI

Client_ Thangi
Design Firm_ Cappelli Identity Design
Designers_ Emanuele Cappelli, Andrea Fiori
Country_ Italy

The design of the Thangi logo is inspired by the morphology and colors of the region of Kashmir, where the landscape is reflected and multiplied by the water. The agency also took its inspiration from the art of tailoring, where ability meets the softness of fabrics. Two different versions of the main logo were created, differentiating the male and female product lines through medical images of genitalia.

THANGI
cashmere

THANGI
cashmere

THANGI
cashmere

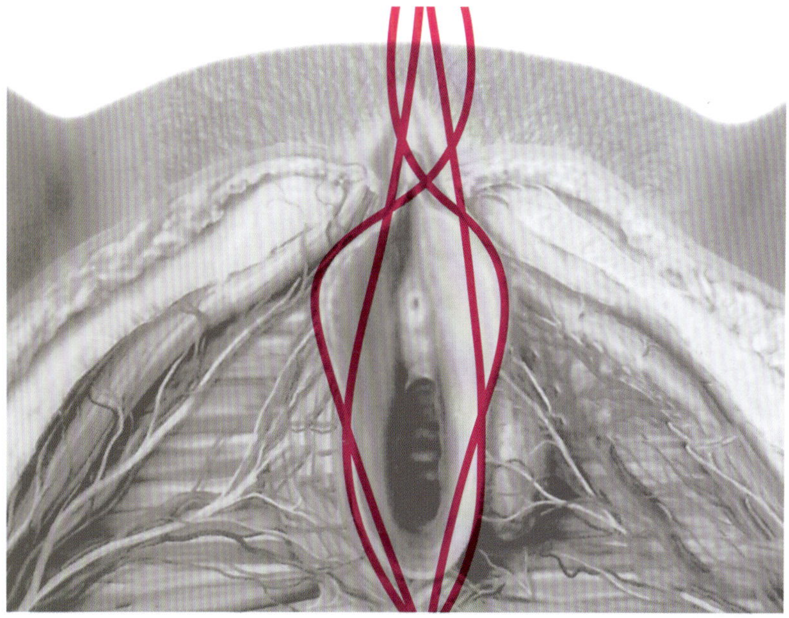

Female

THANGI
cashmere

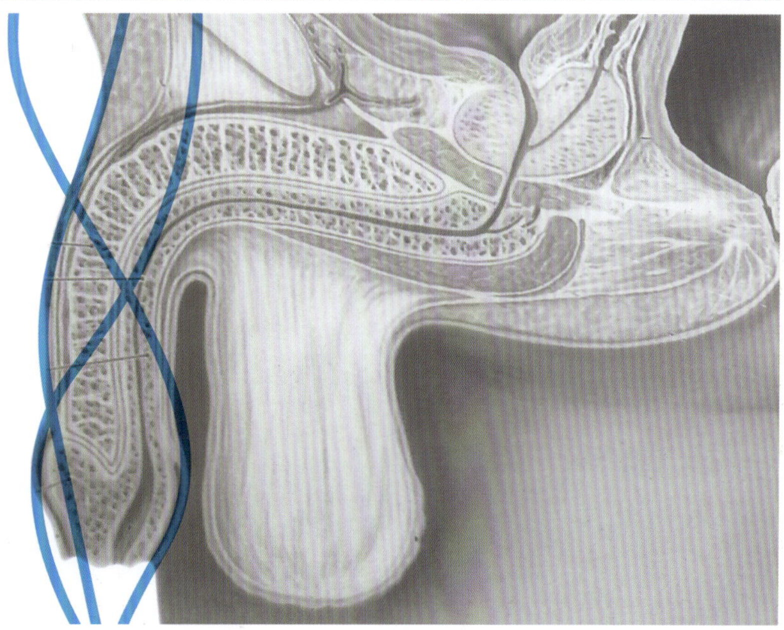

Male

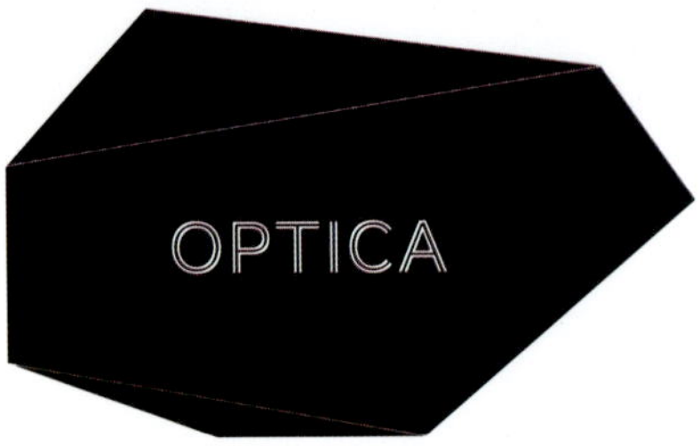

Client_Personal Work
Designer_Vlad Likh
Country_Russia

"Optica" is an identity project for an eyeglasses store. The designer loves simple solutions based on a bright graphic idea. He used three-dimensional models shown at different angles to vary the rhythm. "Optica" is an excellent example of a visual identity that showcases the designer's ability to create some new graphic forms without losing letter recognition.

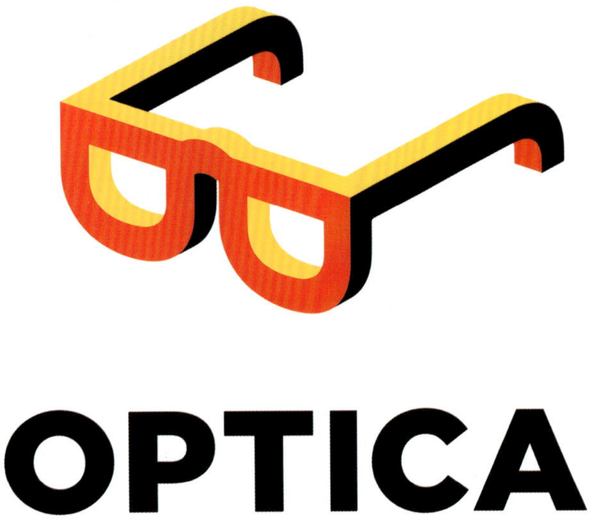

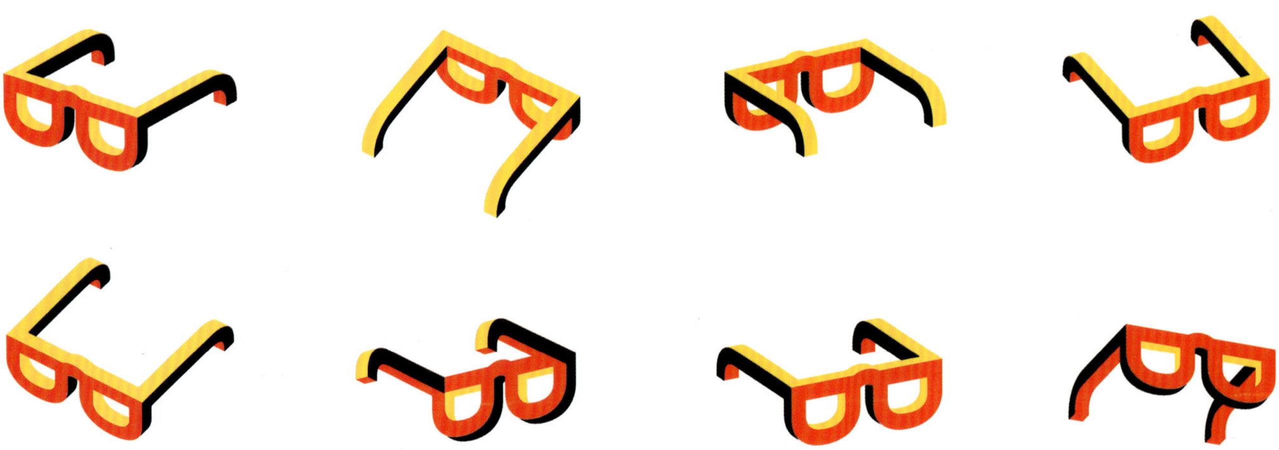

DON'T MISS
YOUR CHANCE
SALES

OPTICA
+7 495 457-71-38 | 37 Tverskaya st., Moscow 117154

IZABELA KLEMENSKA HAIR SALON

Client_ Izabela Klemenska Hair Salon
Creative Director_ Dagny Janowska
Designer_ Dagny Janowska
Country_UK/Poland

Izabela Klemenska is a hair salon located in Poland's seaside city of Sopot. In a place filled with art deco and art nouveau architecture, it was a necessity for the hair salon to fit in to the stylish surroundings. The essence of the art is caught in the decorative typographic symbol, which also captures the femininity of the salon. Towards the top the letters are extended to form a female head with only subtle lips illustrated, thus forming a very unique graphic shape to represent the brand. The logo is also used as the base of a series of graphic elements, where each gives the female head a different hairstyle.

Izabela Klemenska
zaklad fryzjerski

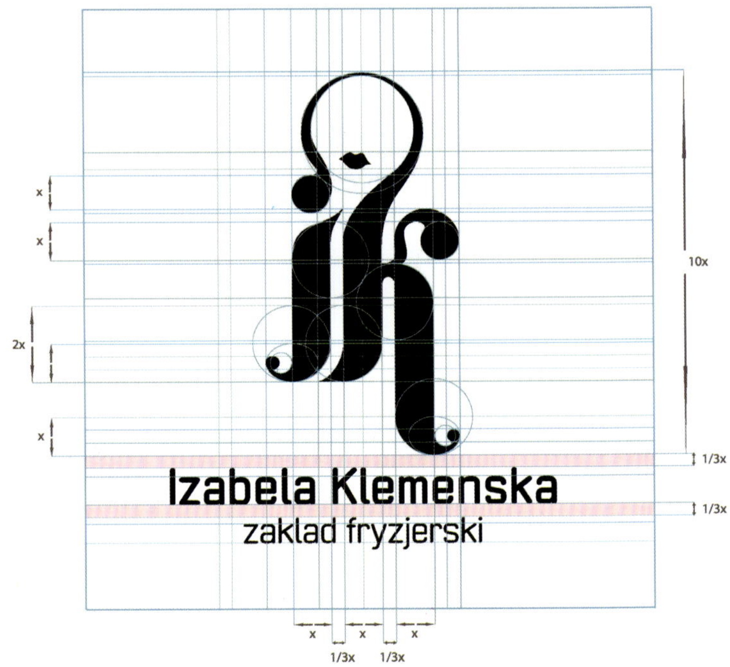

IZABELA KLEMENSKA. Zakład Fryzjerski.

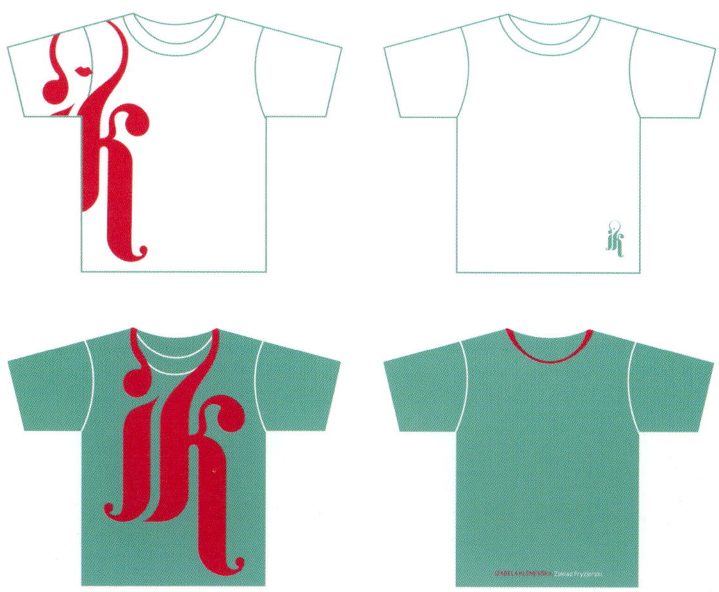

Client_ Takeda Russia
Design Firm_ Charsky Studio
Creative Director_ Eugene Charsky
Designer_ Ekaterina Voronina
Country_ Russia

The Swiss pharmaceutical company Nycomed teamed with Japan's Takeda in 1993. The goals of this project were to use Takeda's corporate colors in a celebratory identity, to create a dynamic feel, and to include a Russian symbol. Designers chose the square as a very simple form and introduced it to the dynamics. From dark blue to red — from Nycomed to Takeda! A logo can be as many colors as in this Takeda example, and should be easy to use with promotional materials of any kind.

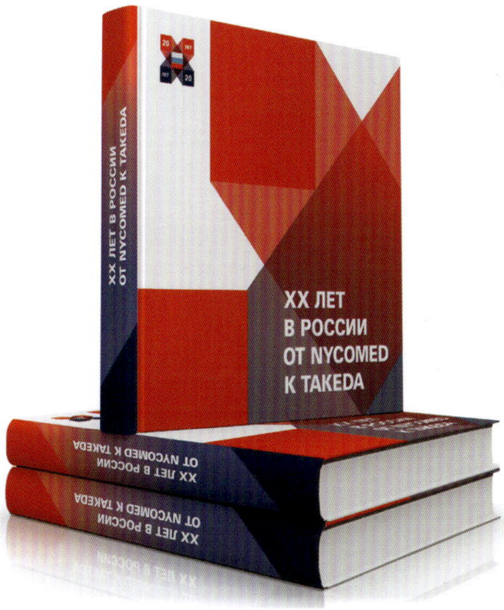
XX ЛЕТ
В РОССИИ
ОТ NYCOMED
К TAKEDA

Открытие филиала
компании никомед
в Москве
1913
год –
XX ЛЕТ В РОССИИ
ОТ NYCOMED К TAKEDA
XX ЛЕТ В РОССИИ
ОТ NYCOMED К TAKEDA

20 ЛЕТ
XX ЛЕТ
В РОССИИ
ОТ NYCOMED
К TAKEDA

CULTURE

ART

EVENT

AG2R LA MONDIALE—LA TRANSAT

Client_AG2R LA MONDIALE
Design Firm_ Studio Dumbar
Designer_ Rejane Dal Bello
Country_ France

In 2009, French insurance companies AG2R and La Mondiale merged to form AG2R LA MONDIALE. Studio Dumbar created complete visual identities for ALM's sponsorship of a Tour de France team and the annual international yacht race — Le Transat and its 20th anniversary celebration. Studio Dumbar's award-winning design program reinvigorated the visual landscape of an industry so often bereft of inspirational branding. The new visual identity is simple yet iconic with expressive typography, engaging photography and a vibrant, versatile color palette.

JCDecaux
JCDecaux
TRANSAT
20
ANS

AG2R LA MONDIALE
TRANSAT
20 ANS

LA TRANSAT
AG2R LA MONDIALE
CONCARNEAU
SAINT-BARTH

TRANSAT 20 ANS

AXIS OF CULTURE IN KATOWICE

Client_ Academy of Fine Arts in Katowice
Designer_ Ola Krupa
Country_ Poland

On the site of a former coalmine, Katowice is creating a culture space. The polymorphic identity will both link and differentiate all the institutions at the same time. The logo was built on a triangular, isometric grid (which originated from a hexagon form, a symbol of coal). Each color in the project is connected to one type of cultural activity.

OŚ KULTURY
strefa sztuki

OŚ KULTUR
strefa tańca

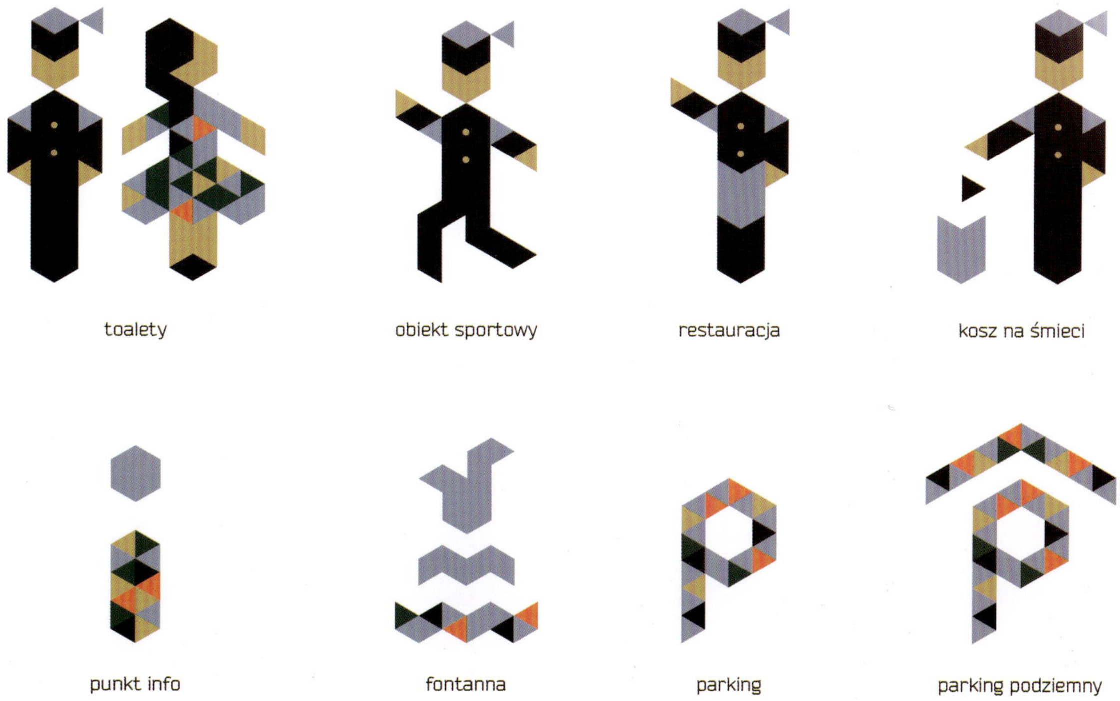

OŚ KULTURY
księga znaku | 2012

OŚ KULTURY

piktogram
logotyp
OŚ KULTURY

toalety

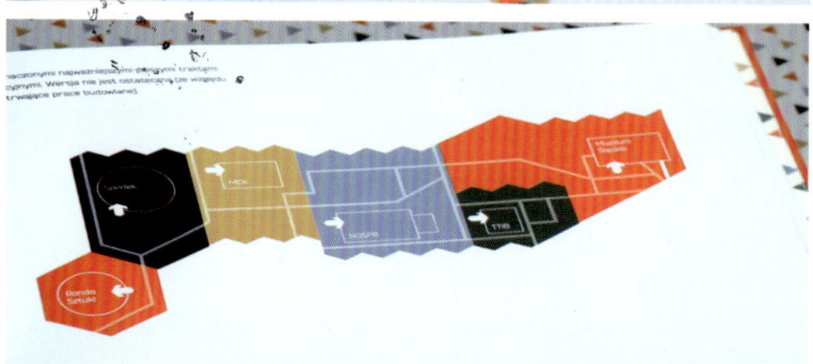

OŚ KULTURY
OŚ KULTURY

OŚ KULTURY
OŚ KULTURY

OŚ KULTURY
tu jest relaks!
OŚ KULTURY
tu jest natura!

OŚ KULTURY
Tu jest. relaks!

DAMA BOOK & DESIGN STORE

Client_DAMA Book & Design Store
Design Firm_ Cappelli Identity Design
Designers_ Emanuele Cappelli, Francesco Di Muro
Country_ Italy

When designing the brand DAMA (Design, Art, Multimedia and Architecture), the design agency chose to play with the name DAMA (Italian for "checkers"). The logo tries to extract from the checkers game the element of time: It is made up of letters that wedge one in another, giving a rhythm to the whole composition. The idea of rhythm is also found within the alternating colors of orange and white. This play with colors and shapes will be used on the whole DAMA image; on corporate material, textures and images.

DAMA
BOOK & DESIGN STORE

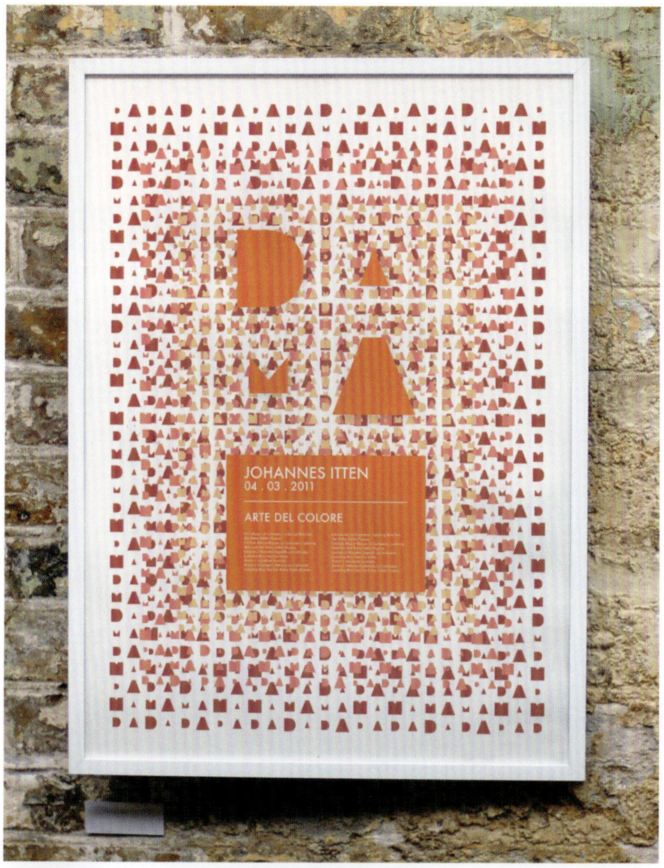
JOHANNES ITTEN
04 . 03 . 2011
ARTE DEL COLORE

MARCEL BREUER
04 . 03 . 2011
FUTURE OF ARCHITECTURE

DE OLHO

Client_ IdeaFixa
Design Firm_ Pianofuzz Design Studio
Country_ Brazil

"De Olho — A Photographic Manifesto" is a publication that gathers portraits of 100 personalities around one question: Who's KEEPING AN EYE ON problems in Brazil? And, more than that, who is willing to show his face for this idea? In this project, designers used geometric figures combined with a black-and-white palette, displaying its conciseness and variety.

OLHAR CRÍTICO PARA SOCIEDADE
PONTO DE ATENÇÃO

Crítico
Social
Foco
Atenção

ACESSÍVEL
SISTEMA ABERTO

Solidário
Transparente
Aberto
Livre

CRITICAL LOOK AT SOCIETY
ATTENTION POINT

Critical
Social
Focus
Attention

ACCESSIBLE
OPEN SYSTEM

Solidary
Transparent
Open
Free

MANIFESTO
FOTOGRÁFICO

DE
OLHO

DE OLHO
MANIFESTO
FOTOGRÁFICO

MANIFESTO
FOTOGRÁFICO
DE OLHO

DE OLHO
MANIFESTO
FOTOGRÁFICO

PERSONALIDADES
IDENTIFICAÇÃO
CREDIBILIDADE

Personalities
Identification
Credibility

JEONJU INTERNATIONAL FILM FESTIVAL

Client_ Jeonju International Film Festival
Design Firm_ Studio Fnt
Country_ South Korea

JIFF (Jeonju International Film Festival) is one of the three leading film festivals in Korea, and takes place every spring. The designers have used the "butterfly wing" as the festival's motif for this season. The new festival identity was designed using the flap of a butterfly's wings as an inspiration for form, and flower blossoms for the color range. The flexibility of the new design system and kaleidoscopic extendibility symbolize the movie projector's light and the endless flapping of the butterfly's wings. More importantly, it represents the festival's spirit — a small step bringing a big change.

JIFF JIFF JIFF JIFF

Graphic Device - Pattern

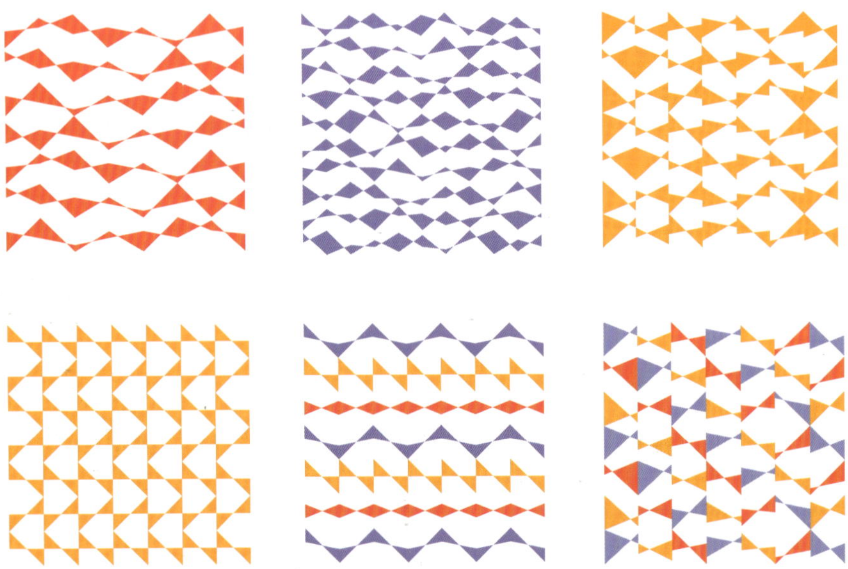

Graphic Device - Linear Pattern

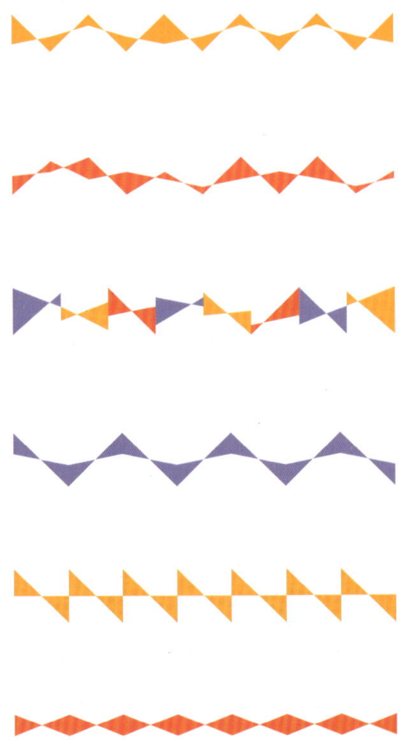

14
JEONJU
INTERNATIONAL
FILM FESTIVAL
2013. 4. 25. - 5. 3.
전주
국제영화제
www.jiff.or.kr
JIFF

14
www.jiff.or.kr
JIFF
전주국제영화제
JEONJU INTERNATIONAL
FILM FESTIVAL

JIFF

14
JIFF
모 악 당
MOAK HALL
전주국제영화제

JEWISH MUSEUM & TOLERANCE CENTER

Client_ Jewish Museum & Tolerance Center
Design Firm_ Flëve Design Consultancy
Creative Director_ Vit Abramov
Designer_ Olya Balina
Country_ Russia

Jewish Museum & Tolerance Center is one of the most technologically advanced museums in Russia. Its identity should make the museum stand out and resonate with today's young people, both Jewish and non-Jewish, and also integrate this identity into the museum space and signage system. The idea behind this identity is based on the notion of three modalities (contact, penetration and inclusion) as ways of the assimilation of two cultures, as well as two histories (Russian and Jewish) interacting with one another.

Jewish Museum & Tolerance Center

Еврейский музей и центр толерантности

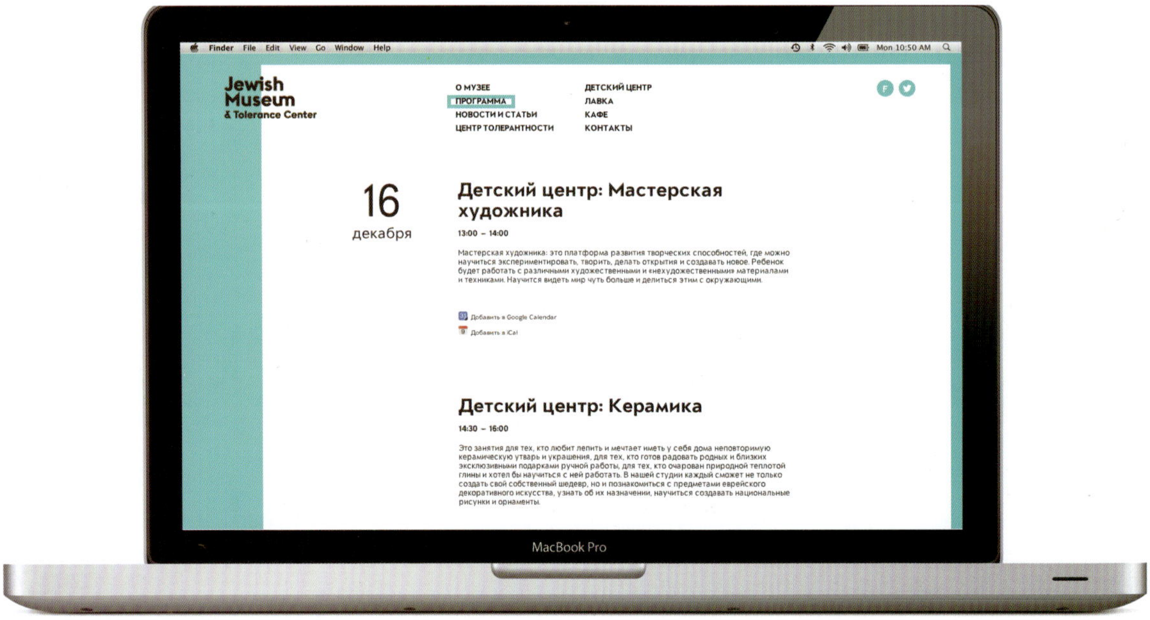

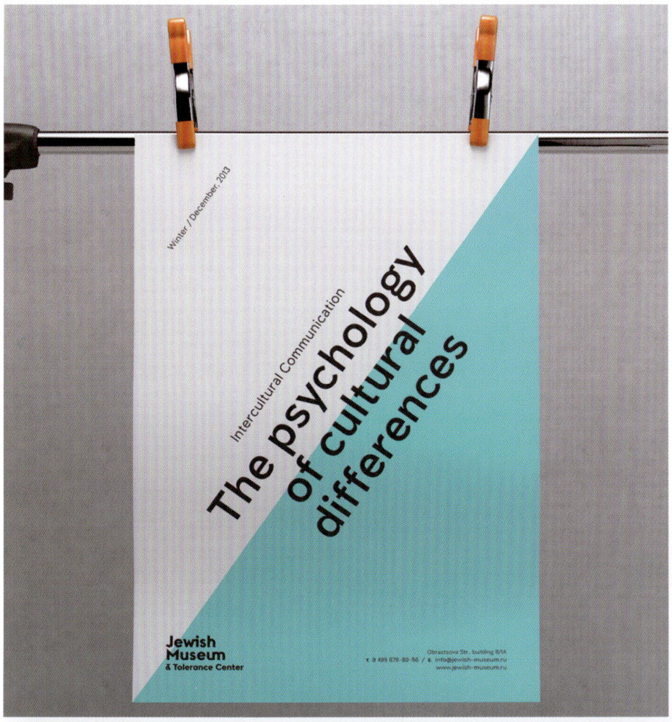
Winter / December, 2013
Intercultural Communication
The psychology of cultural differences
Jewish Museum & Tolerance Center

Jewish Museum & Tolerance Center

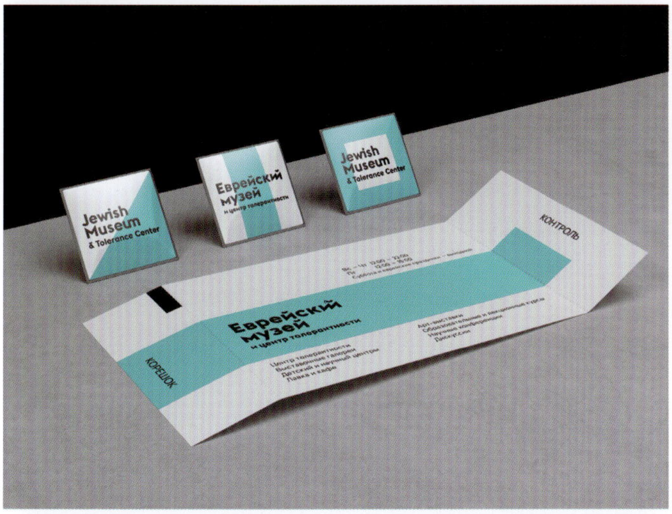
Jewish Museum & Tolerance Center
Еврейский музей и центр толерантности
Контроль
Корешок

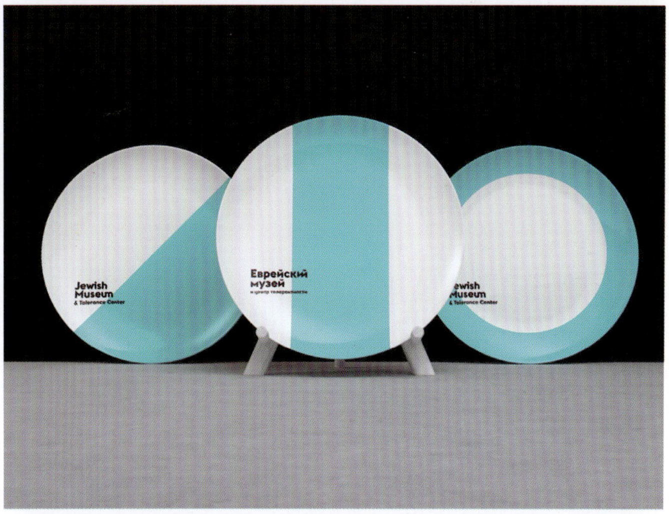
Jewish Museum & Tolerance Center
Еврейский музей и центр толерантности

Moscow will teach tolerance in a new way
Intercultural Communication
The psychology of cultural differences
SCHOOL OF CONTEMPORARY ART

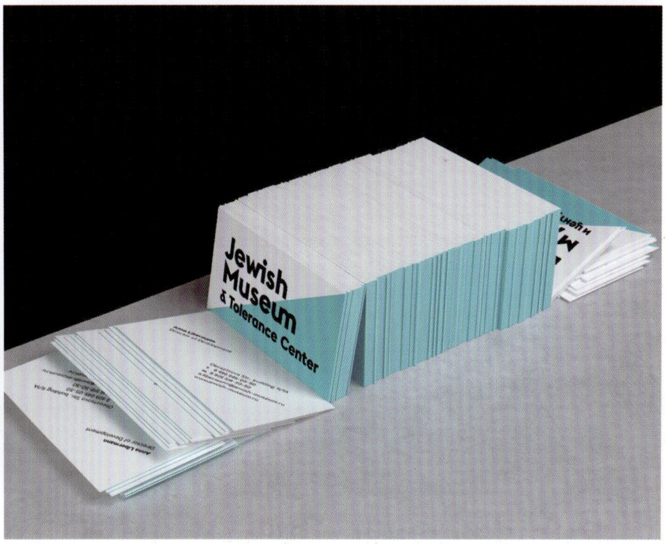
Jewish Museum & Tolerance Center

MAIN UND MEE(H)R

Client_ Stadt Schweinfurt
Design Firm_ Marco Moccia
Creative Directors_ Marco Moccia, Meike Adler
Designers_ Marco Moccia, Meike Adler
Country_ Germany

In 2013 the "Bayerische Landesausstellung" (Bavarian State Examination) took place in Schweinfurt. This exhibition occurs every year in a different city in Bavaria. The task was to design an identity for the supporting program "Main und Mee(h)r" (Main and Sea). The topic was "water." The exhibition is very well-rounded. Because of the mass of performances and their individuality, designers chose the identity to be modular and dynamic. The key visual has the shape of a water molecule that can be shown as different and individual as the program itself.

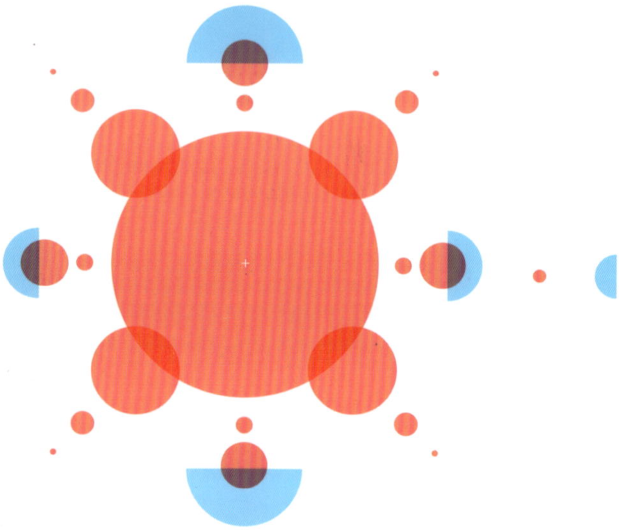

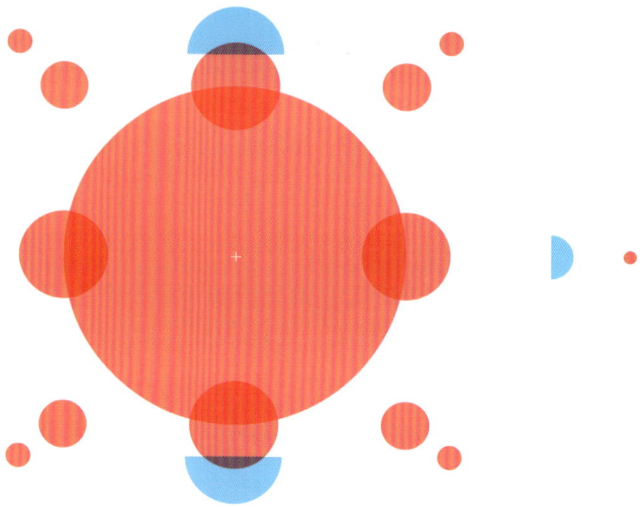

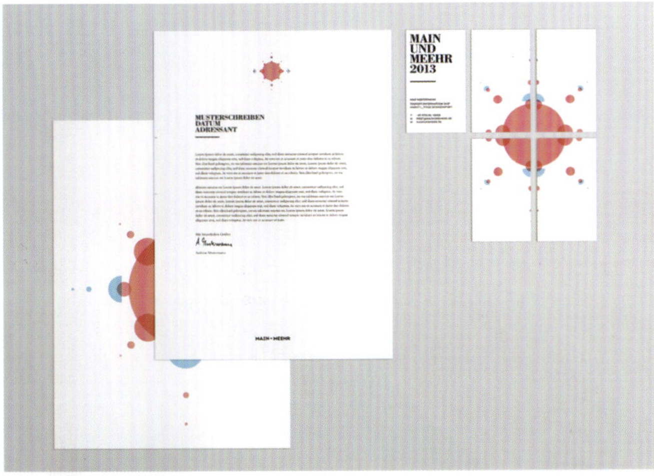
MAIN
UND
MEEHR
2013
MUSTERSCHREIBEN
DATUM
ADRESSANT

MAIN
UND
MEEHR
2013

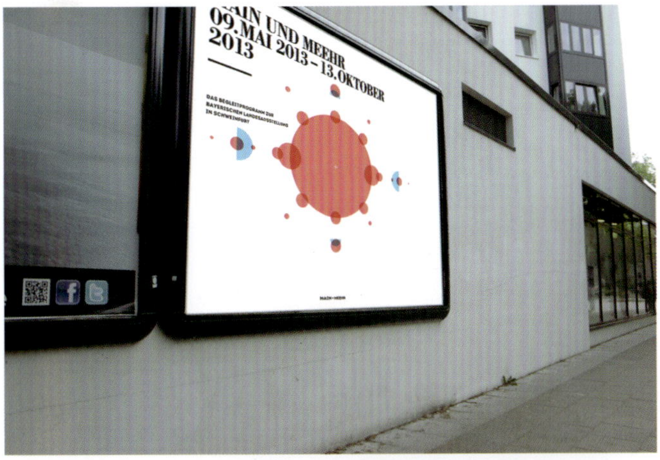

AUSSTELLUNGEN
UND MEEHR

STRÖER
MAIN UND MEEHR
09. MAI – 13. OKTOBER
2013

MUSEUM OF ARCHITECTURE AND DESIGN

Client_ Museum of Architecture and Design
Design Firm_ IlovarStritar
Creative Directors_ Robert Ilovar, Jernej Stritar
Designers_ Robert Ilovar, Jernej Stritar, Miha Kosmač, Kaja Kopitar
Country_ Slovenia

Muzej za arhitekturo in oblikovanje (MAO, "Museum of Architecture and Design" in English) is the central Slovenian museum institution in the field of architecture, urbanism, industrial and graphic design, and photography. It functions as a museum as well as an architectural and design center having a task of enabling exchange of ideas and knowledge as well as establishing dialogue. The purpose of the visual identity was to interpret the visual form of the museum as the framework, which brings different views and highlights various fields covered by the museum.

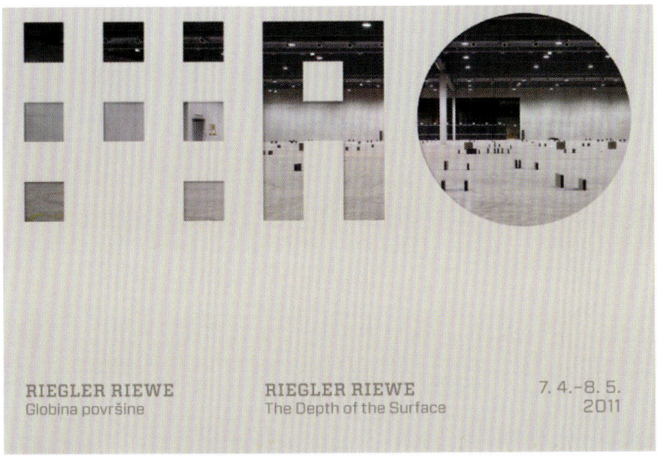
RIEGLER RIEWE
Globina površine
RIEGLER RIEWE
The Depth of the Surface
7. 4.–8. 5.
2011

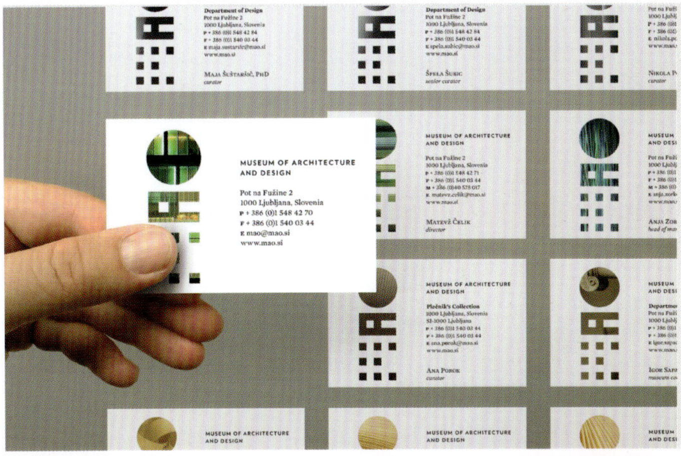
MUSEUM OF ARCHITECTURE AND DESIGN
Pot na Fužine 2
1000 Ljubljana, Slovenia
P + 386 (0)1 548 42 70
F + 386 (0)1 540 03 44
E mao@mao.si
www.mao.si

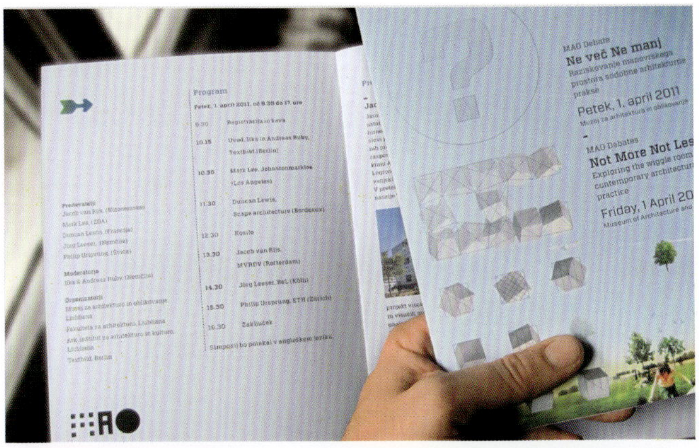
Ne več Ne manj
Petek, 1. april 2011
Not More Not Les
Friday, 1 April 20

Arhitektura Oblikovanje Fotografija
Architecture Design Photography
Št. vstopnice
Ticket n°
3 €

ODPRTI DEPOJI:
predstavitev zbirk Muzeja za arhitekturo in oblikovanje
OPEN DEPOT:
Introducing the Collections of the Museum of Architecture and Design
3. 2.–20. 3.
2011

NOVA GORSKA KOČA
1. 3.–1. 4. 2012

GLENN MURCUTT
GLENN MURCUTT
22. 3.–10. 6.

MTV BRAZIL

Client_MTV Brazil
Design Firm_ Pianofuzz Design Studio
Country_ Brazil

The studio Pianofuzz has developed one of the collections of licensed products for MTV Brazil for the year of 2010. The challenge of this collection was to develop a geometric aesthetic line, such as the 1960s' optical art, but with a contemporary style. This project includes illustrated prints, patterns, icons, and two exclusive type families.

MUZEON ARTS PARK

Client_ Muzeon Arts Park, Moscow
Design Firm_ Charsky Studio
Creative Director_ Evgeny Charsky
Designer_ Ekaterina Voronina
Country_ Russia

Park museum is a truly unique place. Exhibitions' appearances change constantly as the sun traverses the sky during the day, and through different seasons. It is lit by sunlight and presents the antagonist — the shadow. The new Muzeon logo symbolizes this duality of light and shadow, being opposites but parts of a whole. Light and shadow play a very special and important role in fine arts. Thus the new logo naturally delivers the historically established image of Muzeon as a place where various artists meet.

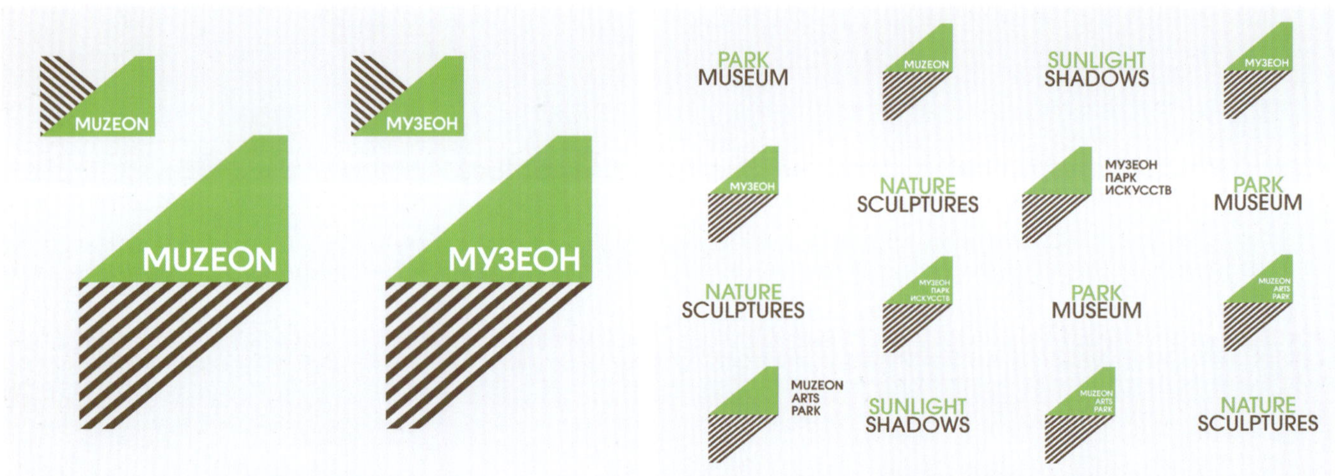

МУЗЕОН
Фонтан
Fountain
Туалет
WC
Вход
Entrance

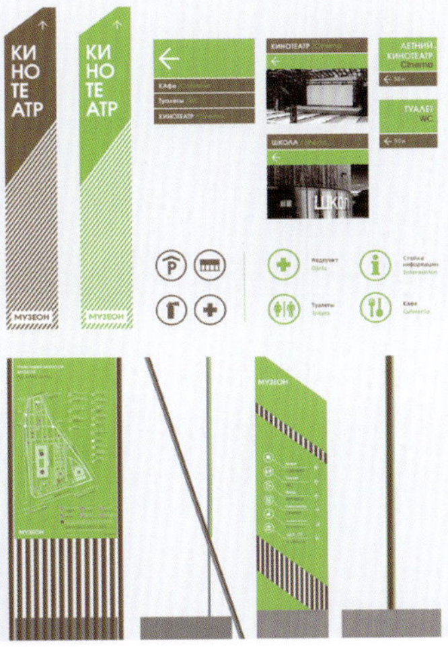
КИ
НО
ТЕ
АТР
КИ
НО
ТЕ
АТР

СКУЛЬПТУРЫ
SCULPTURE
МУЗЕОН
ЙОГА В ПАРКЕ
YOGA
МУЗЕОН
ВЫСТАВКА-ПРОДАЖА РАСТЕНИЙ
PLANTS MARKET
МУЗЕОН
МАРКЕТ
В ПАРКЕ
с 09:00 до 22:00

EXHIBITION
PROJECT
VERA
MUKHINA
31 АВГУСТ – 23 ОКТЯБРЯ
МУЗЕОН
МУЗЕО

THE
SINGER
The Inspedor Cluzo /
12 June /
Park Museon
МУЗЕОН
THE
SINGER
The Inspedor Cluzo /
12 June /
Park Museon
МУЗЕОН
YO
GA
MAR
KET

МУЗЕОН
приглашение
на праздничное
мероприятие
МУЗЕОНУ
20 ЛЕТ
ПАРК
ИСКУССТВ
МУЗЕОН
СПЕЦ
ПОКАЗ
приглашение
ТВОРЧЕС
КИЙ ВОРК
ШОП
МУЗЕОН

МУЗЕОН
КИНО
POSTER
NUMBER
ONE
POSTER
NUMBER
TWO
POSTER
NUMBER
THREE
ПОДВЕДЕНИЕ ИТОГОВ
STUDENT ART PROM
THE
SINGER
The Inspector Cluzo /
12 June /
28 июля
20:00
AMIINA
(Iceland)
МУЗЕОН

МУЗЕОН

TOUR'S PLAN
ARTS PARK
PAVILION SHKOLA
Monu ments of the Soviet era
МУЗЕОН

In Museon
31 АВГУСТ – 23 ОКТЯБРЯ
VERA MUKHINA
EXHIBITION PROJECT
МУЗЕОН

13-16 JUNE
MU SES
OF THE ARTISTS
Every Thursday Tour «Monuments of the Soviet period»
ARTS PARK
EVERY THURSDAY
MONUMENTS OF THE SOVIET PERIOD
CINE MA
IN MUSEON
SUM MER PROG RAM
МУЗЕОН

13-16 JUNE
MU SES
OF THE ARTISTS
Every Thursday Tour «Monuments of the Soviet period»
МУЗЕОН
MUSEON
АВГУСТ – 23 ОКТЯБРЯ
VERA MUKHINA
EXHIBITION PROJECT
THURSDAY
PERIOD

MUZEUM NARODOWE W WARSZAWIE

Client_ Personal Work
Designer_ Dawid Cmok
Country_ Poland

Muzeum Narodowe w Warszawie (The National Museum in Warsaw) is a national institution of culture, one of the largest museums in Poland and the largest in Warsaw. The structure of the museum includes four different branches. The designer created a distinctive image of the museum based on a functional design that would be easily recognized and would be distinguished among other museum institutions in the world. He created a wide variety of elements in a multi-layer corporate identity: a dynamic logotype system — four branches, each with letterheads, envelopes, visiting cards, folders, company cars, badges, and identity books.

MUZEUM NARODOWE
W WARSZAWIE

MUZEUM NARODOWE
W WARSZAWIE

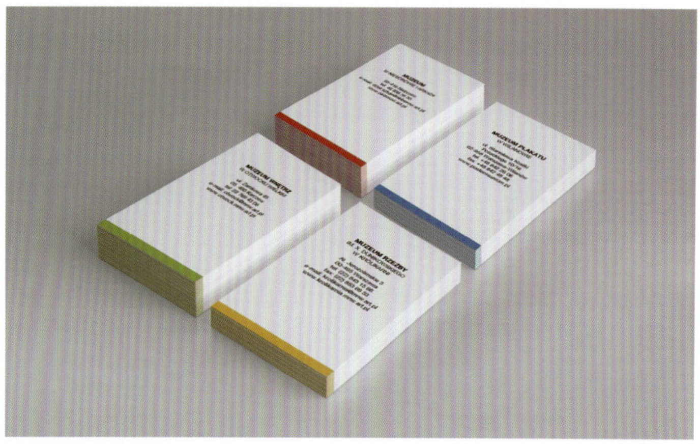

NIMUS

Client_ Nimus
Designers_ Silvia Acerbi, Matilde Arduini, Paola Berardelli, Mikele Corradini
Country_ Italy

Nimus, an international contemporary opera festival, is located in Istanbul, Turkey. The dynamic logo expresses the changing soul of music. Designers analyzed the geometric decorations that cover Topkapi Palace (the festival location): They used the shapes to create a basic form and created the logo from the principle of kaleidoscopes; changing the shape and rotating the basic form, they built 180 different logos that relate to each other, but are always different.

nimus
contemporary opera festival

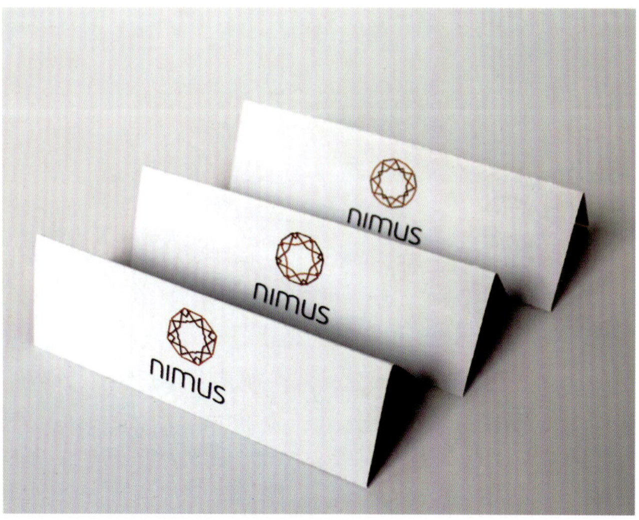

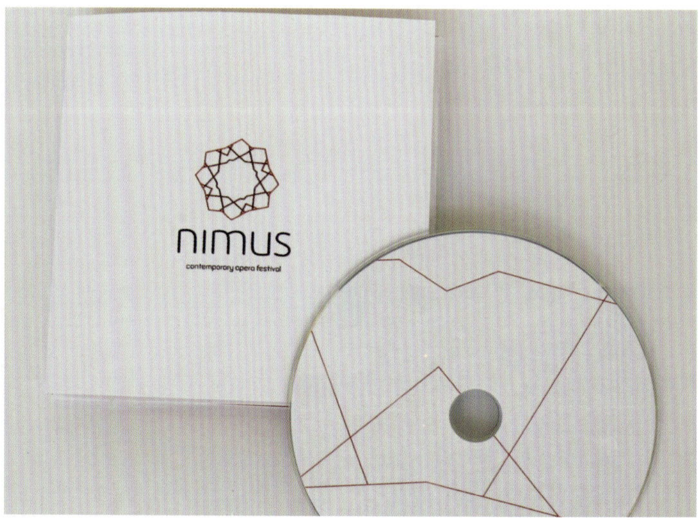

nimus
nimus
nimus
nimus
contemporary opera festival

GUEST pass
VIP pass
PRESS pass

LOREM IPSUM
CONCEPTAM NE EAIIM
nimus
THE ISTANBUL
CONTEMPORARY
OPERA
FESTIVAL

LOREM IPSUM
CONCEPTAM NE EAIIM
nimus
THE ISTANBUL
CONTEMPORARY
OPERA
FESTIVAL

nimus
contemporary opera festival

TOPKAPI PALACE
01.09.2011 - 15.09.2011
DIE
ZAUBERFLÖTE
nimus
contemporary opera festival

TOPKAPI PALACE
01.09.2011 - 15.09.2011
DIE
ZAUBERFLÖTE
nimus
contemporary opera festival

FESTIVAL PROGRAMME
PALACE MAP

NIMH
The Nimus Opera Magazine
FOCUS ON OPERA

CATALOGUE 2011
DIE ZAUBERFLÖTE
nimus

CATALOGUE 2011

DIE ZAUBERFLÖTE
MOZART
01/15 . 09 . 2011
TOPKAPI PALACE
Cum. 11/09/2011 saat 21.00
Galeri "vivaldi" - yer 3
TUM 400,00 tr
nimus

Client_Schism
Design Firm_b2s6
Creative Director_Alexander Pomidor
Designer_Alexander Pomidor
Country_Russia

Schism is a music festival. It is tailored for the widest audience: from rock-music fans and extreme sportsmen, to the fans of e-sport and yoga. This flexible and expressive logo provides the whole market with the game temperament.

The logo is divided into separate elements, differentiated and metamorphosed, but it is always recognizable — on-screen applications, souvenirs, advertising, navigation signage and documents.

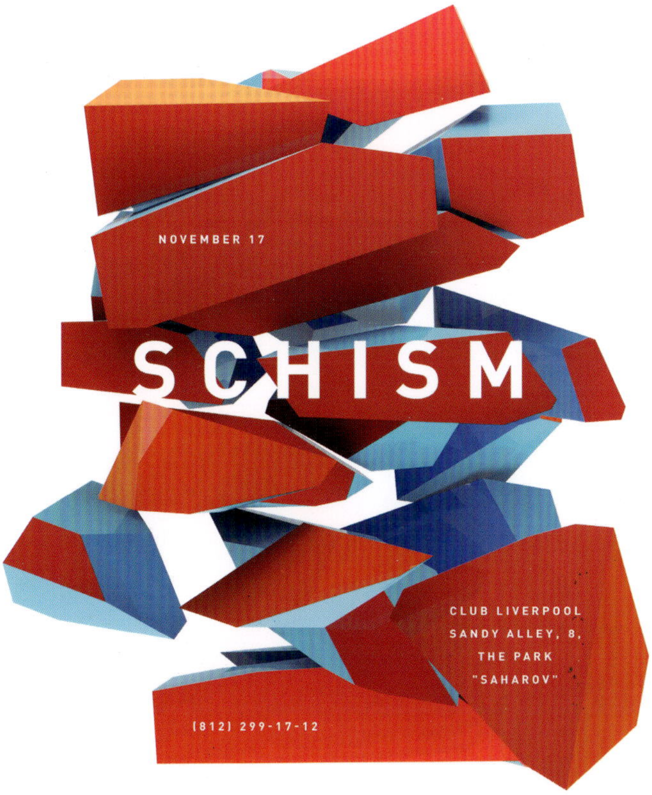
NOVEMBER 17
SCHISM
CLUB LIVERPOOL
SANDY ALLEY, 8,
THE PARK
"SAHAROV"
(812) 299-17-12

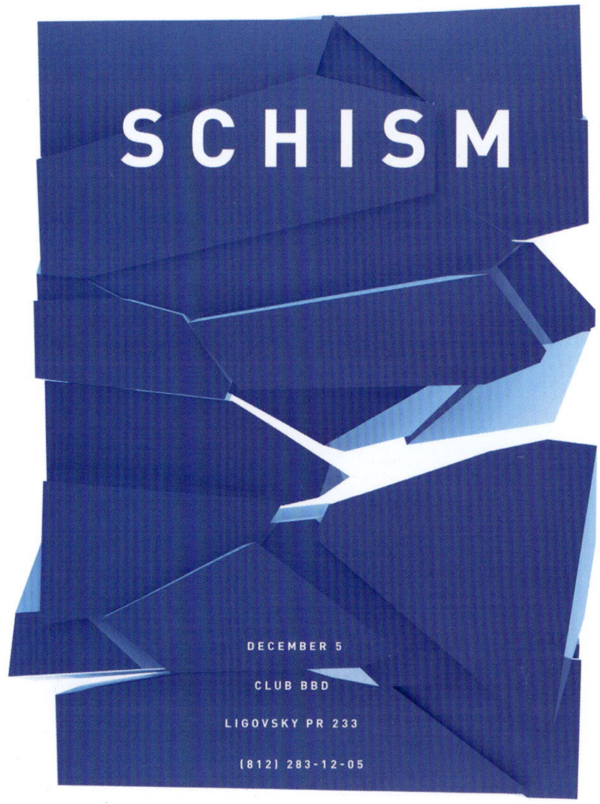
SCHISM
DECEMBER 5
CLUB BBD
LIGOVSKY PR 233
(812) 283-12-05

SCHISM
MUSIC FESTIVAL

SCHISM
MUSIC FESTIVAL

SPAIN ARTS & CULTURE

Client_ Embassy of Spain, Washington
Design Firm_ Toormix
Creative Directors_ Oriol Armengou, Ferran Mitjans
Designer_ Gerard Marin
Country_ Spain

Spain Arts & Culture is a new brand born to reflect all the expressions of Spain, and to convey the cultural variety of the country. Spain is a combination of living cultures. It is a stone that is continuously shaped and polished in different ways by the constant influences and the many creators that form it. An evolving stone is the new symbol that moves, almost alive, and that evolves constantly and shows new expressions with each step it takes.

ARCHITECTURE/
DESIGN/FILM/FOOD/
HERITAGE/KIDS/
LITERATURE/
PERFORMING ARTS/
SKETCHING THE
FUTURE/URBAN
CULTURE/
VISUAL ARTS/
From Spain

2011

NEW YORK
CONCRETE IMPROVISATIONS
ARTBUS
ANTÓN CABALEIRO
ELECTRICA
PEN WORLD VOICES
JAUME PLENSA
ABOUT FACE
CREA+S

A GEM
TO BE
DISCO-
VERED

SPAIN
arts &
culture
MEET
THE LATEST
MUSIC
& CULTURAL
TRENDS
From Spain
www.spainculture.us
MUSIC/ARCHITECTURE/DESIGN/
FILM/FOOD/HERITAGE/KIDS/
LITERATURE/PERFORMING ARTS/
SKETCHING THE FUTURE/URBAN
CULTURES/VISUAL ARTS
Also follow us on:
Facebook.com/SpainArtsCulture
@SpainCultureUSA

SPAIN
arts &
culture
VISUAL ARTS/
WASHINGTON D.C.
MARE-
MAGNUM
BY
JORDI
SOCÍAS
A visual journey through the last four decades in Spain and Europe guided by an icon of photographic journalism.
November 9 – February 11
Mexican Cultural Institute
2829 16th Street N.W.
www.spainculture.us
GOBIERNO DE ESPAÑA
AC/E
ACCIÓN CULTURAL ESPAÑOLA
SPAIN/USA/
Foundation/
LUNWERG

TEATRO CIRCO PRICE

Client_ Teatro Circo Price
Design Firm_ Toormix
Creative Directors_ Oriol Armengou, Ferran Mitjans
Designer_ Gerard Marin
Country_ Spain

The studio developed this new graphic project for Teatro Circo Price, a theatre and former circus in Madrid. As the programming and public opening changed, it became necessary to change the identity. The project therefore is the culmination of this new philosophy. The new image revolves around the idea of the interior space, a building with a 360-degree shape and the circles, which create its format.

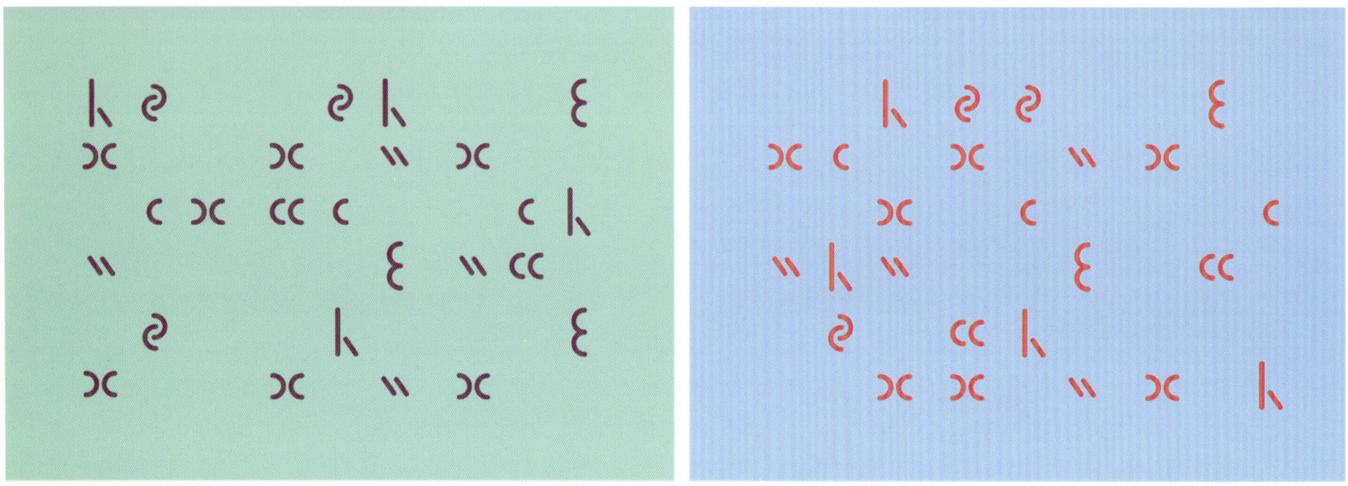

TEATRO CIRCO
PRICE
MADRID
ROMANèS
CIRQUE
TZIGANE
9
25

TEATRO CIRCO
PRICE
MADRID
"UN ESPECTÁCULO
AÉREO DE DANZA
Y MÚSICA BRUTAL"
FORZA
BRUTA
9
25

TEATRO CIRCO
PRICE
MADRID
FESTIVAL CIRCOS
PEQUEñO
FORMATO
17
27
LES COLPORTEURS
THEATRE D'UN JOUR
EIA
7 DOIGTS DE LA MAIN

TEATRO CIRCO
PRICE
MADRID
CNAC
"THIS IS THE END"
30
3

TEATRO CIRCO
PRICE
MADRID
CIRCA
9
25
"VUELVE
EL GRAN ÉXITO
DEL 2011"

TEATRO CIRCO
PRICE
MADRID
AL FILO
2012
9
25

EA2
ABCDEFGHIJKL
MNOPQRSTUVWXYZ
0123456789
Gravur
FESTIVAL
CIRCOS

CRECE
v.20.11
DEL
21
SEPTIEMBRE
AL
30
SEPTIEMBRE
CREACIóN DE CIRCO
CONTEMPORáNEO

TEATRO CIRCO
PRICE
MADRID

THE FLOATING EYE

Client_The Sydney Pavilion, Shanghai Biennale 2012
Design Firm_RE
Creative Director_Jason Little
Designers_Alexis Waller, Erin Hoffman, Jason Little, Mick Boston, Sam Byrnes, Sam Mcguinness
Country_Australia

"The Floating Eye" was the curatorial theme of the Sydney Pavilion in the Shanghai Biennale, the largest international art event in mainland China. The challenge was to convey the theme of varied perspectives of the city's transforming reality observed through its demographics, geography, history, politics, and society. Its identity should create standout recognition amongst hundreds of pavilions, whilst appealing to an international audience. Designers built a visual language of symbols, combined and intertwined through a shifting graphic lens interpretation that avoided the need for wordy articulation.

THE FLOATING EYE
东张西望
SYDNEY PAVILION

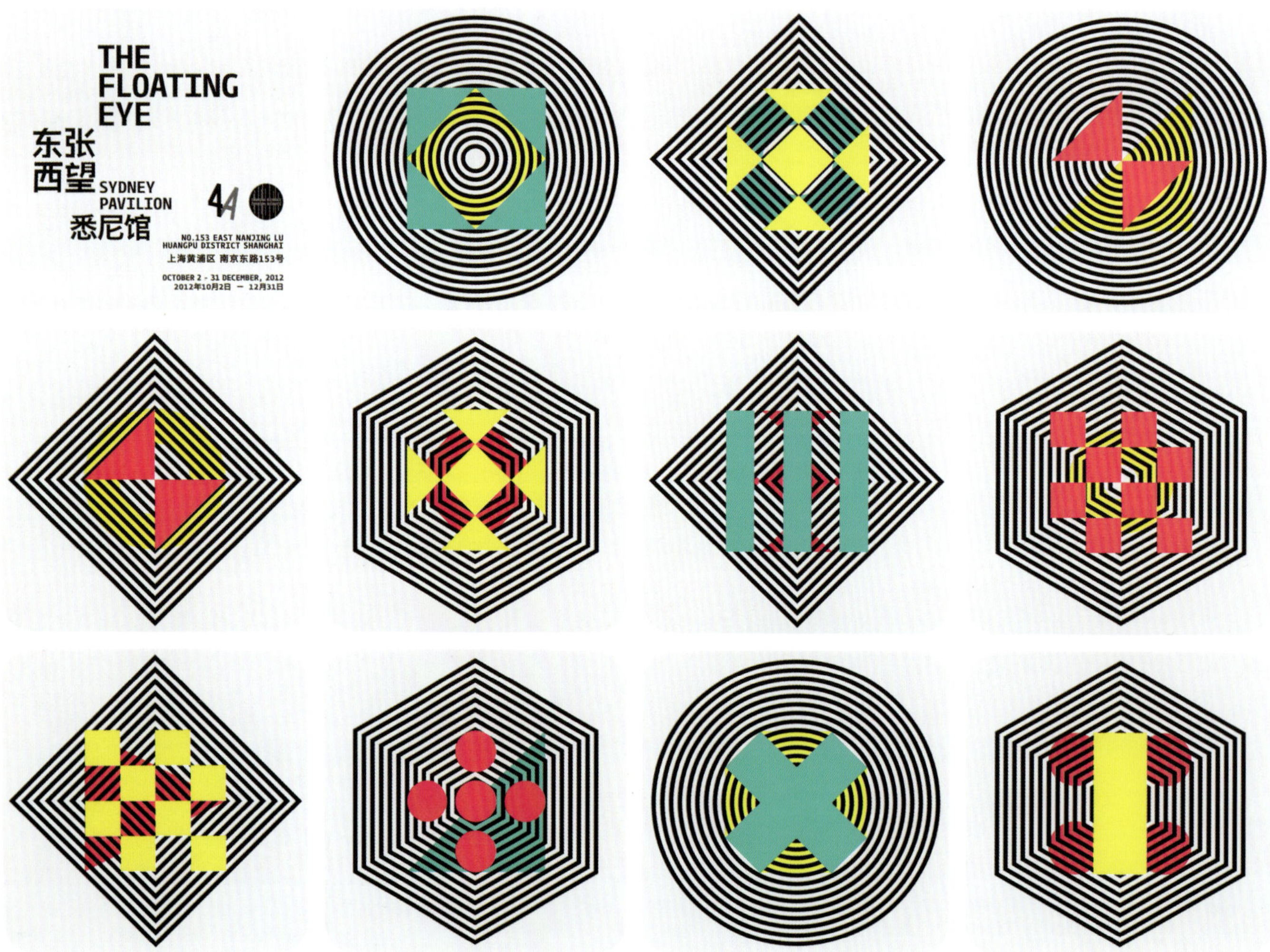

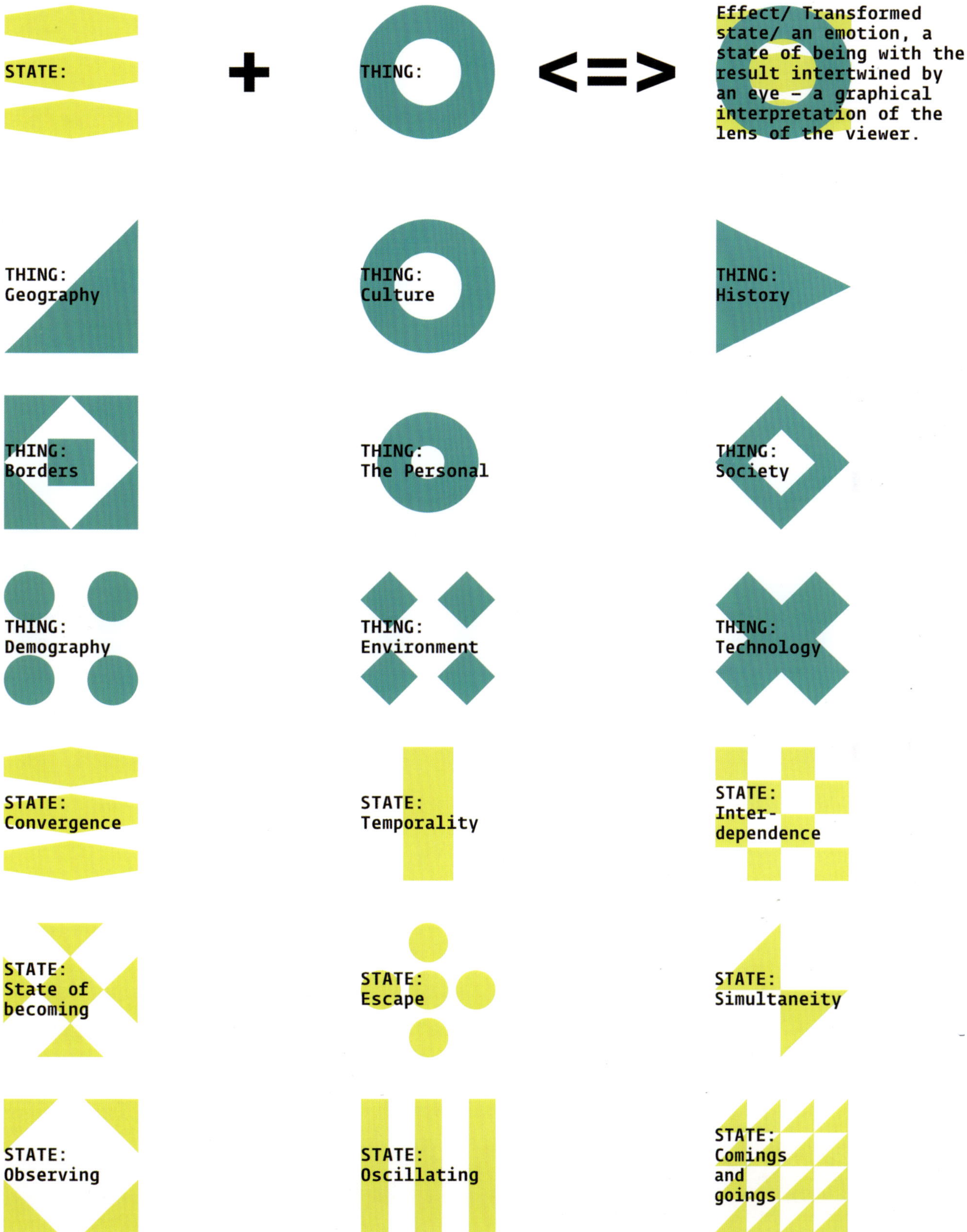
STATE:
+
THING:
<=>
Effect/ Transformed state/ an emotion, a state of being with the result intertwined by an eye – a graphical interpretation of the lens of the viewer.
THING: Geography
THING: Culture
THING: History
THING: Borders
THING: The Personal
THING: Society
THING: Demography
THING: Environment
THING: Technology
STATE: Convergence
STATE: Temporality
STATE: Inter-dependence
STATE: State of becoming
STATE: Escape
STATE: Simultaneity
STATE: Observing
STATE: Oscillating
STATE: Comings and goings

东张西望
THE
FLOATING
EYE
悉尼馆
上海黄浦区南京东路153号
2012年10月2日 - 12月31日
THE FLOATING EYE
东张西望
SYDNEY PAVILION

东张西望
THE
FLOATING
EYE
悉尼馆
上海黄浦区南京东路153号
2012年10月2日 - 12月31日
THE FLOATING EYE
东张西望
SYDNEY PAVILION

THE FLOATING EYE
东张西望
SYDNEY PAVILION
NO.153 EAST NANJING LU, HUANGPU DISTRICT, SHANGHAI
OCTOBER 2 - 31 DECEMBER, 2012
东张西望
THE
FLOATING
EYE
悉尼馆

东张西望
THE
FLOATING
EYE
悉尼馆
上海黄浦区南京东路153号
2012年10月2日 - 12月31日
THE FLOATING EYE
东张西望
SYDNEY PAVILION

东张西望
THE
FLOAT
EYE
黄浦区南京东路153号
2012年10月2日 - 12月31日

THE FLOATING EYE
东张西望
SYDNEY PAVILION
悉尼馆
NO.153 EAST NANJING LU HUANGPU DISTRICT SHANGHAI
上海黄浦区 南京东路153号
OCTOBER 2-21 DECEMBER, 2012
HOME
ABOUT | 关于
ARTISTS | 艺术家
RESOURCES | 资源
东张西望
SYDNEY PAVILION
CENTRE FOR CONTEMPORARY ASIAN ART
TWITTER UPDATES
PHOTO GALLERY

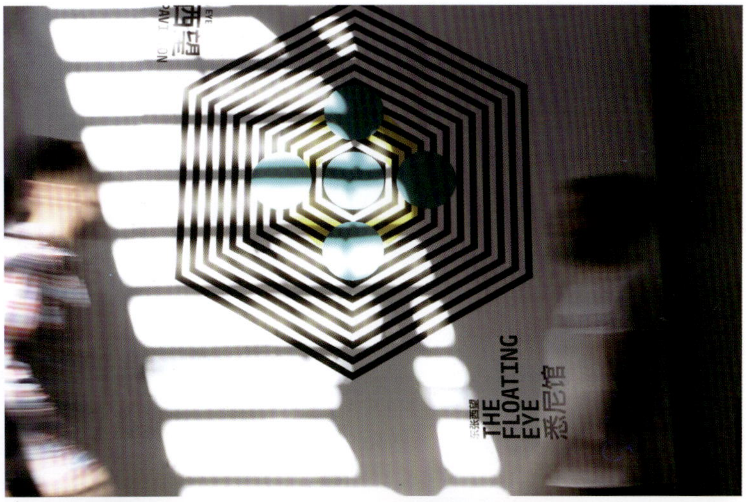
东张西望
THE FLOATING EYE
悉尼馆

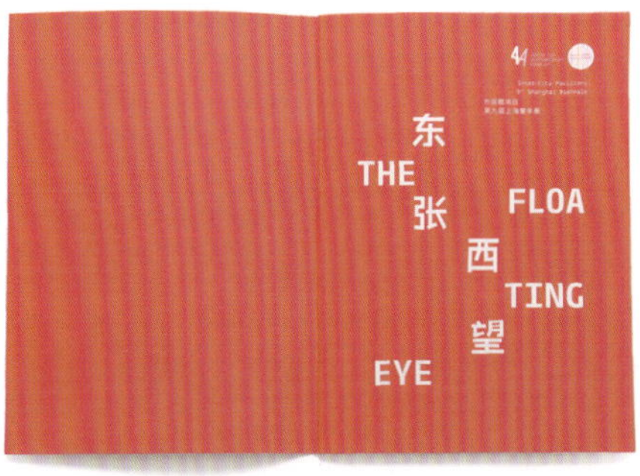
东
THE
张
FLOA
西
TING
望
EYE

BABABA INTERNATIONAL
国际BABABA

沈少民
SHEN SHAOMIN

LIST OF WORKS
作品列表

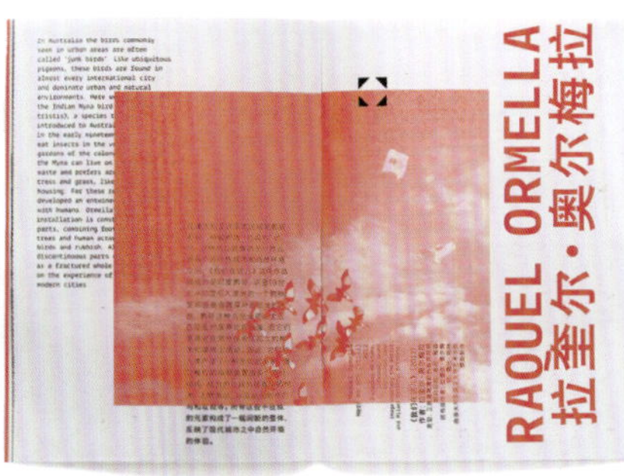
RAQUEL ORMELLA
拉奎尔·奥尔梅拉

KHALED SABSABI
卡莱德·萨布萨比

VANCOUVER ABSTRACT MUSEUM

Client_ Personal Work
Creative Director_ Luis Francisco
Designer_ Luis Francisco
Country_ Brazil

This is a school project for a new museum in Vancouver. The solution was a dynamic identity, based on Rorschach tests, that adapts to the featured event or artist, expressing their personality. A custom symbol set, and later an algorithm, were created with which users could input the artist or event name and have a logo shape based upon the selection. Thus, the brand can constantly renew itself and have infinite graphic possibilities for communication pieces, and even for the museum's souvenirs.

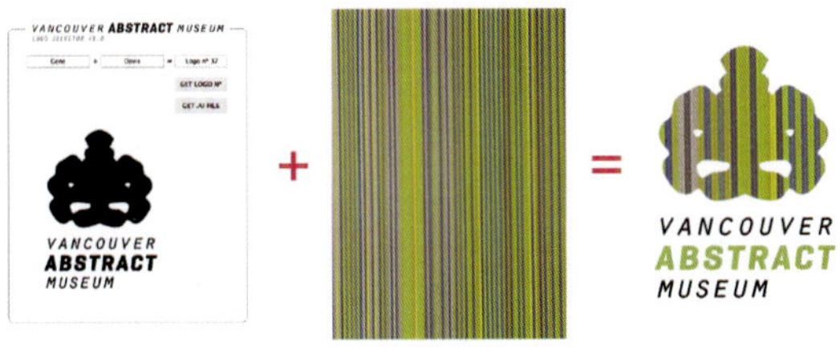
VANCOUVER ABSTRACT MUSEUM
+
=
VANCOUVER
ABSTRACT
MUSEUM

VANCOUVER ABSTRACT MUSEUM
+
=
VANCOUVER
ABSTRACT
MUSEUM

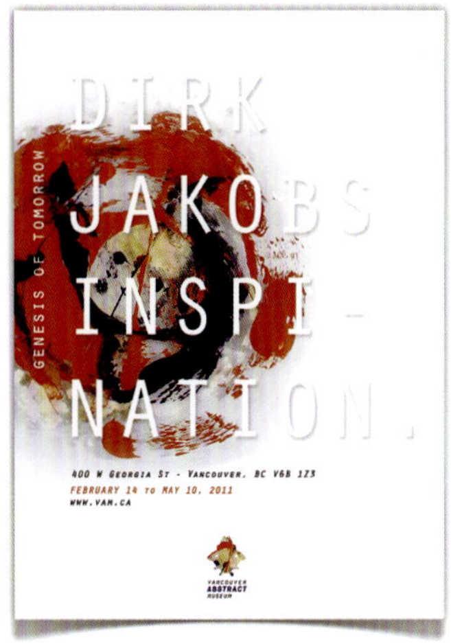
DIRK
JAKOBS
INSPI-
NATION.
GENESIS OF TOMORROW
400 W GEORGIA ST - VANCOUVER, BC V6B 1Z3
FEBRUARY 14 TO MAY 10, 2011
WWW.VAM.CA

With Compliments

VANCOUVER ABSTRACT MUSEUM

VANCOUVER
ABSTRACT
MUSEUM

VANCOUVER ABSTRACT MUSEUM
VANCOUVER
ABSTRACT
MUSEUM
COUTINHO
MARIA
KENNEDY

YOUNG LIONS ITALY 2013

Client_ Giovani Leoni
Creative Directors_ Lumen Bigott, Alessandro Lapetina
Designer_ Lumen Bigott
Country_ Italy

Giovani Leoni "Young Lions" is a competition for young designers and copywriters to create projects freely. This identity was created for the competition itself. It was inspired by the element that differentiates a young lion from an older one, its mane. In nature, the mane grows larger and darker with the lion's age. The Young Lions competition represents an opportunity for talented designers to get more experience and let their metaphorical mane grow larger. Each one of the four colors represents a category of the competition.

GIOVANI LEONI
GIOVANI LEONI

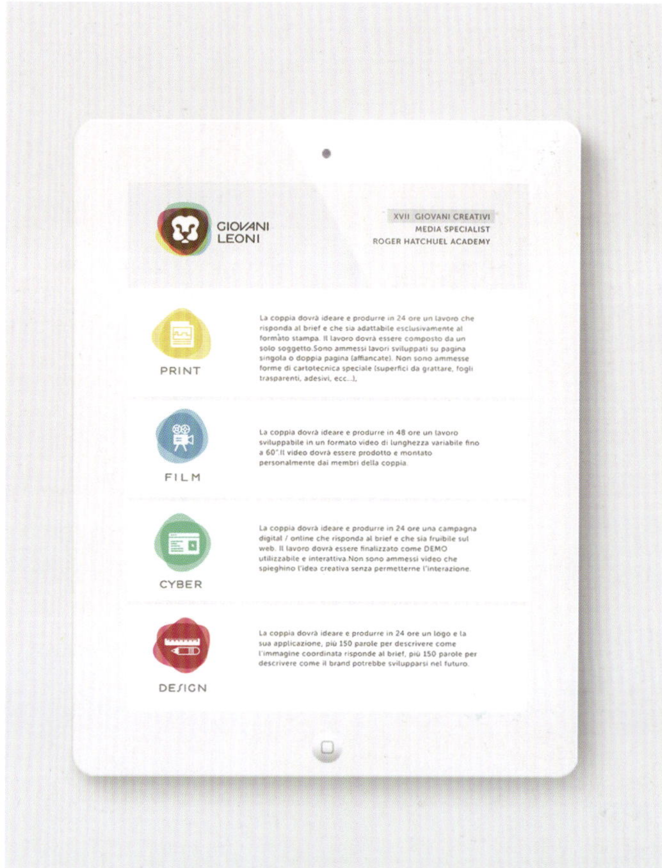
GIOVANI LEONI
XVII GIOVANI CREATIVI
MEDIA SPECIALIST
ROGER HATCHUEL ACADEMY
PRINT
La coppia dovrà ideare e produrre in 24 ore un lavoro che risponda al brief e che sia adattabile esclusivamente al formato stampa. Il lavoro dovrà essere composto da un solo soggetto.Sono ammessi lavori sviluppati su pagina singola o doppia pagina (affiancate). Non sono ammesse forme di cartotecnica speciale (superfici da grattare, fogli trasparenti, adesivi, ecc...),
FILM
La coppia dovrà ideare e produrre in 48 ore un lavoro sviluppabile in un formato video di lunghezza variabile fino a 60".Il video dovrà essere prodotto e montato personalmente dai membri della coppia.
CYBER
La coppia dovrà ideare e produrre in 24 ore una campagna digital / online che risponda al brief e che sia fruibile sul web. Il lavoro dovrà essere finalizzato come DEMO utilizzabile e interattiva.Non sono ammessi video che spieghino l'idea creativa senza permetterne l'interazione.
DESIGN
La coppia dovrà ideare e produrre in 24 ore un logo e la sua applicazione, più 150 parole per descrivere come l'immagine coordinata risponde al brief, più 150 parole per descrivere come il brand potrebbe svilupparsi nel futuro.

GIOVANI LEONI
Sipra e ADCI sono lieti di invitare tutti i leoni di primo e secondo pelo alla premiazione finale che si terrà in Design Library a Milano in data 14 aprile, 2013 dalle 8.30 PM.
gettyimages
www.giovanileoni.it

GIOVANI LEONI

MEDIA

FILM & TELEVISION

INTERNET

CHANNEL 4

Client_ Channel 4 Television
Design Firm_ Rudd Studio
Creative Director_ Matthew Rudd
Designers_ Matthew Rudd, Oscar Gonzalez, Sylvie Minois
Country_UK

The object of this rebranding was to make the iconic logo center-stage again. Designers wanted to show Channel 4 as confident and irreverent, so they made the logo very big. It is always moving and never sits on a grid. The logo is viewed in a cubist way — from multiple angles, creating an intriguing atmosphere.

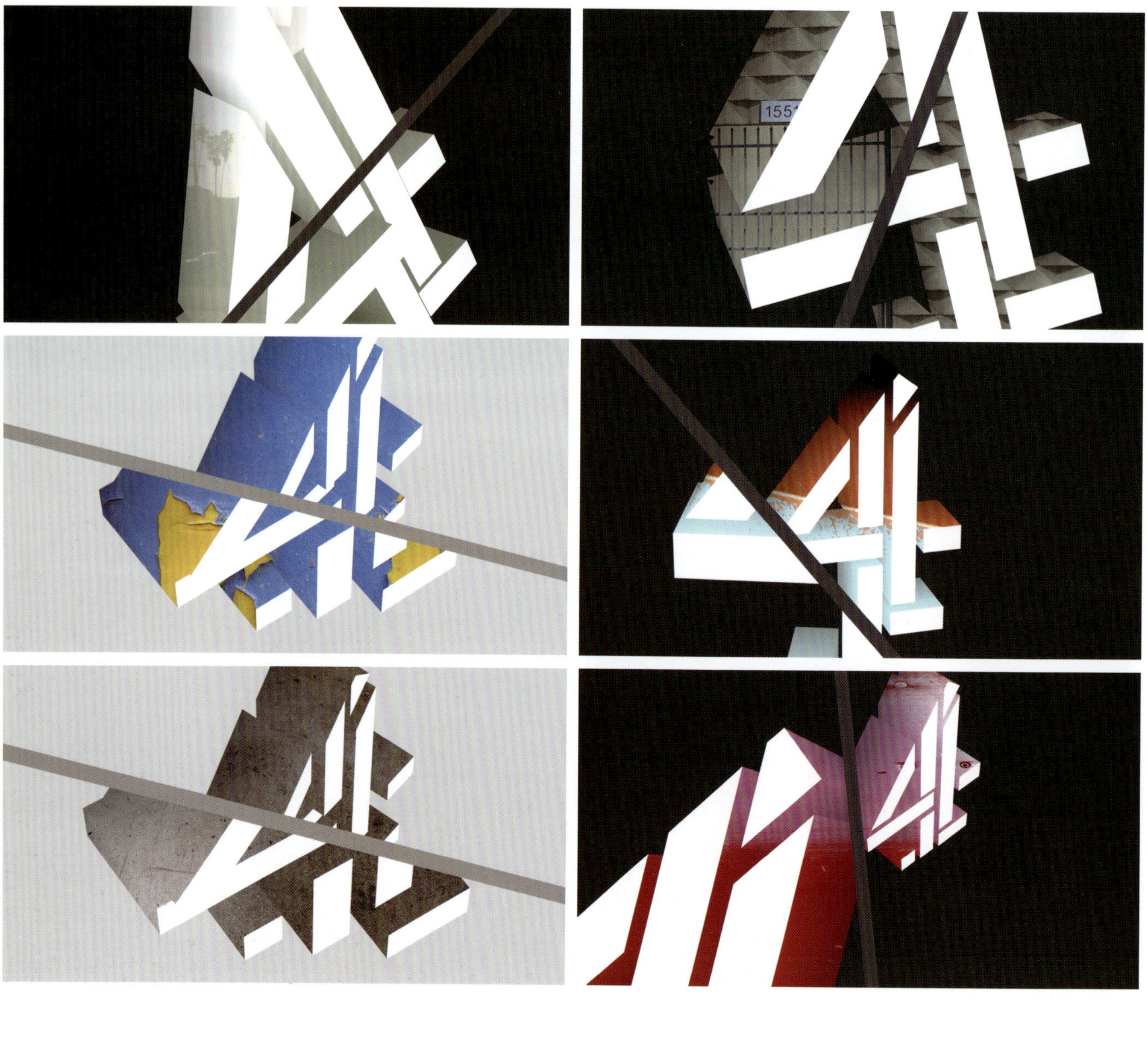

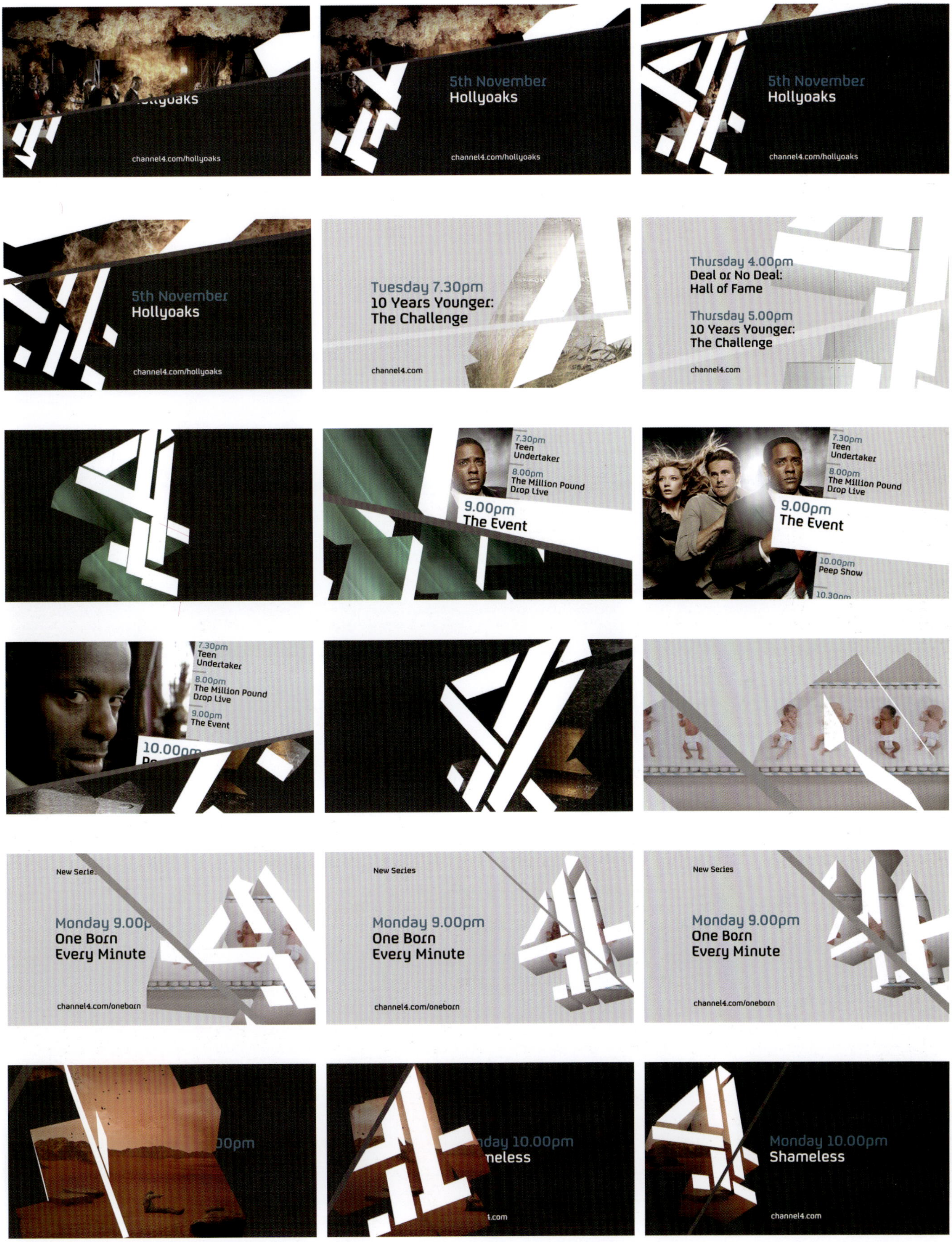

channel4.com/hollyoaks
5th November
Hollyoaks
channel4.com/hollyoaks
5th November
Hollyoaks
channel4.com/hollyoaks
5th November
Hollyoaks
channel4.com/hollyoaks
Tuesday 7.30pm
10 Years Younger:
The Challenge
channel4.com
Thursday 4.00pm
Deal or No Deal:
Hall of Fame
Thursday 5.00pm
10 Years Younger:
The Challenge
channel4.com
7.30pm
Teen
Undertaker
8.00pm
The Million Pound
Drop Live
9.00pm
The Event
7.30pm
Teen
Undertaker
8.00pm
The Million Pound
Drop Live
9.00pm
The Event
10.00pm
Peep Show
7.30pm
Teen
Undertaker
8.00pm
The Million Pound
Drop Live
9.00pm
The Event
New Series
One Born
Every Minute
channel4.com/oneborn
New Series
Monday 9.00pm
One Born
Every Minute
channel4.com/oneborn
New Series
Monday 9.00pm
One Born
Every Minute
channel4.com/oneborn
Monday 10.00pm
Shameless
channel4.com

THE JUICE AGENCY

Client_ The Juice Agency
Design Firm_ Art & Science
Creative Director_ Kirk Clyne
Designer_ Jovan Rocanov
Country_ Canada

Inspired by natural and organic processes, the visual identity of The Juice Agency centers on a "droplet" of juice. This core logo mark forms the basis for all visual manifestations of the brand. This mark was designed to allow the agency to tailor its message for various contexts while remaining true to the brand. The business cards feature eight different icons on the back, like the "social bee" or the "strategic dart." This variety allows people to choose the card they like best, ensuring some personal affinity with the brand.

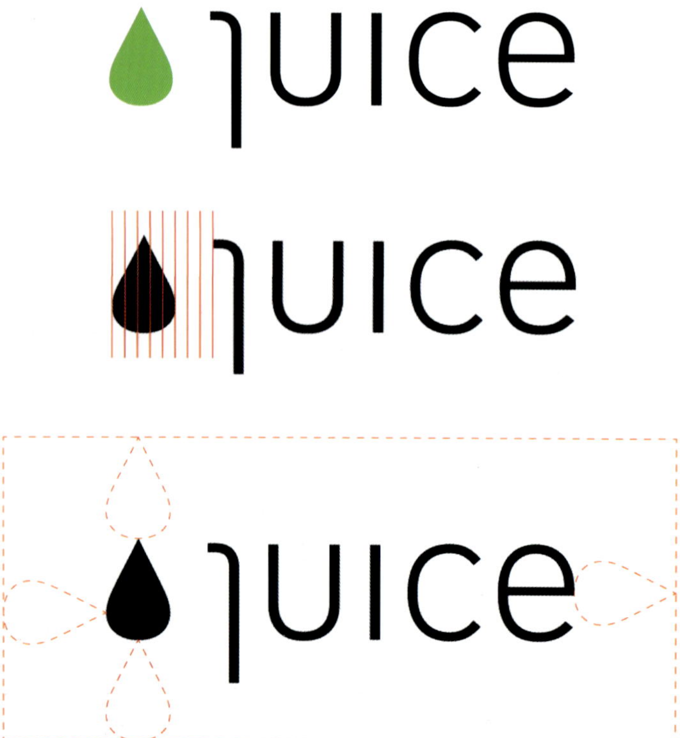

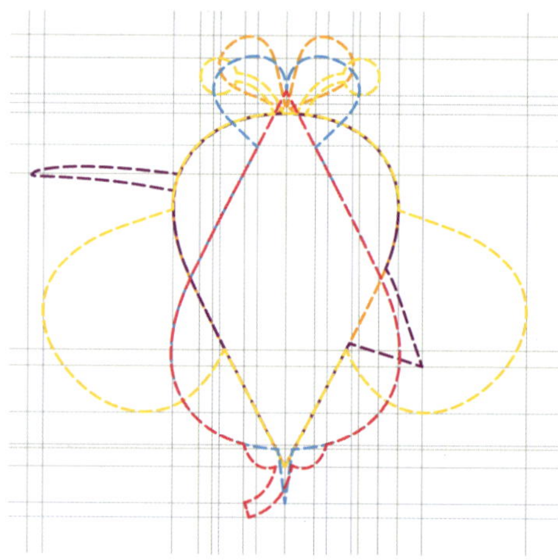

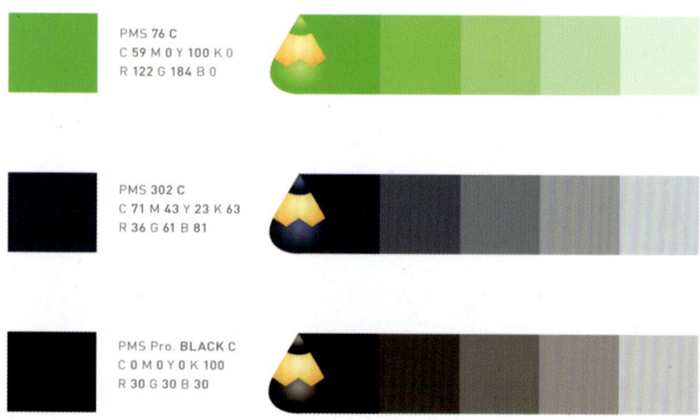

thejuiceagency.ca
thejuiceagency.ca
thejuiceagency.ca
thejuiceagency.ca

CARAT

Client_ Aegis Group
Design Firm_ North
Country_ Worldwide

Carat is the world's leading independent media planning and buying agency, comprising of more than 5,000 people in 70 countries worldwide. A dynamic, animated identity was created to reflect the ever-changing world of global media. The vibrant color spectrum further reinforced the fluid and transformative nature of the business.

Reasons to Believe
Why we can achieve our vision.
4

Media choices are multiplying exponentially.
Consumers are in control.
They demand content whenever and wherever they want it.

Viewers sat back and watched the ads.
Mass media advertising was king.
But times have changed.

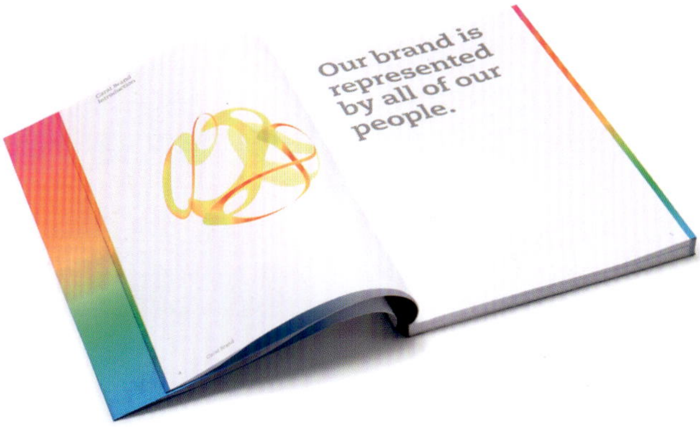
Our brand is represented by all of our people.

Design examples
Presentations & reception areas
Collaborate
Transforming Communications
Change
92
Carat Identity
Collaborate
Transformation
Transforming Communications

CRYSTALET

Client_ Crystalet
Design Firm_ b2s6
Creative Director_ Alexander Pomidor
Designer_ Alexander Pomidor
Country_ Russia

Crystalet is a provider of digital television. The studio created a dynamic form of the logo, which displays the diversity of the company's content. Crystalet's identification system opens unlimited potential for creation — any image can be projected onto the form of the logo.

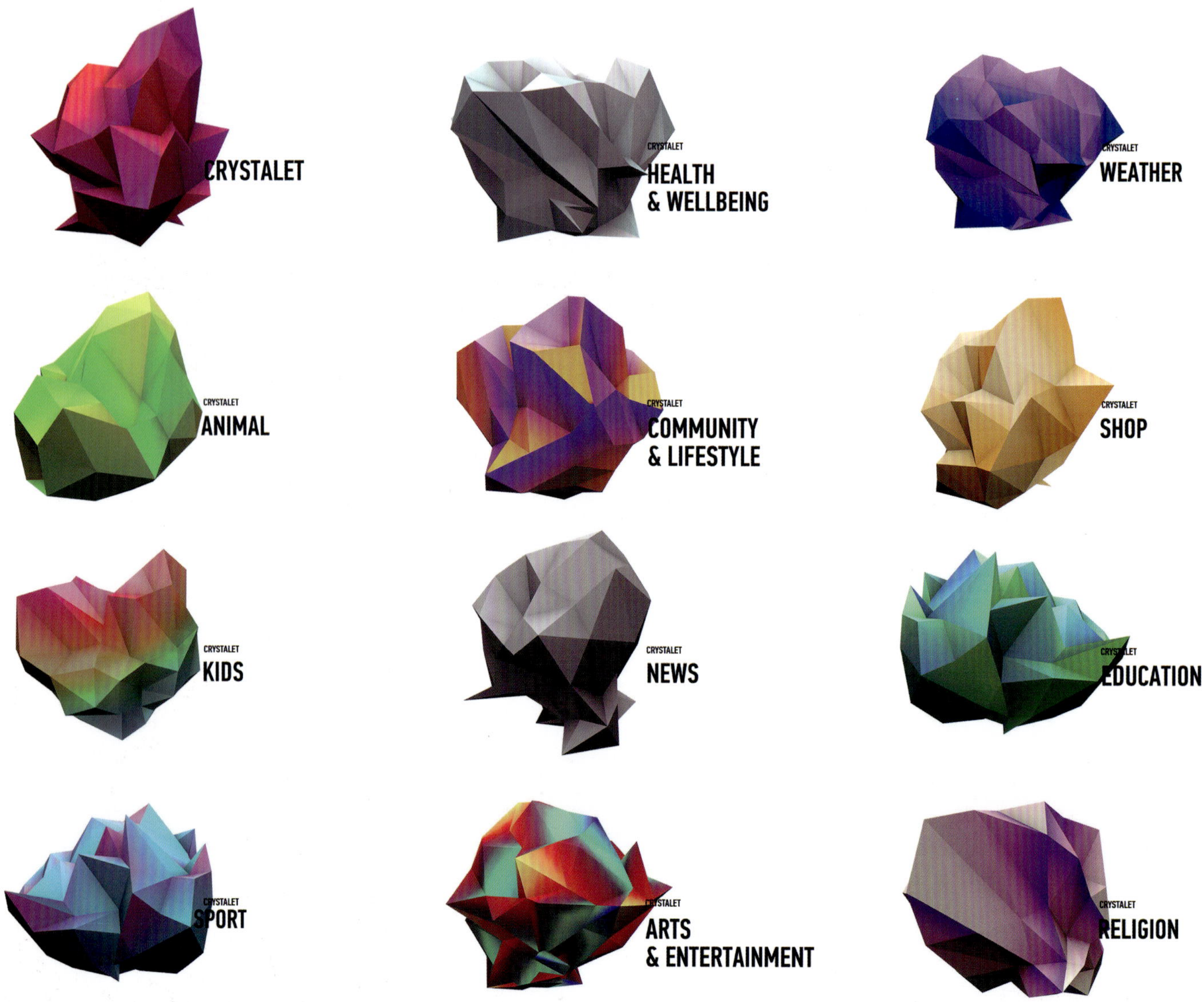

EUGÈNE DELACROIX

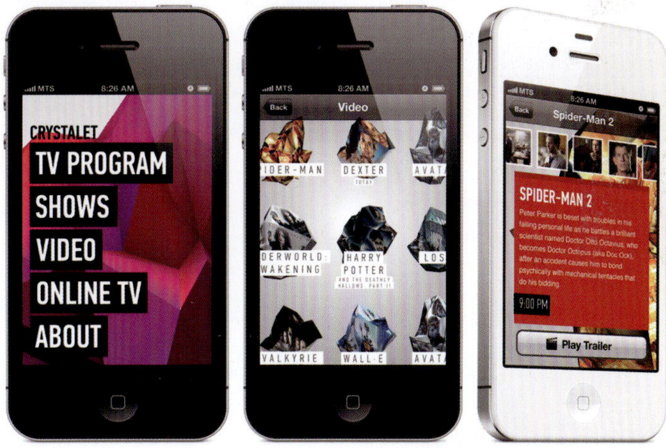
CRYSTALET
TV PROGRAM
SHOWS
VIDEO
ONLINE TV
ABOUT
Video
DEXTER
HARRY POTTER
SPIDER-MAN 2
Play Trailer

TV PROGRAM
SHOWS
VIDEO
ONLINE TV
ABOUT
CRYSTALET
SPIDER-MAN 2
9:00 PM
TOMORROW
SHREK
4:30 PM
VALKYRIE
9:30 PM
Tomorrow

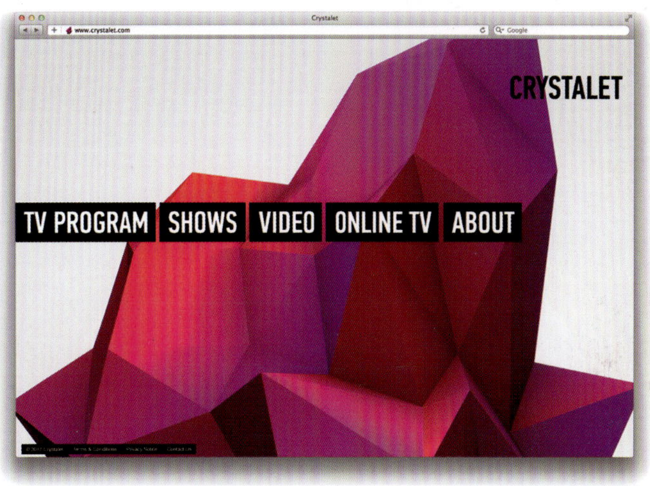
CRYSTALET
TV PROGRAM
SHOWS
VIDEO
ONLINE TV
ABOUT

GUSTO VIDEO PRODUCTION

Client_ Gusto
Design Firm_ Another Day
Creative Director_ Yorick de Vries
Designer_ Yorick de Vries
Country_ Netherlands

Gusto is a young talented and energetic video production company. Another Day created the new visual dynamic world of Gusto. The logo is based on the frames of a video. In editing a movie, there can be magical occurrences between the frames. The logo is divided into separate frames. Among these frames is space for playful elements; the logo continues to grow in the visual language through all the design's elements.

GUSTO
VIDEO PRODUCTIES
THIS! IT'S
BEAUTIFUL!

GUSTO PRODUCTIES
GUSTO PRODUCTIES
GUSTO PRODUCTIES
GUSTO PRODUCTIES

SELL ICE
WATER
IN THE

THIS
ISN'T REAL,
THIS
ISN'T REAL,
THIS
RICHARD
PARKER,
COME
OUT YOU
HAVE
TO SEE
THIS! IT'S
WHAT
A DAY
FELT LIKE I
COULDN'T
SELL ICE
WATER
IN THE

GUSTO
VIDEO PRODUCTIES
GUSTO
VIDEO PRODUCTIES
GUSTO
VIDEO PRODUCTIES
GUSTO
VIDEO PRODUCTIES

MY NAME IS FILMS

Client_ My Name Is Films
Creative Director_ Rafael Bessa
Designer_ Rafael Bessa
Country_ Brazil

My Name Is Films is a film production company based in Brazil. The main idea of this branding was to present the plurality of audiovisual work using the tricky company name. The complement of the"My name is" sentence is anything the brand can deliver through its rich visual projects. This concept was extended to all the identities, making the dynamic possibilities present in business card, website and other materials.

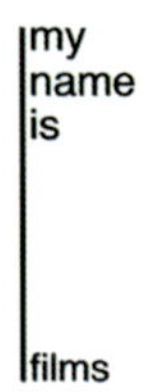

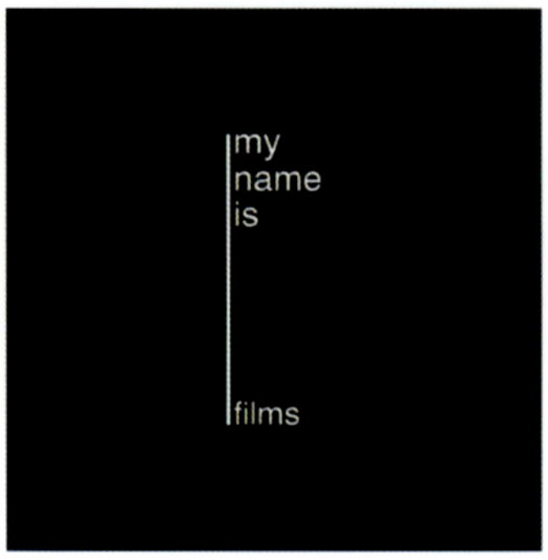

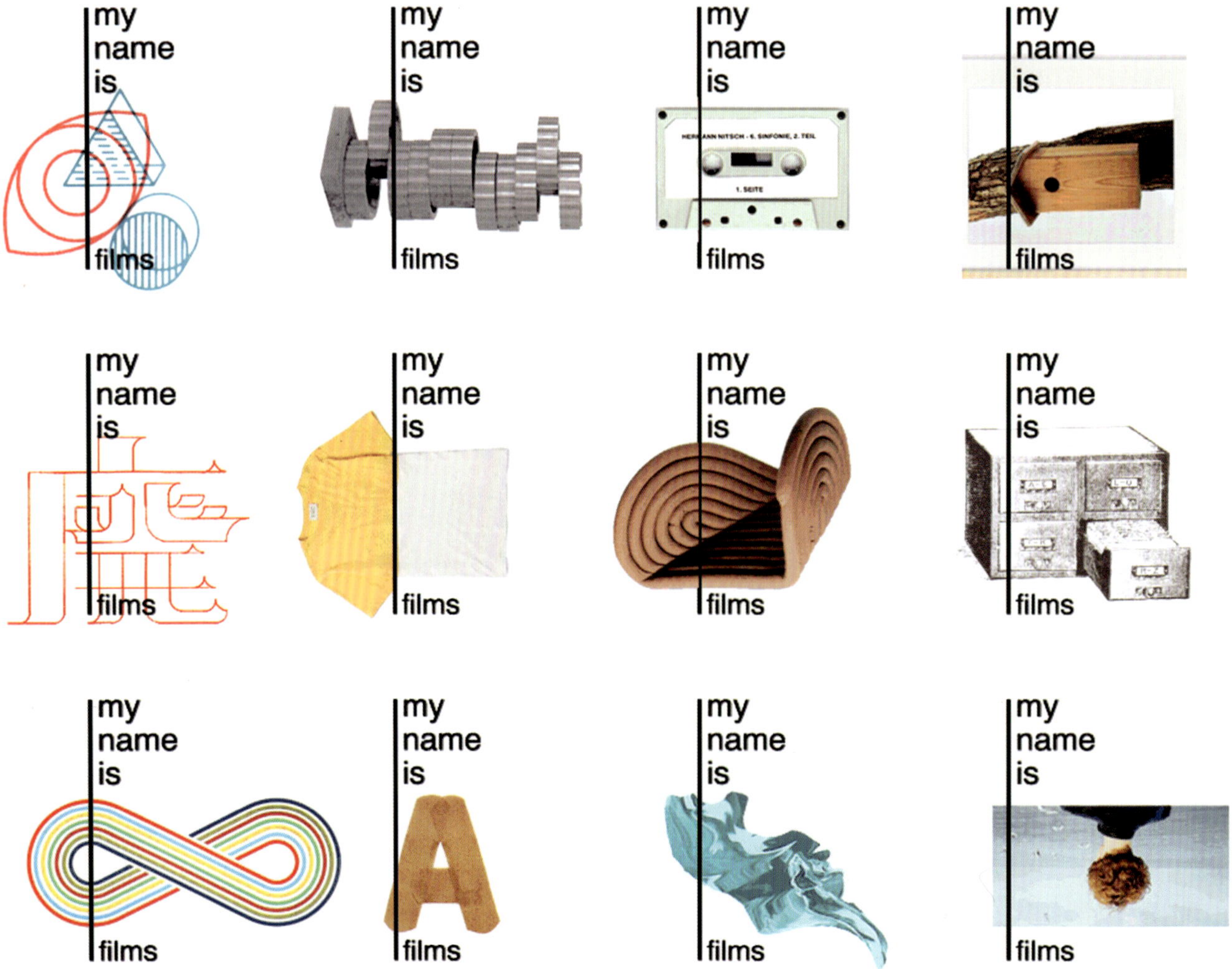

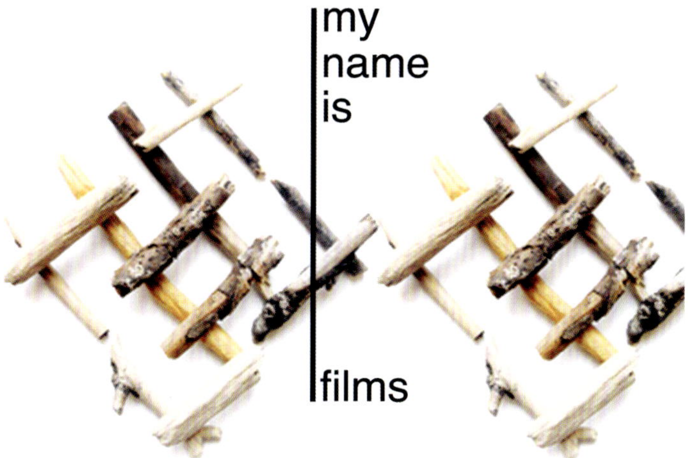
my
name
is
films

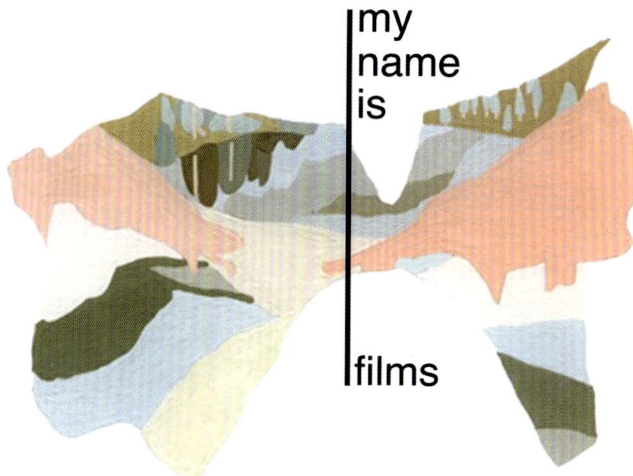
my
name
is
films

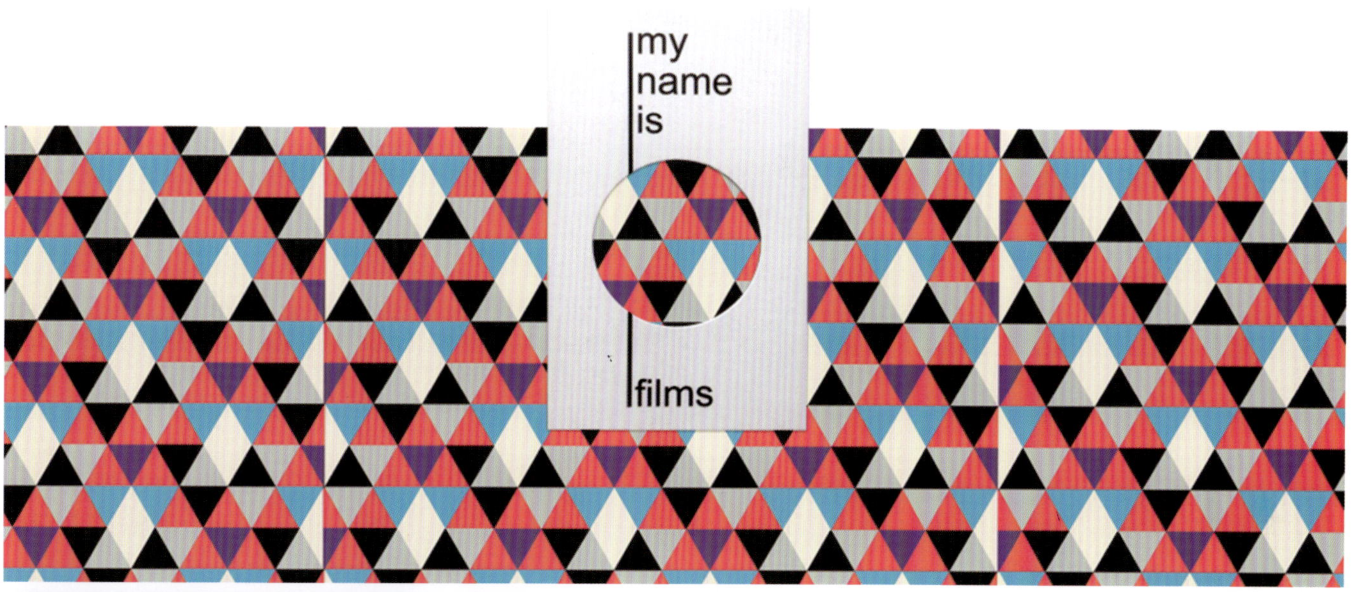
my
name
is
films

my
name
is
films

my
name
is
films

my
name
is
films

STYRIA DIGITAL

Client_Styria Media Group
Design Firm_Moodley Brand Identity
Creative Director_Mike Fuisz
Designer_Kurt Glänzer
Country_Austria

The new corporate design of Styria Digital Holding states clearly how much fun it is to go digital — if it is well done: Friendly colors, nice icons and lots of energy and feeling must be included. The different colors and forms reflect the wide portfolio of the umbrella brand and serve as a differentiation. They are also used for the logo that — depending on the business segment — slightly diverges in form and color.

sd styria digital

Hey, we are
styria digital
styria digital holding gmbh
schönaugasse 64, 8010 Graz
styria-digital.com
sd
styria digital

elena hartner
sd
styria digital
transactions
& marketplaces

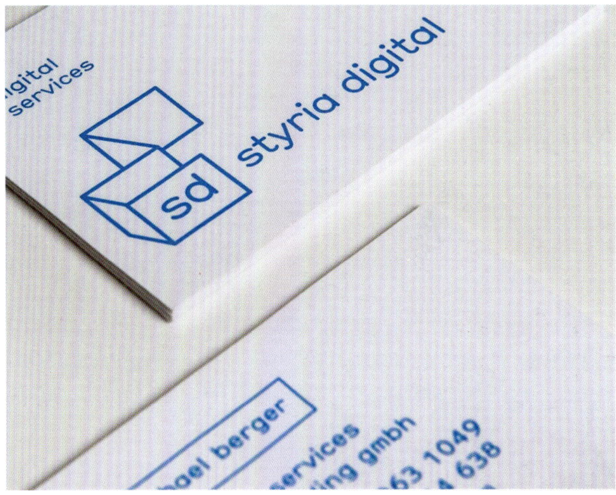
sd
styria digital

we are
styria digital
sd
styria digital
sd
styria digital
sd
styria digital

sd
styria digital
dr. christian buchs

TESS MANAGEMENT

Client_ Tess Management
Design Firm_ Mind Design
Country_UK

This identity was created for a London-based model agency. Tess represents well-established names such as Naomi Campbell and Erin O'Connor from the UK. The identity uses several logo variations based on a modular system of Art Deco-inspired elements. The same elements are being used for frames (which overlap images of the models) on various printed applications and on the website. The design was created in collaboration with Simon Egli from Zurich.

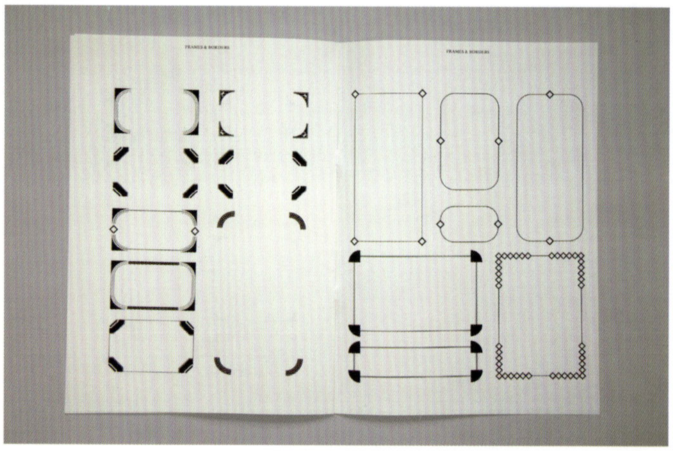

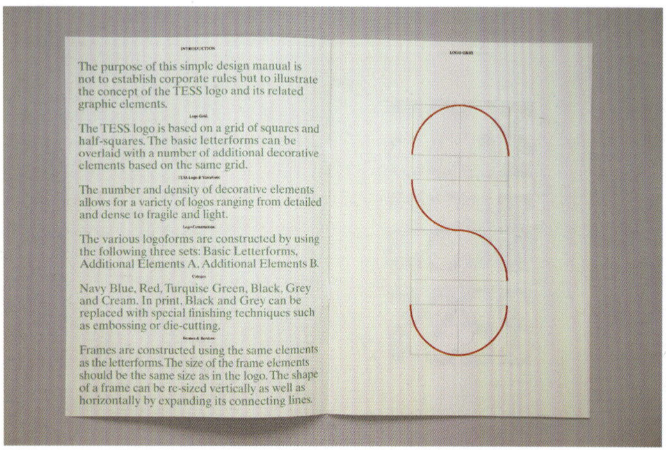

TESS

TESS Management
4TH Floor, 9–10 Market Place
London W1W 8AQ
T +44 (0)20 7557 7100
F +44 (0)20 7557 7101
info@tessmanagement.com
www.tessmanagement.com

TESS

TESS
Logo & Graphic Elements

TESS
TESS Management
info@tessmanagement.com • www.tessmanagement.com

TESS
IS
MORE

NAOMI CAMPBELL
TESS

SYN

Client_ Syn K.K.
Design Firm_ North
Country_ Japan

Syn is a creative agency comprising of four divisions: Syn Create, Songs, Studios and Entertainment. Vibrant colors were chosen to represent each of these disciplines and incorporated into the architecture, which was created by the renowned designer Marc Newson. Signage was also developed to reflect both the interior design and the building's footprint.

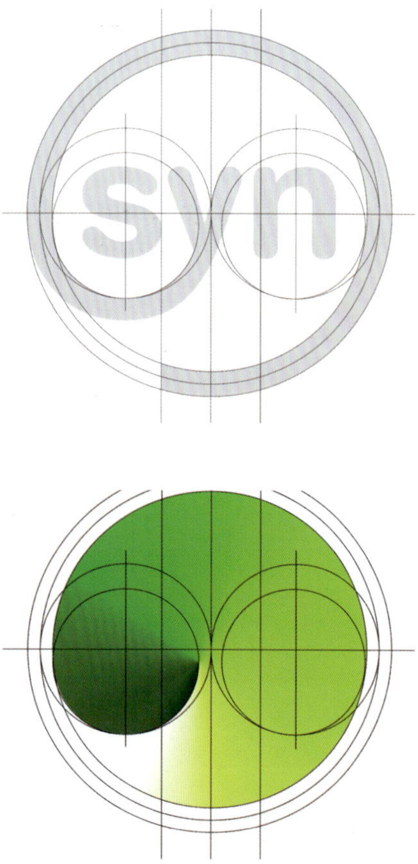

Syn Songs Yellow
Pantone 109 / RGB 255/222/002

Syn Studios Green
Pantone 375 / RGB 119/218/033

Syn Entertainment Blue
Pantone 306 / RGB 000/185/229

Syn Create Purple
Pantone 266 / RGB 125/000/240

syn
syn
syn
syn
syn
syn

YG ENTERTAINMENT

Client_YG Entertainment
Design Firm_ Plus X
Creative Directors_ Myungsup Shin, Sabum Byun, Seungwon Huh
Designers_ Uisun Jung, Dongwoo Lee, Jiyoung Yoon, Jihoon Kim, Junhyuck Chun, Hyerim Kim, Jihye Park, Yeonsu Kim, Eunock Jung, Hyojin Park, Junggun Park, Jeoonghyun Lee
Country_ South Korea

YG Entertainment is the leading entertainment company in South Korea. YG needed a new identity system to expand their business flexibly. YG's new symbol has maintained most of the existing symbols, which are the company's valuable asset, but improving its formative completeness has been improved.

Designers also created the brand's font, which is based on the forms of the YG logo. To facilitate systematic brand expansion, designers built a unique, complete brand identity system, including sub-brand symbols in combination with YG logo and YG's brand font.

YG MUSIC

YG CONCERT

YG ON AIR

YG FAMILY CONCERT

KARAOKE SCHOOL

KARAOKE SCHOOL

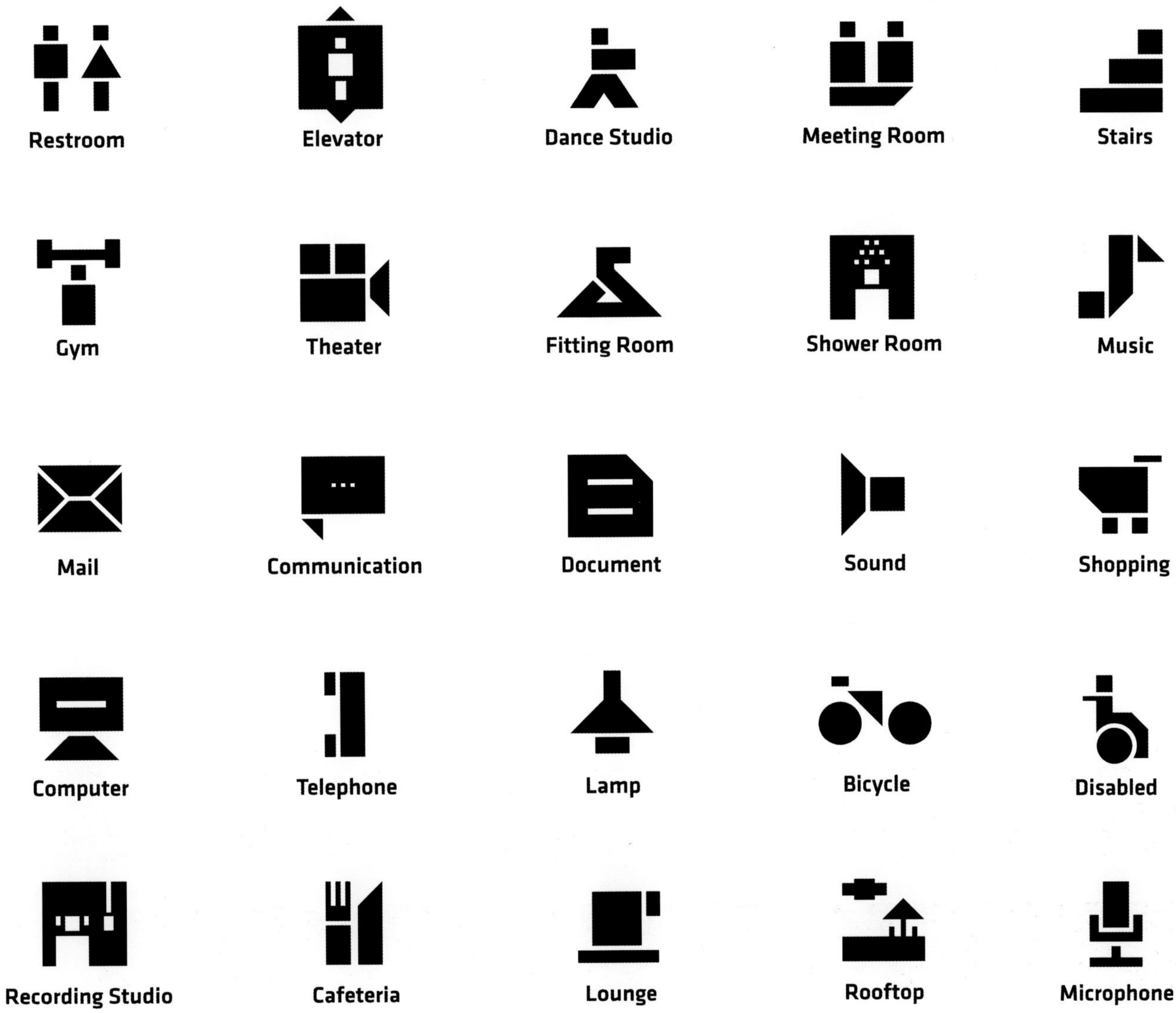

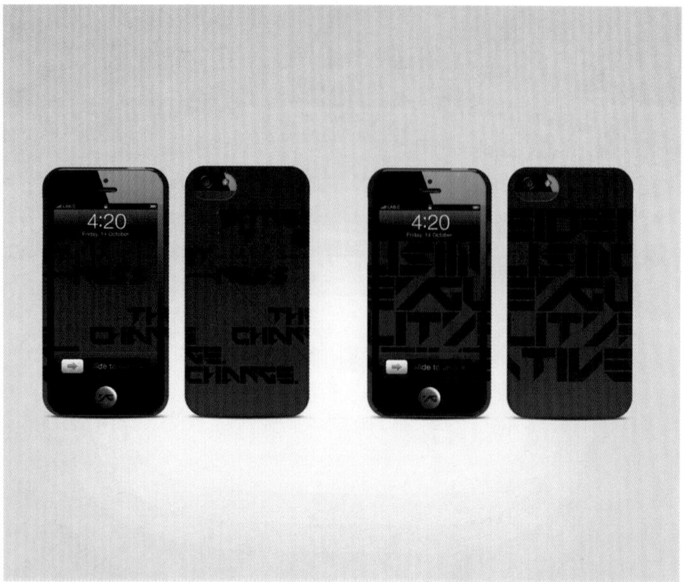
4:20
4:20

Kim, Seul Ki
김 슬 기
Associate
사원
Production Division / Design
YG ENTERTAINMENT

DEMO Recording
DEMO Recording

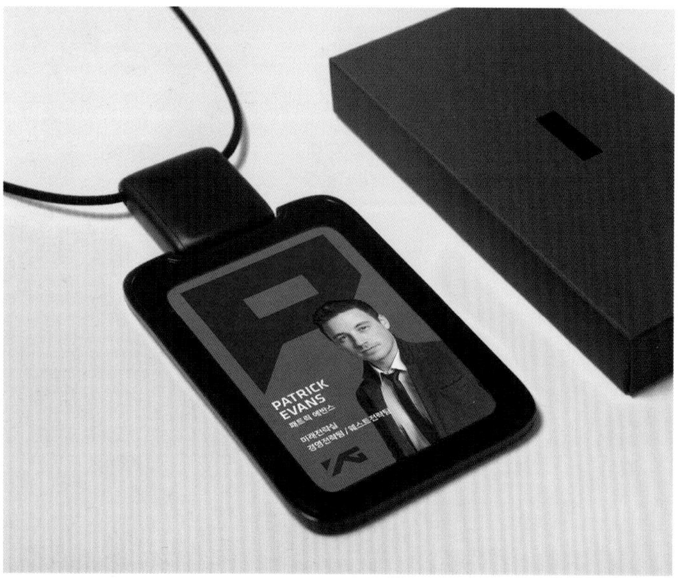
PATRICK
EVANS
패트릭 에반스

WITNESS
THE CHANGE

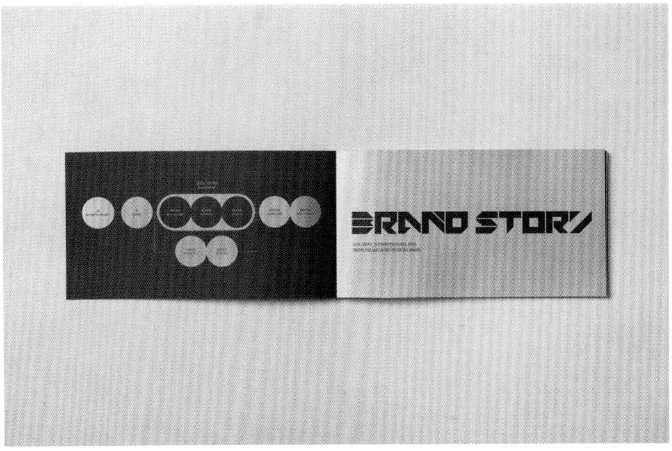
BRAND STORY

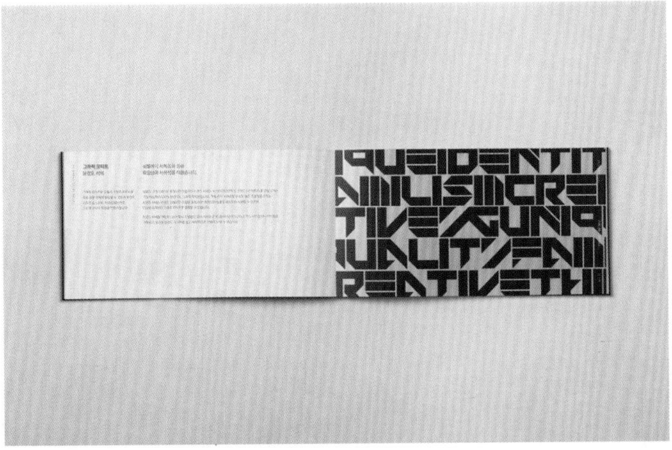

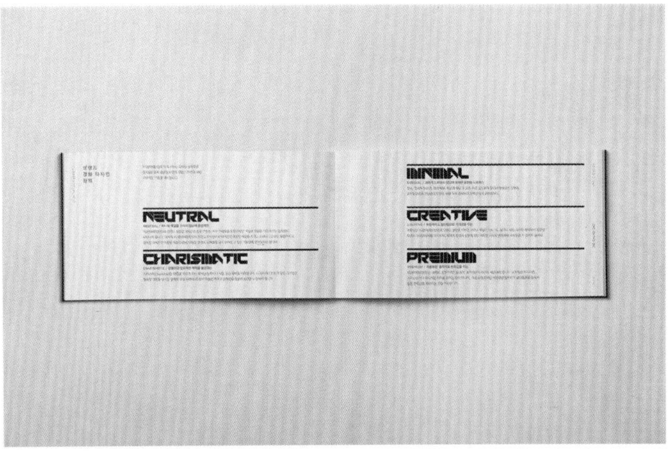
NEUTRAL
CHARISMATIC
MINIMAL
CREATIVE
PREMIUM

브랜드 정신과
핵심가치
YG BRAND STORY BOOK
YG SPIRIT
YG
SPIRIT

Client_ Arcade
Design Firm_ Zebra
Creative Directors_ Michelle Tranter, Martin Maher
Designers_ Michelle Tranter, Martin Maher
Country_ Singapore

Moodmakr is an app that aims to satisfy the mood of consumers with an instant, hyper-relevant offer. Zebra designed the overall look and feel for the brand. The idea was to give Moodmakr a personality of its own, one that changes and morphs depending on the mood or state-of-mind of the consumer. This is reflected in the brand's specific "tone of voice," which was developed to reflect the friendly, fun nature of the brand.

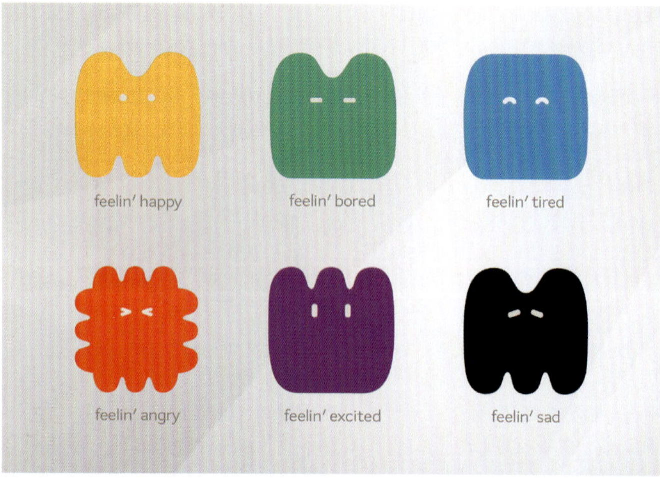

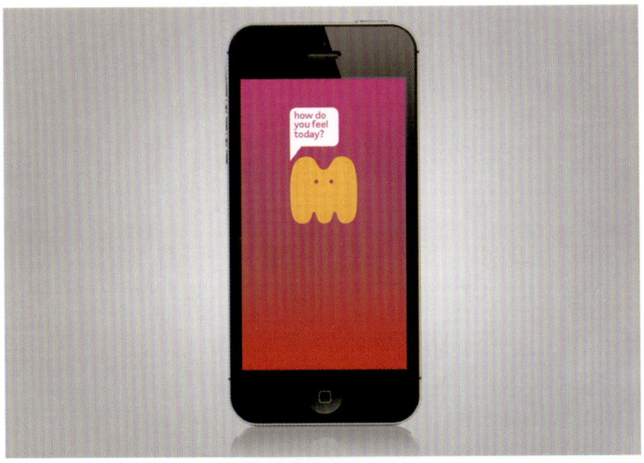
how do
you feel
today?

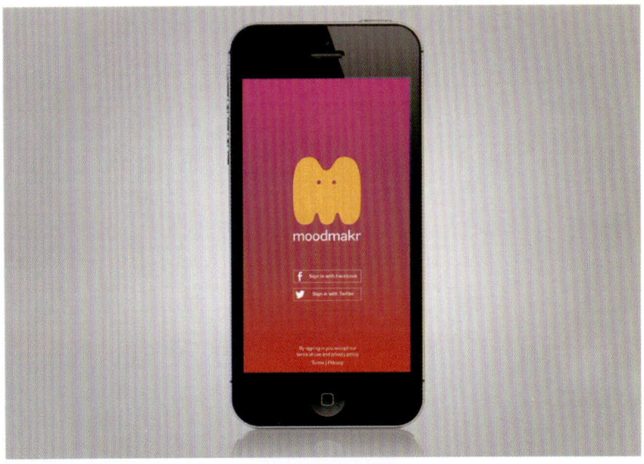
moodmakr

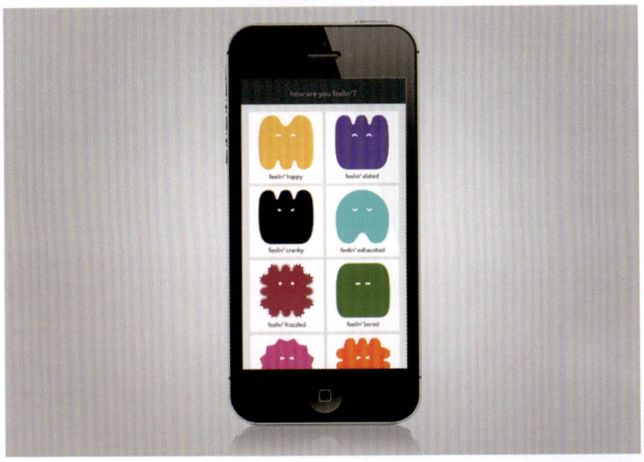
how are you feelin'?
feelin' happy
feelin' elated
feelin' cranky
feelin' exhausted
feelin' frazzled
feelin' bored

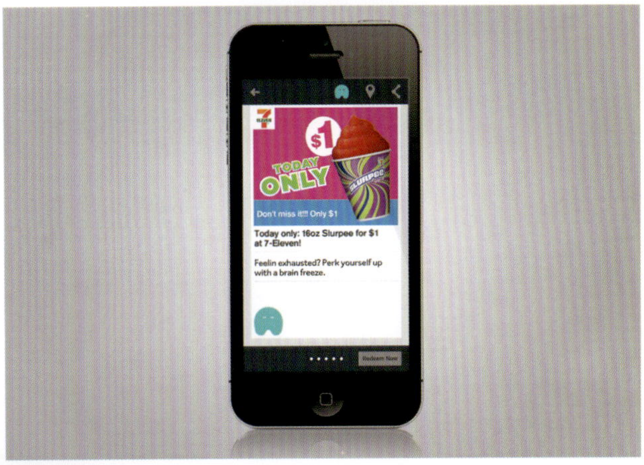
$1
TODAY ONLY
SLURPEE
Don't miss it!!! Only $1
Today only: 16oz Slurpee for $1 at 7-Eleven!
Feelin exhausted? Perk yourself up with a brain freeze.

What's your mood?
gloomy
happy
angry
puzzled
fancy a coke?
moodmakr
moodmakr creates the perfect market by satisfying moods with instant, hyperrelevant offers.

KAKAO GAME PARTNERS FORUM

Client_KAKAO
Design Firm_ Plus X
Designers_ Bohyun Sin, Myungsup Shin, Jiyoung Yoon, Jihoon Kim, Velosh
Country_ South Korea

KAKAO Game platform is a mobile game platform using the social graph of KakaoTalk. This project was created for its branch KAKAO Game Partners Forum. Designers defined the forum as a place for finding new opportunities and communicating with game partners. The artists created KAKAO's brand identity with yellow as the main color, and using simple and witty designs. Designers also used aspects of the games as design elements to accentuate the characters of the game forum.

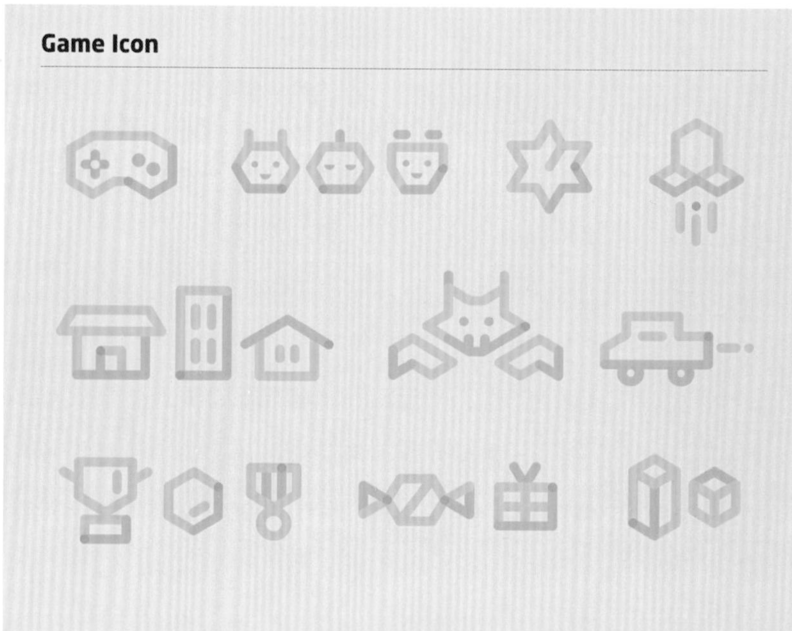

KAKAO
Game
Partners
Forum
2013

KAKAO
Game
Partners
Forum
2013
KAKAO

KAKAO
Game
Partners
Forum
2013

KAKAO
Game
Partners
Forum
2013

Convenience Store
KAKAO
Game
Partners
Forum
2013
Date
2013. 05.10. Fri
AM 10:00-PM17:30
Place
COEX 4F
Conference Room (South)

KAKAO
Game
Partners
Forum
2013
Welcome!

KAKAO
Game
Partners
Forum
2013

KAKAO
Game
Partners
Forum
2013
Date
05.10. Fri
AM 10:00-
PM17:30
Place
COEX 4F
Conference
Room (South)

Client_Worldeka
Design Firm_Landor Associates
Creative Directors_Jason Little, Mike Staniford
Designers_Joao Peres, Serhat Ferat, Jason Little
Country_Australia

Worldeka is a social networking site and platform of collaboration for the greater good. Worldeka, which means "one world" in Sanskrit, is driven by the belief that collectively people can accomplish anything. In reducing the signature identity down from Worldeka to the abbreviated "WE," which represents "Warriors Embracing," "Wireless Entrepreneurs," "Working Effectively," "Warranty Extended" and "Welcome Enterprise." The many "WE" logotypes prevent the brand from "standing still" amid global movement. The illustration becomes the signature style of the brand, allowing its revolutionary spirit to be clearly expressed.

we
worldeka
worldeka
Warranty
Extended

worldeka
charlie cox
m: 07870 680 421
d: +44 (0) 1343 813 552
e: charlie@worldeka.com
www.worldeka.com
worldeka
sophie cox
m: 07885 326 876
d: +44 (0) 1343 813 551
e: sophie@worldeka.com
www.worldeka.com

working
effectively

wireless
entrepreneur

warranty
extended

we
worldeka
working effectively
WORK
ING
EFFECT
IVELY

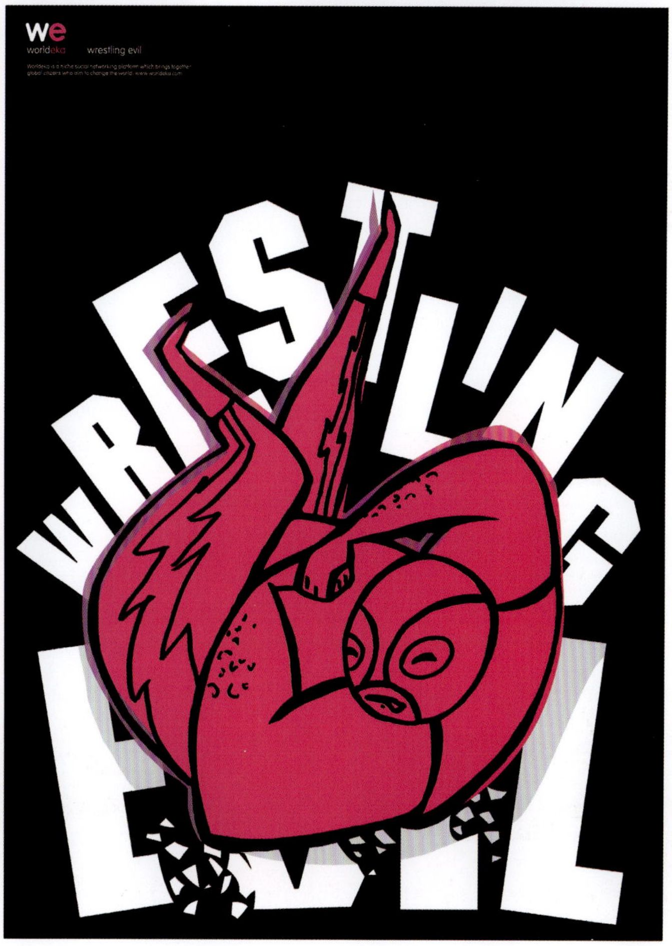
we
worldeka
wrestling evil
WRESTLING
EVIL

FASHION CLUB

Client_ Fashion Club
Design Firm_b2s6
Creative Director_ Alexander Pomidor
Designer_ Alexander Pomidor
Country_ Russia

Fashion Club is a young, ambitious, and successful Internet project that offers designer clothes and accessories from across the globe. The studio has created a bright and catchy image that is closely related to the modern lifestyle. While working, the designer came to the idea of explosion, which symbolizes the flow of new trends and pushes the brand to constant development.

FASHION
CLUB

FASHION CLUB

Урусхан Сампиев / генеральный директор
FASHION
CLUB
+7 911 285-06-85 / u.sampiev@fashioncult.ru / www.fashionclub.ru

FASHION
CLUB

Урусхан Сампиев
Генеральный директор
+7 911 285-06-85
u.sampiev@fashionclub.ru
www.fashionclub.ru

ПЛАТОК KIST
Шерсть 100%
Размер, см 125x125+/-3
Арт. 1CH123-3UU
4 606453 849072

Client_ria.ru
Design Firm_Notamedia
Designer_Maxim Pavlov
Country_Russia

This project is an identity for PublicPost, which is a new information portal with editorial content, blogging and social networking elements. Each section of the portal (news, stories, blogs, info graphics, photos and videos) has its own version of the logo. All these make the identity fluid and flexible.

PublicPost

НОВОСТИ ОПРОСЫ ТЕМЫ БЛОГИ ВИДЕО ФОТО

ИНФОГРАФИКА

PublicPost

СМИ
НОВОГО
ПОКОЛЕНИЯ
PublicPost

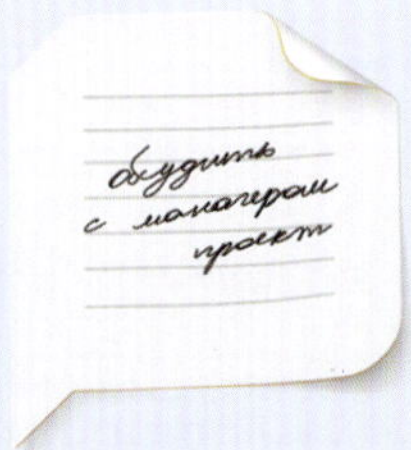

PublicPost
СМИ НОВОГО ПОКОЛЕНИЯ

PublicPost

TALKING HEADS (GOGOL)

Client_ Gogol.tv
Design Firm_ Notamedia
Designer_ Maxim Pavlov
Country_ Russia

"Talking Heads" is a project for Gogol.tv. Gogol's head profile became the basis of the logo. Besides the Gogol logo, this project contains seven other characters who symbolize sections of the site (Lenin — politics, Gagarin — progress, Pushkin — culture, etc.). There is common man's head profile inside each of them. These heads gradually transform into profiles of "gurus," the main symbols of the site.

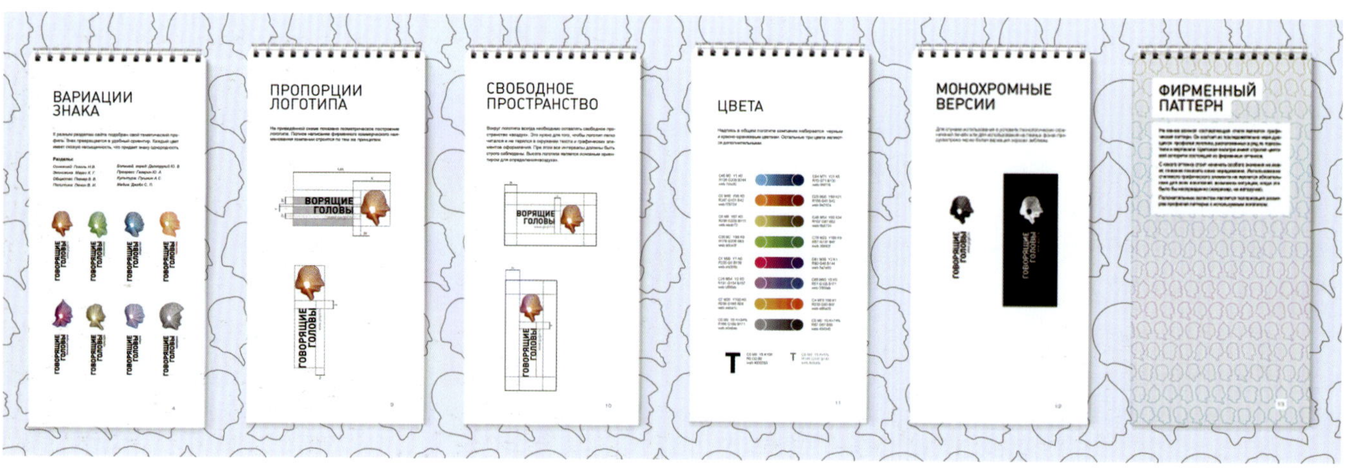

политика

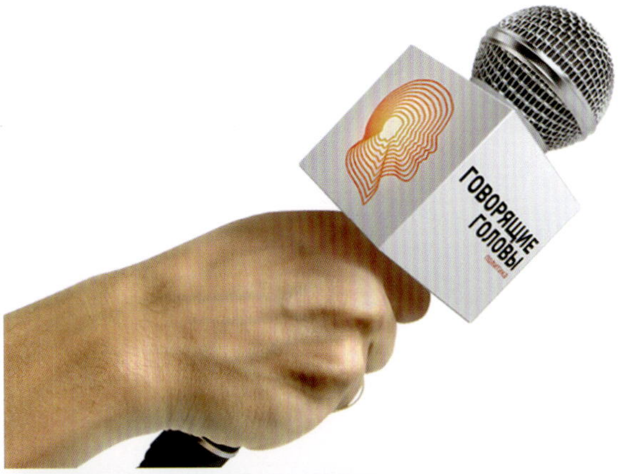

прогресс

ORGANIZATION
INSTITUTION
PUBLIC SPACE

Client_ Citysocializer
Graphic Designer_ Elvire Delanote
Creative Strategist_ Fiona Mandos
Country_ Belgium

This is a brand new logo project for Citysocializer, which is about getting together, sharing social experiences and enjoying good times with laid-back people. The "C" from Citysocializer stands for challenging, creativity and communicative; for "Cmiley" happy people that want to meet up, expand their circle of connections, and socialize in the city of London. From enjoying tacos and tequila after work to exploring the central square market and biking around the city ..., it's 360° Citysocializer.

c0m85y85k0 CITYSOCIALIZER

CITYSOCIALIZER c0m20y0k80

c65m10y10k0 CITYSOCIALIZER

CITYSOCIALIZER c0m10y10k50

CITYSOCIALIZER
CITYSOCIALIZER

CITYSOCIALIZER

EVOLVING LOGO

Client_Personal Work
Design Firm_Michael Schmitz Interaktive Gestaltung
Creative Director_Michael Schmitz
Designer_Michael Schmitz
Country_Germany

"Evolving Logo" is a generative system using the principles of evolution to adapt and enhance a company's logo according to its current state. Different variations of the logo reproduce while their genes randomly mutate and recombine — the population lives in constant change and only the fittest stay to reproduce. "Evolving Logo" was put into practice for the Max Planck Institute of Molecular Cell Biology and Genetics Dresden, which studies how cells form tissue. However, the concept could have been used for any other company.

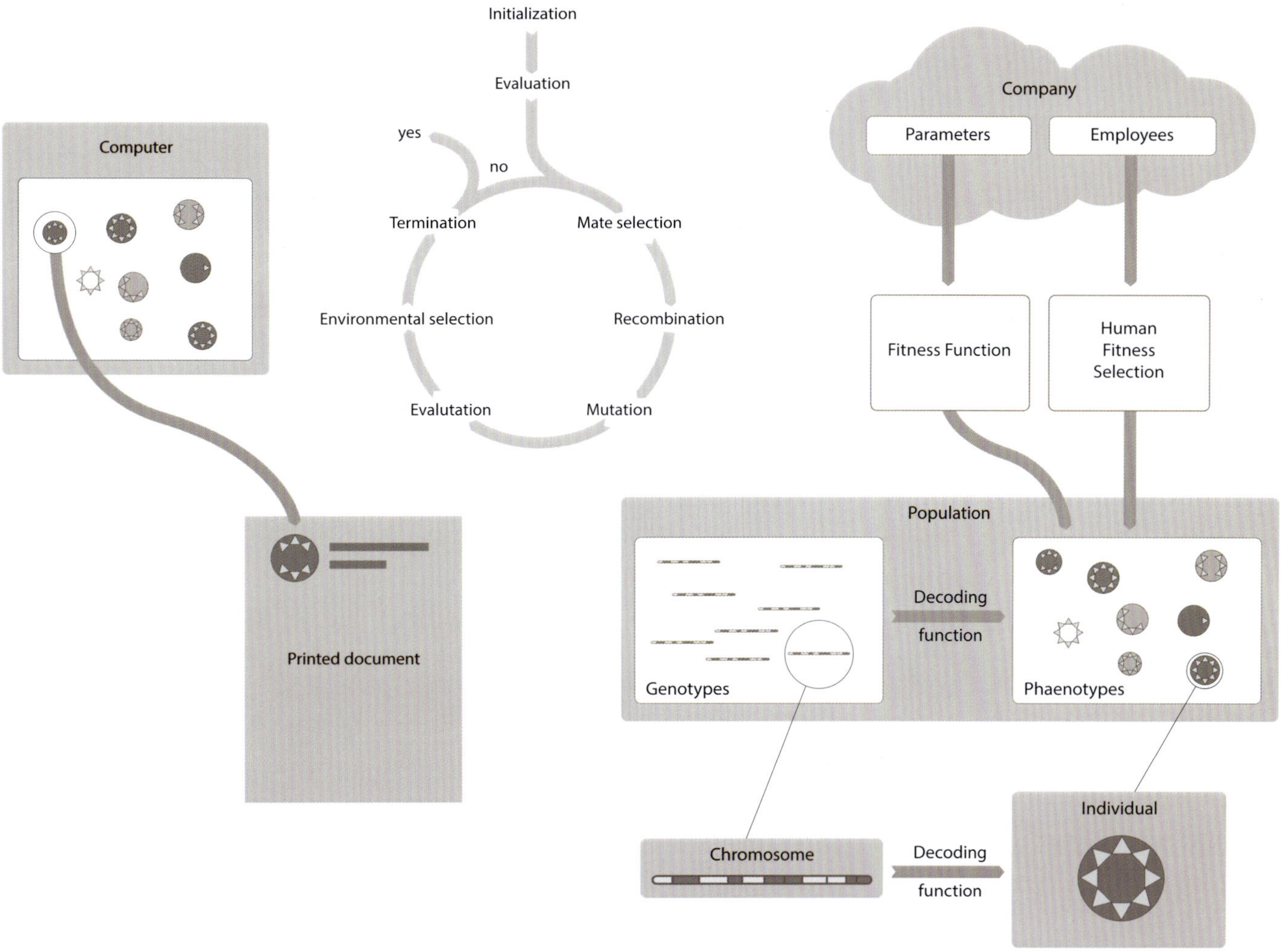
Computer
Printed document
Initialization
Evaluation
yes
no
Termination
Mate selection
Environmental selection
Recombination
Evalutation
Mutation
Company
Parameters
Employees
Fitness Function
Human
Fitness
Selection
Population
Genotypes
Decoding
function
Phaenotypes
Chromosome
Decoding
function
Individual

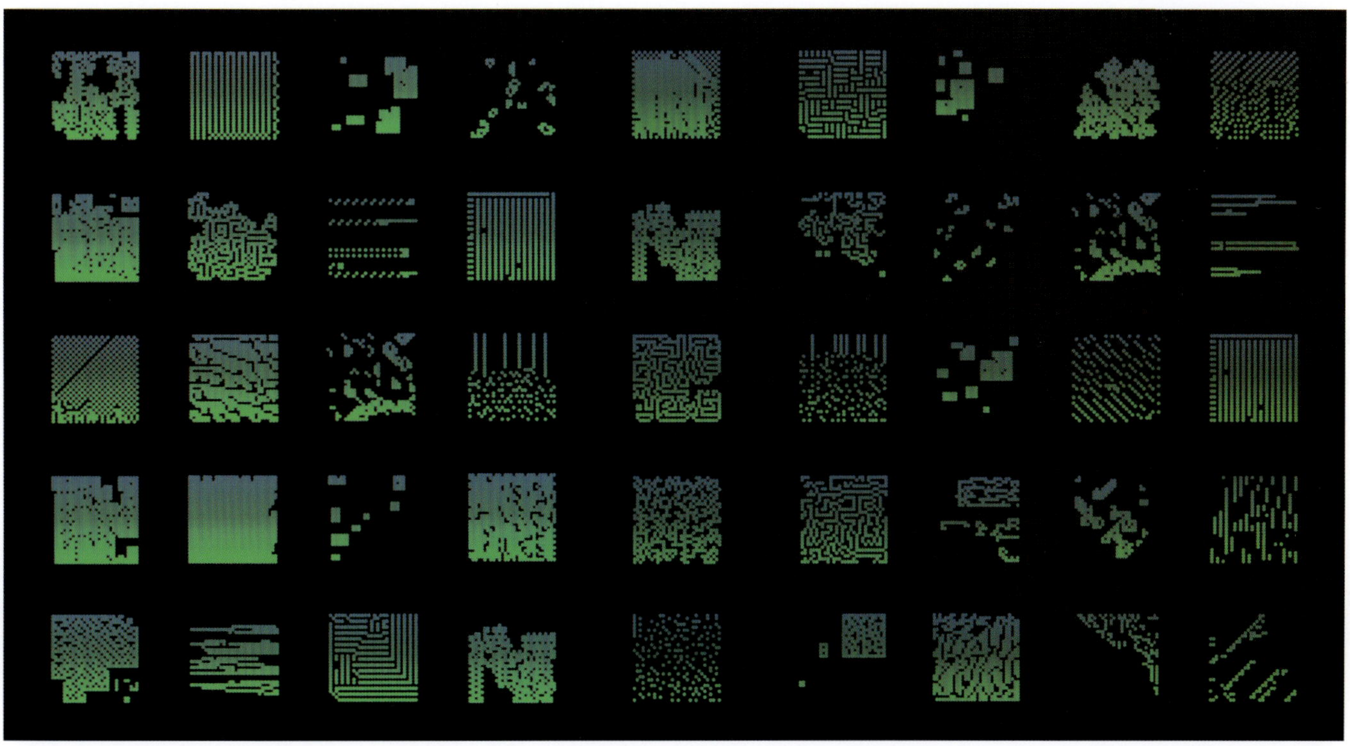

FEDERAÇÃO ACADÉMICA DO DESPORTO UNIVERSITÁRIO

Client_ Federação Académica do Desporto Universitário (FADU)
Design Firm_ Gen Design Studio
Designers_ Catarina Correia, Leandro Veloso
Photography_ Leandro Veloso
Country_ Portugal

FADU, the Academic Federation for University Sports in Portugal, represents dynamism, union, intelligence, and competitiveness. The studio proposed to create a system that structures FADU and conveys professionalism and dedication. Each modality has a signature attached, creating a structure to the level of an Olympic organization. Such an approach allows the identity to grow and communicate efficiently. Combining those concepts above with a representative element of sport and success, designers were able to develop a strong and dynamic shape inspired by the laurel wreath geometry.

F.A.D.U.
PORTUGAL

fadu
portugal
university sports

fadu
portugal
basquetebol

fadu
portugal
remo

fadu
portugal
tiro com arco

fadu
portugal
natação

fadu
portugal
esgrima

fadu
portugal
ginástica

logotipo integral
logotipo integral (dimensões mínimas)
fadu
portugal
university sports
logotipo preto (dimensões mínimas)
fadu
portugal
university sports

fadu
portugal
university sports

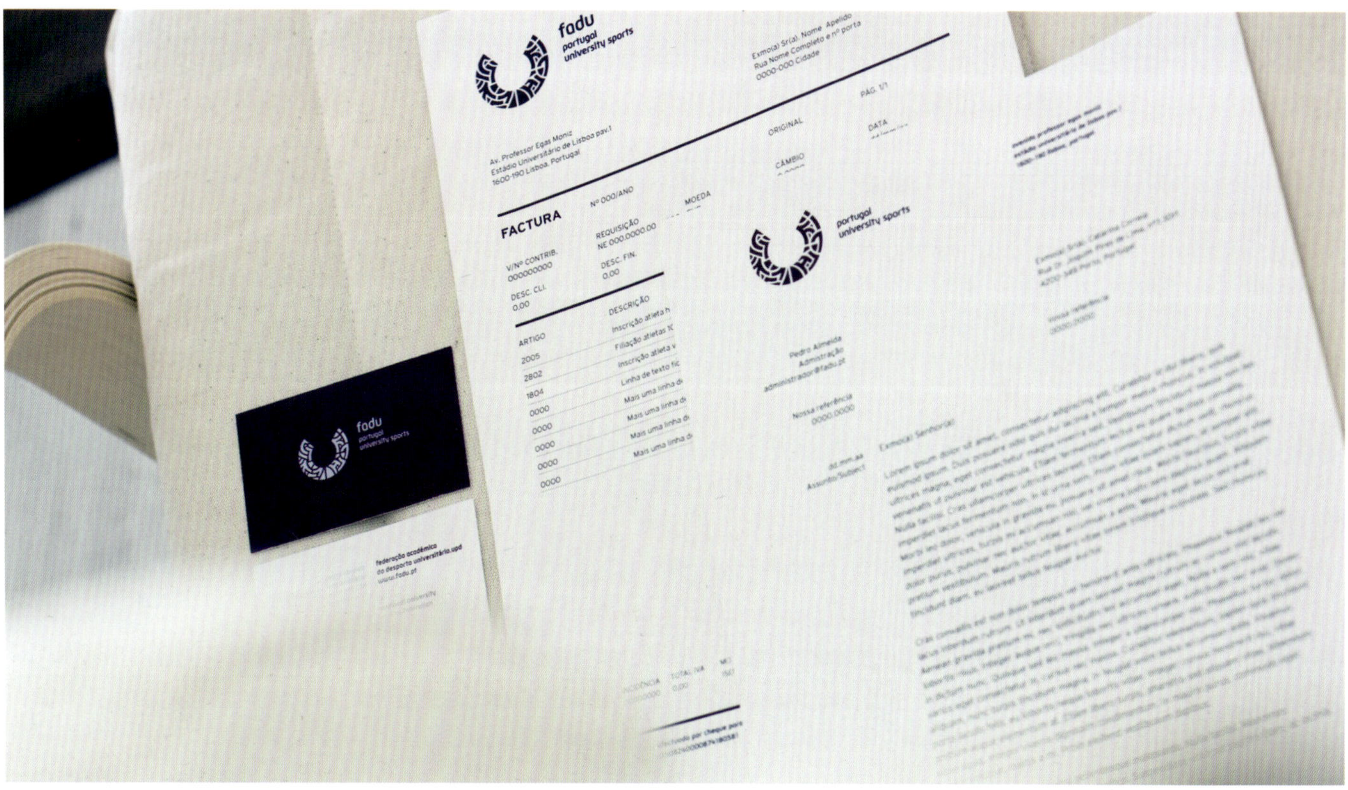

fadu
portugal
university sports
FACTURA
fadu
portugal
university sports
portugal
university sports

i am
a sports
lover
fadu

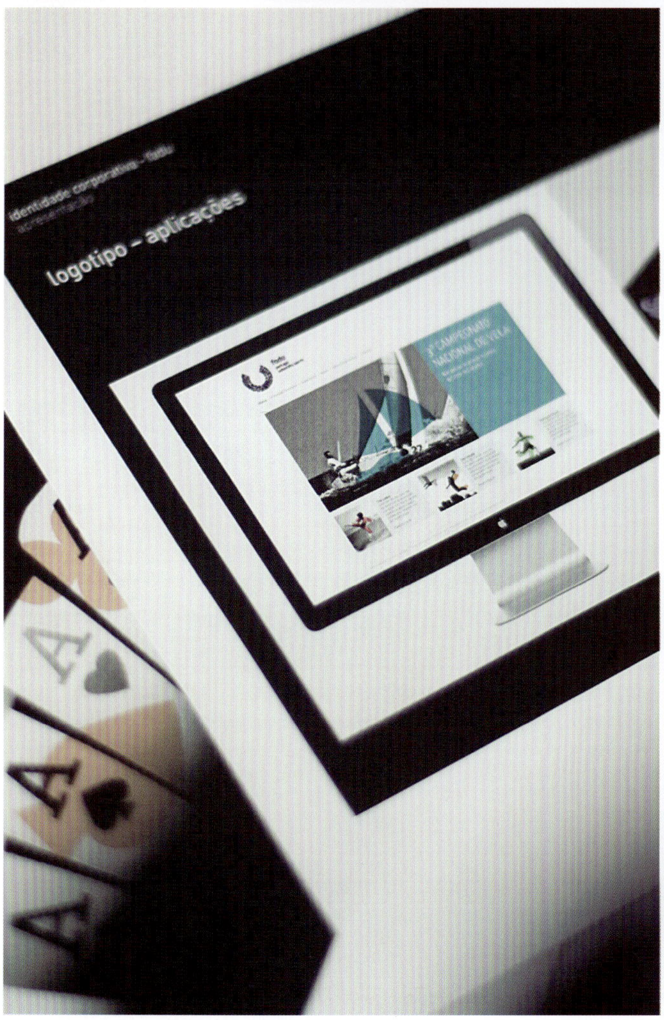
logotipo - aplicações

fadu

Client_FDM
Design Firm_b2s6
Creative Director_ Alexander Pomidor
Designer_ Alexander Pomidor
Country_ Russia

Every year hundreds of seminars, lectures, master classes of various directions take place in FDM. In the identification system the designer demonstrated the process visually: dozens of rays that rush from one fixed point in different directions. Due to the natural dynamics the logo works on different types of media; its character changes but its reconcilability always remains.

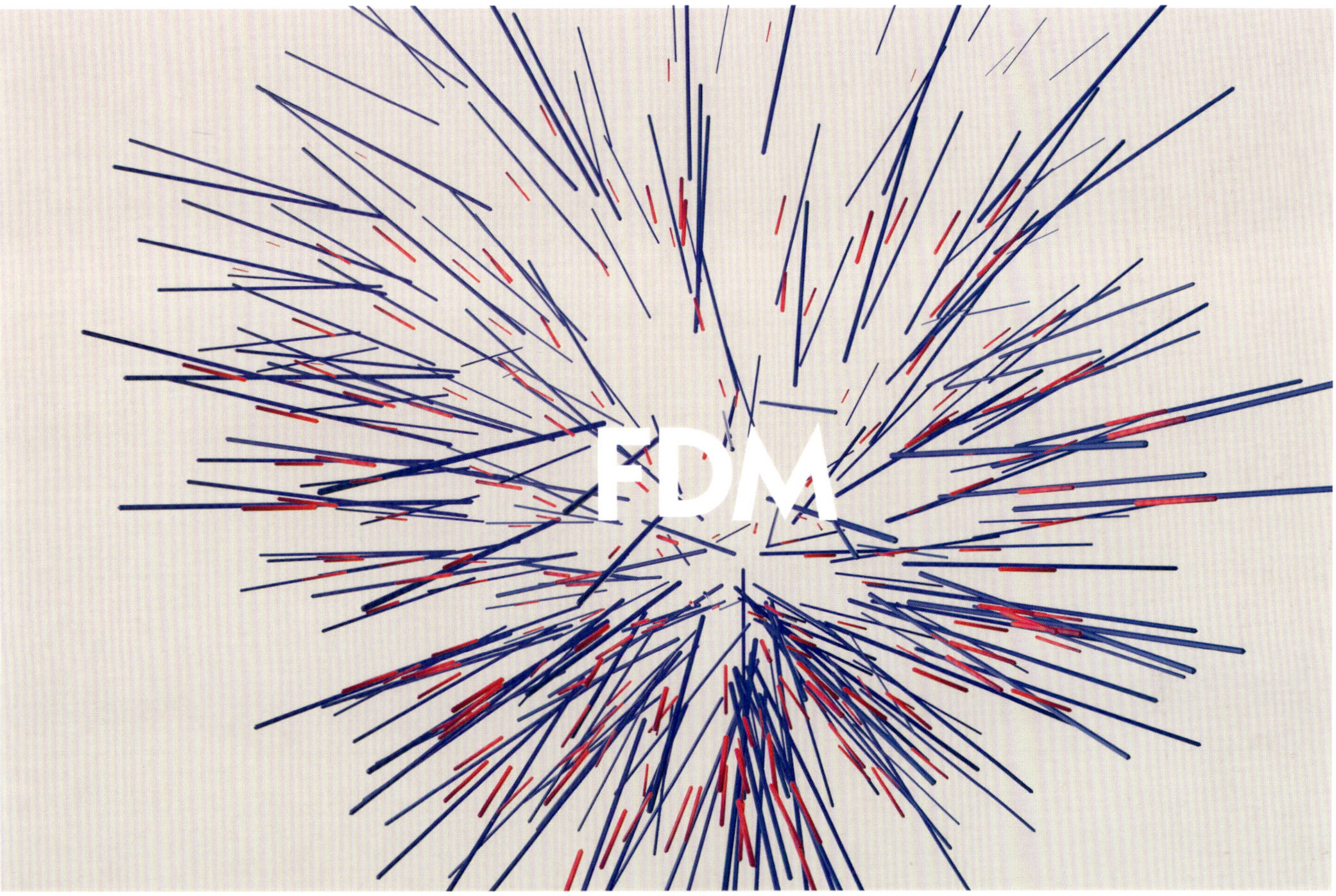
FDM

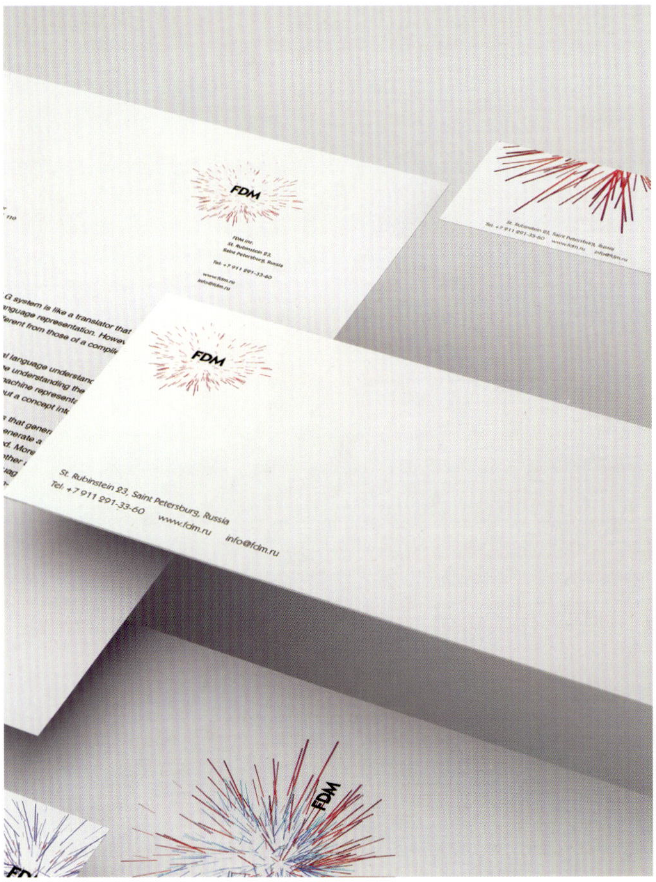
FDM
St. Rubinstein 23, Saint Petersburg, Russia
Tel: +7 911 291-33-60 www.fdm.ru info@fdm.ru

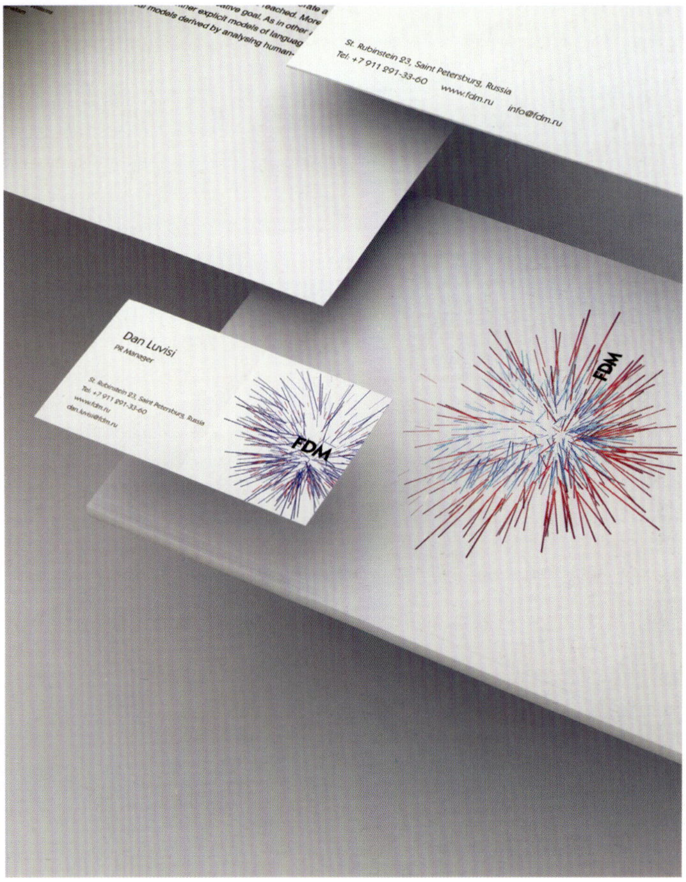
St. Rubinstein 23, Saint Petersburg, Russia
Tel: +7 911 291-33-60 www.fdm.ru info@fdm.ru
Dan Luvisi
PR Manager
FDM

Client_ Geores
Design Firm_ Cappelli Identity Design
Designers_ Emanuele Cappelli, Francesco De Chirico, Francesco Di Muro
Country_ Italy

In order to create an advanced identity system, the agency designed a dynamic brand for Geores. Through a concept that takes its moves from the earth, the designers created an interconnected system in which the various layers influence and enrich each other. This brand has been developed with different layouts, selected from the movement of the main logo, and different applications that change their color depending on the specific area of activity.

geores
Manuale di brand
2012

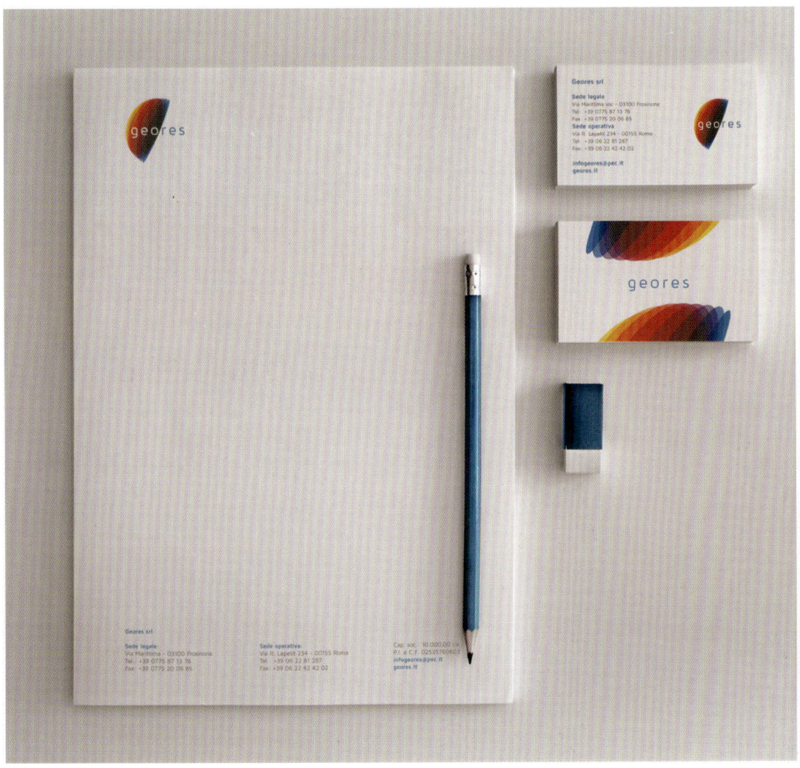
geores
geores
geores

Innovating
Earth experience
Geores fornisce servizi altamente qualificati garantendo alla clientela risultati consistenti ed affidabili mediante la costante attenzione alle esigenze delcommittente, l'elevata expertise dei collaboratori e l'aggiornamento continuo. Geores opera nel campo della **Geofisica**, della **Geotecnica**, della **Geomatica** e dei **servizi geologici per l'Archeologia**, oltre ad eseguire indagini di laboratorio.
geores LAB
Il laboratorio Geores, autorizzato dal Ministero delle Infrastrutture e dei Trasporti a svolgere attività di prova e certificazione su terre (settore A circ. 7618/STC) con Decreto n.160 del 19/04/2011, utilizza un sistema di gestione della qualità e istruzioni tecnico-operative in riferimento alla normativa EN ISO 9001:2008
geores
Tel. +39 06 2281287 +39 0775 871376 info@geores.it www.geores.it

SOFIA BREATHES STREET FESTIVAL

Client_S Communication
Designer_ Boris Bonev
Country_ Bulgaria

The main aim of "Sofia Breathes" is to stop the traffic on main streets in the capital for its duration and thus to transform them into cultural platforms. The visual identity derives from the event's name. The street concept is represented pictographically with the choice of typeface. It is then rethought through the principle of the breathing process including expansion and contraction. This leads to the creation of a secondary typeface coming out of the main one, which complements it.

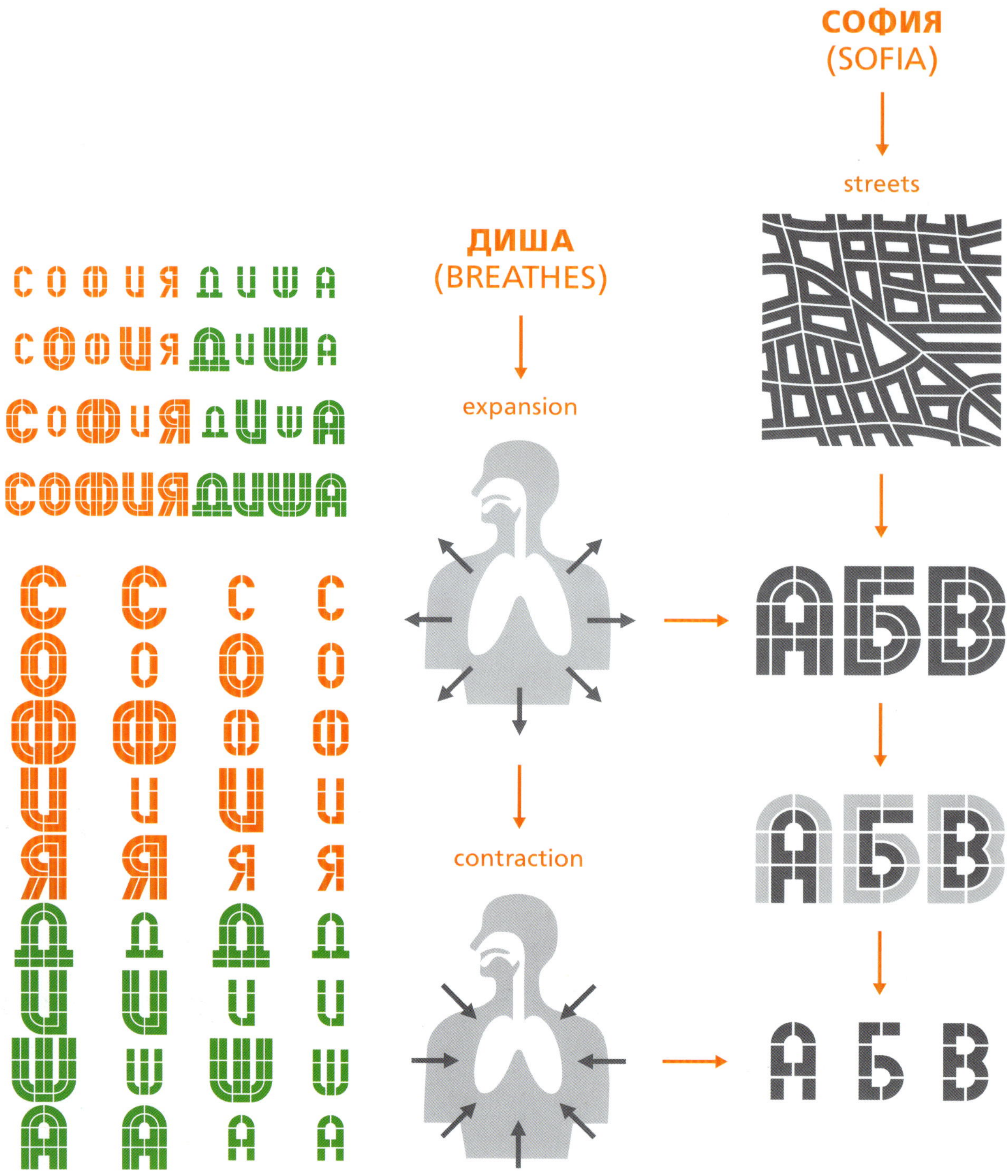

СОФИЯ
ДУША
СОФИЯ
ДУША
СЛОВОТО ЗОВЕ
12.08.12
УЛ. АНГЕЛ КЪНЧЕВ
16.00--21.00Н

СОФИЯ
ДУША
СОФИЯ
ДУША
ПЕСЕНТА НА ТАНЦА
26.08.12 16.00--21.00Н
ПЛ. НЕЗАВИСИМОСТ
(ЛАРГОТО)

ВЕТРОВЕ
ОТ
ЦВЕТОВЕ
СОФИЯ
ДУША
19.08.12
УЛ. ПИРОТСКА
16.00--21.00Н

СОФИЯ
ЗА СЦЕНАТА И ХОРАТА
ДУША
05.08.12 16.00--21.00Н
СОФИЯ
УЛ. ЦАР ИВАН ШИШМАН
ДУША

Client_GNP+
Design Firm_COOEE
Designer_Leon Dijkstra
Country_Netherlands

The Global Network of People Living with HIV and AIDS (GNP+) is an international organization that advocates improving the quality of life of all HIV-positive people. GNP+ also supports the R&D of new prevention technologies (NPT). The continuous development of prevention technologies formed the basis of the NPT identity. Each technology has been translated into a unique symbol in the appearance of a line or dot which visualizes the abstract terminology. This leads to creation of a greater richness, an identity that grows along with the success of developments.

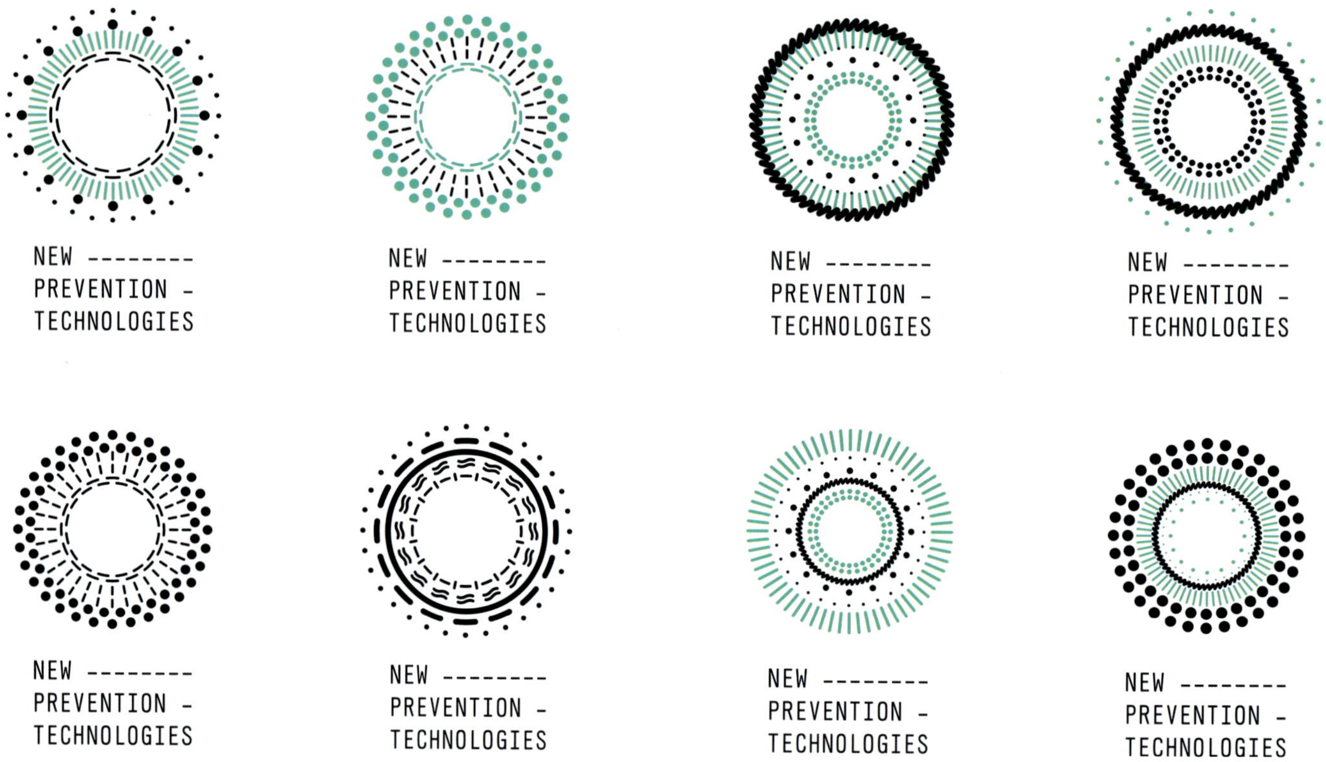

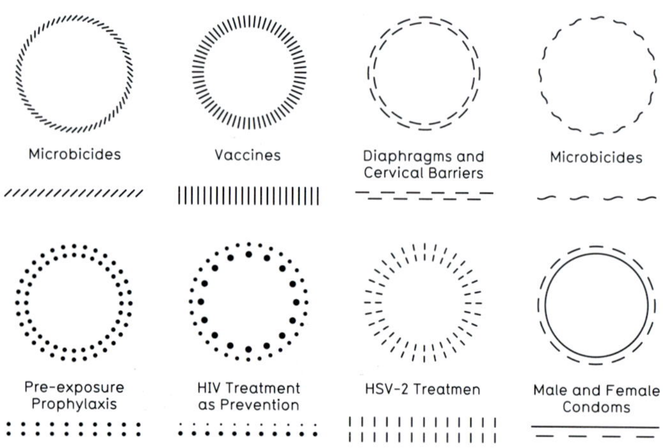

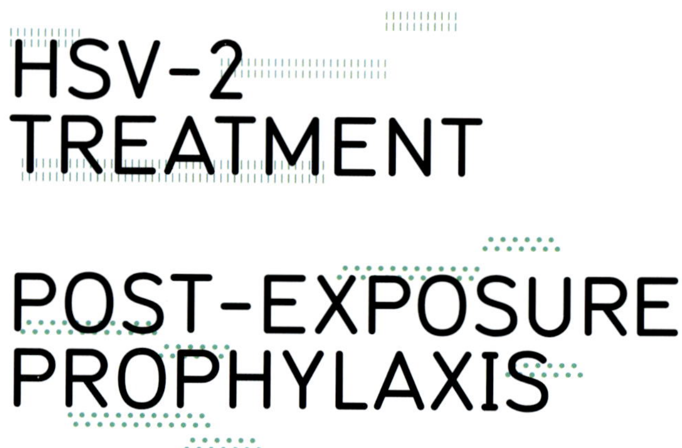

NEW PREVENTION TECHNOLOGIES
What are they and what is their relevance for people living with HIV?

PREVIOUSLY INVESTIGATED TECHNOLOGIES

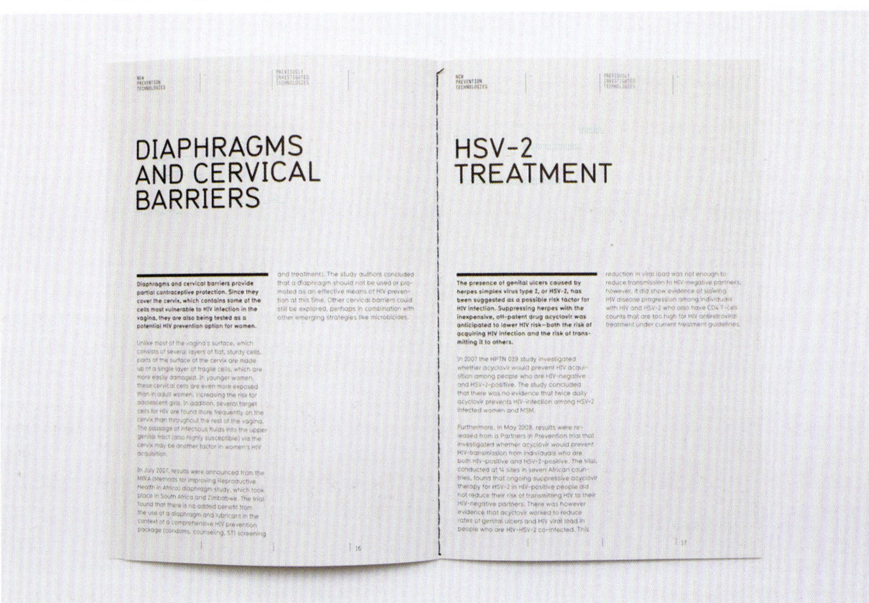
DIAPHRAGMS AND CERVICAL BARRIERS
HSV-2 TREATMENT

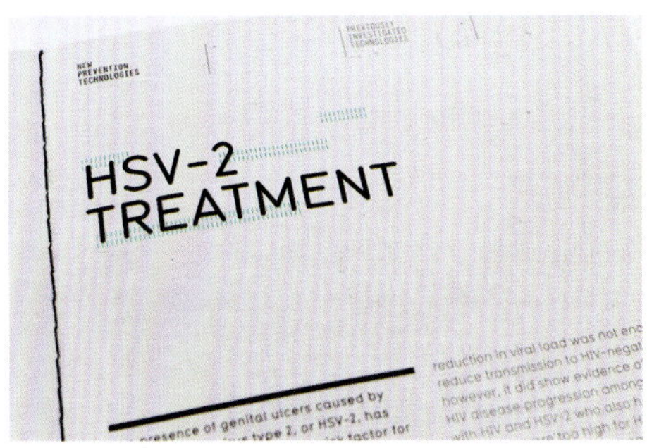
HSV-2 TREATMENT

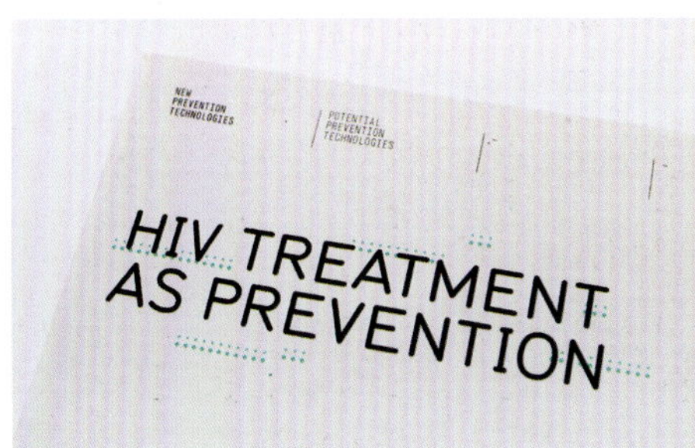
HIV TREATMENT AS PREVENTION

THE BIRTHPLACE

Client_ Birthplace Healthcare Private Limited
Design Firm_NH1 Design
Designer_ Neha Tulsian
Country_ India

The birth of a child gives life to a myriad of relationships. The Birthplace is a cradle for many phenomena. For its identity, designers used a simple, fluid letter "B", which features a line that connects its outer protuberance to a blossoming heart inside, representing the life growing within the mother's womb. The identity in some explorations indicates the progress of the precious life over nine months. The heart motif gradually blossoms in size till birth, when it is no longer inside the letter "B" (womb) but outside, a living, breathing entity.

theBirthplace

theBirthplace
of new relationships

theBirthplace
of a mother

theBirthplace
of a father

theBirthplace
of new dreams

theBirthplace
of fresh ideas

theBirthplace
of new beginnings

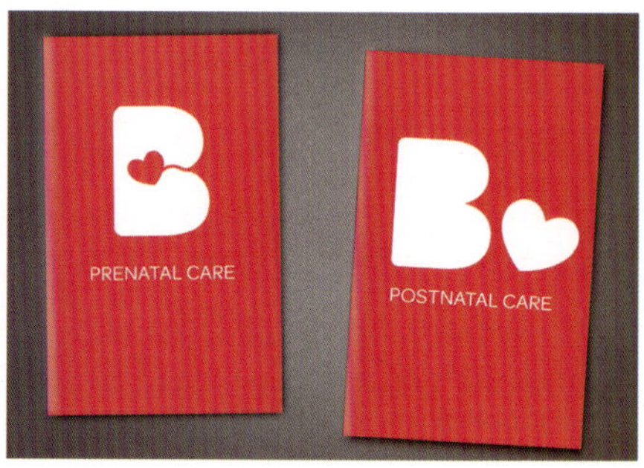

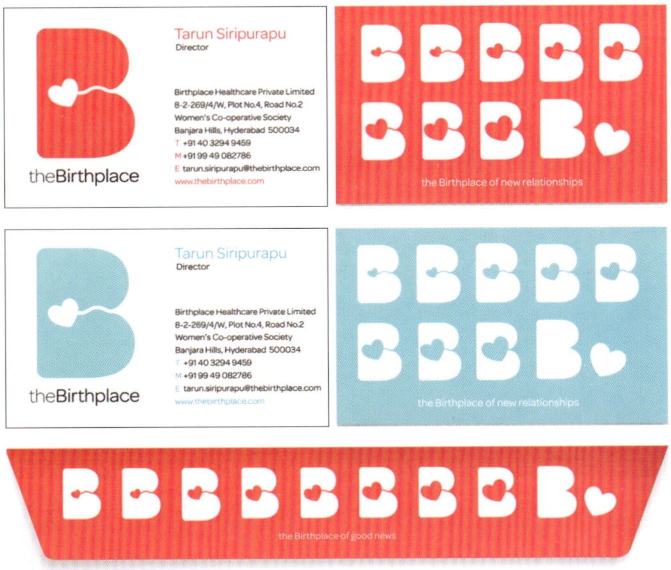
Tarun Siripurapu
Director
Birthplace Healthcare Private Limited
8-2-269/4/W, Plot No.4, Road No.2
Women's Co-operative Society
Banjara Hills, Hyderabad 500034
T +91 40 3294 9459
M +91 99 49 082786
E tarun.siripurapu@thebirthplace.com
www.thebirthplace.com
theBirthplace
the Birthplace of new relationships
the Birthplace of good news

theBirthplace
of a father

theBirthplace

theBirthplace

Just Delivered!

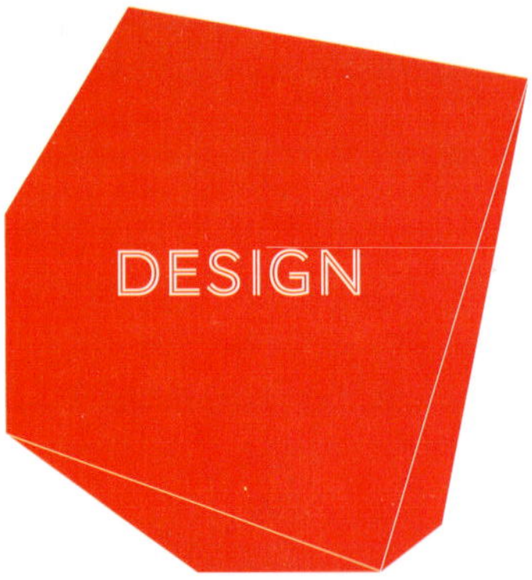

Client_ Design Workshop
Design Firm_ Composition School
Creative Director_ Aleksey Popovtsev
Designer_ Aleksey Popovtsev
Country_ Ukraine

The corporate style was based on the principles of the famous school and the cradle of functional design, Bauhaus. Hence the famous formula by Kandinsky: blue circle, red square, yellow triangle, which makes up the style's basis. Combinatorics of geometric figures and the modular system have once again shown its inexhaustibility. Taking various combinations of these figures one can make different logotype versions. Such combination together with the rhythmic movement of the color elements works for the style's recognizability.

DESIGN
das ist Design
www.dasistdesign.com
mail@dasistdesign.com
057 719 8 719

DISEGNO INDUSTRIALE PALERMO

Client_ University of Palermo
Designer_ Gabriele D'Asaro
Country_ Italy

This project is the outcome of demanding research on dynamic identities, carried out by Professor Dario Russo and the designer. The three shapes of the DIP acronym move inside the hexagonal grid, obtained by a stylized Triskelion, symbol of Sicily. Overlapping in constantly different configurations, they generate a totally dynamic brand, a perfect expression of the vitality and the different aspects of the degree course. The color scheme cross-references the CMYK profile as an immediate connection with the design field.

PANTONE Process Cyan
CMYK 100/0/0/0
RGB 0/160/230
HEX #00a0e6
RAL 5015

PANTONE Process Magenta
CMYK 0/100/0/0
RGB 230/0/125
HEX #e6007d
RAL 4010

PANTONE Process Yellow
CMYK 0/0/100/0
RGB 255/235/0
HEX #ffeb00
RAL 1018

PANTONE Process Black
CMYK 40/40/40/100
RGB 0/0/0
HEX #000000
RAL 9017

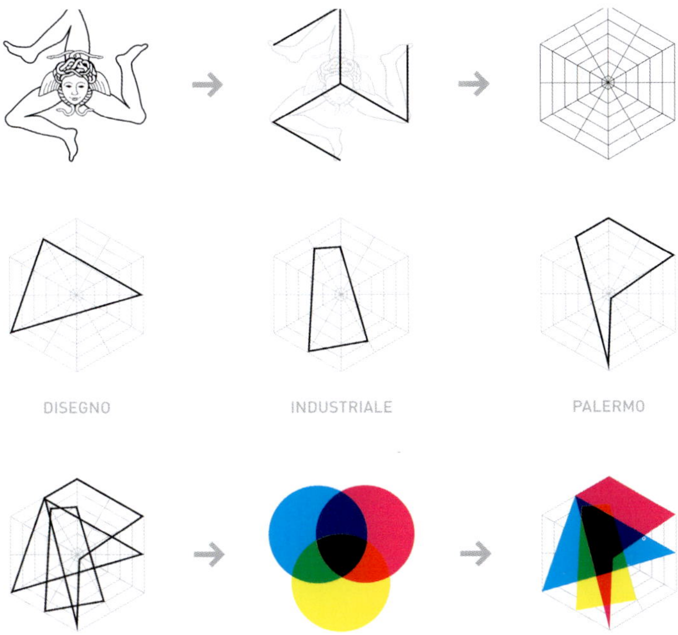
DISEGNO
INDUSTRIALE
PALERMO

DISEGNO
INDUSTRIALE
PALERMO
CALENDARIO DELLE LEZIONI
A.A. 2012-2013 – Anno II – Semestre II
Università di Palermo – Facoltà di Architettura
Lunedi
08.30 - 09.30
09.30 - 10.30
10.30 - 11.30
11.30 - 12.30
12.30 - 13.30
Disegno automatico
A. Mancuso
0.4
14.30 - 15.30
15.30 - 16.30
16.30 - 17.30
17.30 - 18.30
Martedi
08.30 - 09.30
09.30 - 10.30
10.30 - 11.30
11.30 - 12.30
12.30 - 13.30
Semiotica
L. Agnello
4.4
14.30 - 15.30
15.30 - 16.30
16.30 - 17.30
17.30 - 18.30
C.I. Nuove forme dell'abitare (sdoppiato)
G. Marsala
G. Sarta
3.6
3.7
Mercoledi
08.30 - 09.30
09.30 - 10.30
10.30 - 11.30
11.30 - 12.30
12.30 - 13.30
Materiali per il design
Da definire
4.8
14.30 - 15.30
15.30 - 16.30
16.30 - 17.30
17.30 - 18.30
C.I. Nuove forme dell'abitare (sdoppiato)
G. Marsala
G. Sarta
3.6
3.7
Giovedi
08.30 - 09.30
09.30 - 10.30
10.30 - 11.30
11.30 - 12.30
12.30 - 13.30
C.I. Laboratorio di disegno industriale
14.30 - 15.30
15.30 - 16.30
16.30 - 17.30
17.30 - 18.30
Venerdi
08.30 - 09.30
09.30 - 10.30
10.30 - 11.30
11.30 - 12.30
12.30 - 13.30
14.30 - 15.30
15.30 - 16.30
16.30 - 17.30
17.30 - 18.30
DISEGNO
INDUSTRIALE
PALERMO
DISEGNO
INDUSTRIALE
PALERMO

Mark Brooks

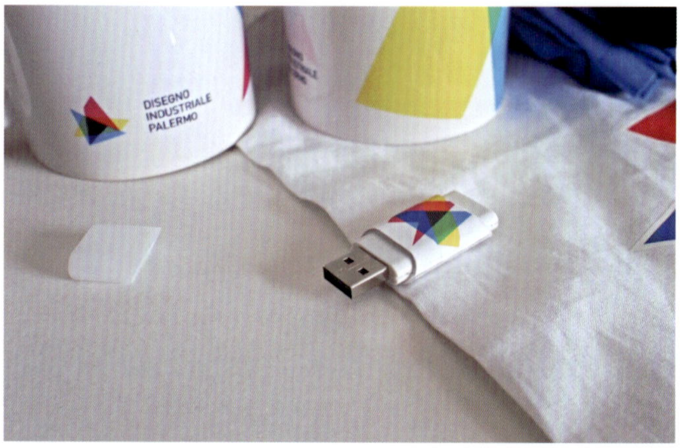
DISEGNO
INDUSTRIALE
PALERMO

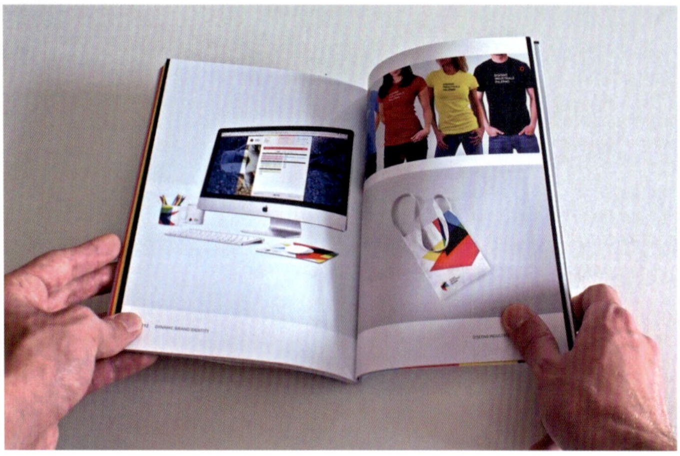

DYNAMIC
BRAND
IDENTITY
DYNAMIC BRAND IDENTITY

DISEGNO
INDUSTRIALE
PALERMO
CALENDARIO DELLE LEZIONI
LOREM IPSUM

DISEGNO
INDUSTRIALE
PALERMO

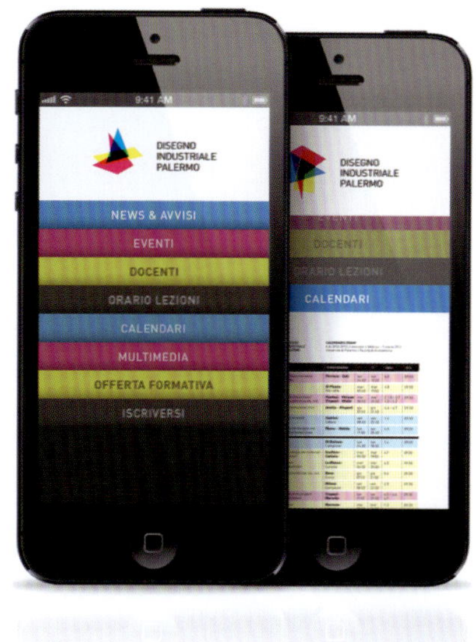
DISEGNO
INDUSTRIALE
PALERMO
NEWS & AVVISI
EVENTI
DOCENTI
ORARIO LEZIONI
CALENDARI
MULTIMEDIA
OFFERTA FORMATIVA
ISCRIVERSI

ORARI LEZIONI

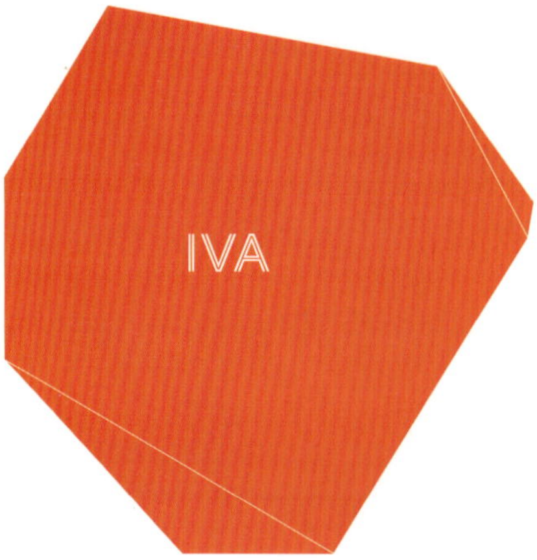

Client_IVA
Design Firm_ Make®
Project Manager_ Caroline Ørsted
Creative Director_ Kristoffer Gudbrand
Designers_ Hans Chan, Louise Brandt Overgaard
Country_ Denmark

This is a new identity for IVA (Det Informationsvidenskabelige Akademi), an educational institution in Denmark. The repositioning should be fundamental and rooted in support from stakeholders. Therefore, the designers employed a transparent process that identified needs and generated understanding from the faculty, students, governmental ministries and funding bodies, and finally produced the core of the brand: "We create connections." It was clearly signaled by a name change to "Det Informationsvidenskabelige Akademi" which removed the word "library" from the Danish version of its name.

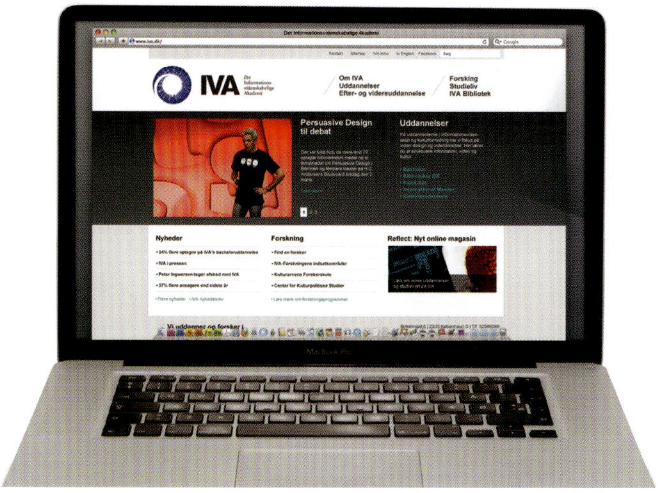
IVA
Om IVA
Uddannelser
Efter- og videreuddannelse
Forsking
Studieliv
IVA Bibliotek
Persuasive Design til debat
Uddannelser
Nyheder
Forskning
Reflect: Nyt online magasin

iva.dk

IVA
TAG EN MASTER PÅ IVA
EN MASTERUDDANNELSE MED TONINGSMULIGHEDER

IVA
MODULER PÅ MASTER UDDANNELSEN

EKSAMENSBEVIS
DIPLOMA
IVA
Det Informations-videnskabelige Akademi

IVA
Det Informations-videnskabelige Akademi

Client_Rose Innovation
Design Firm_b2s6
Creative Director_Alexander Pomidor
Designer_Alexander Pomidor
Country_Russia

Rose Innovation is a unique system that teaches piano playing, turning the learning process into a simple and interesting pastime. In the identification system the designer depicted the mood and harmony of the brand. Graphic associations with harmony, motion and music are the core of the identity.

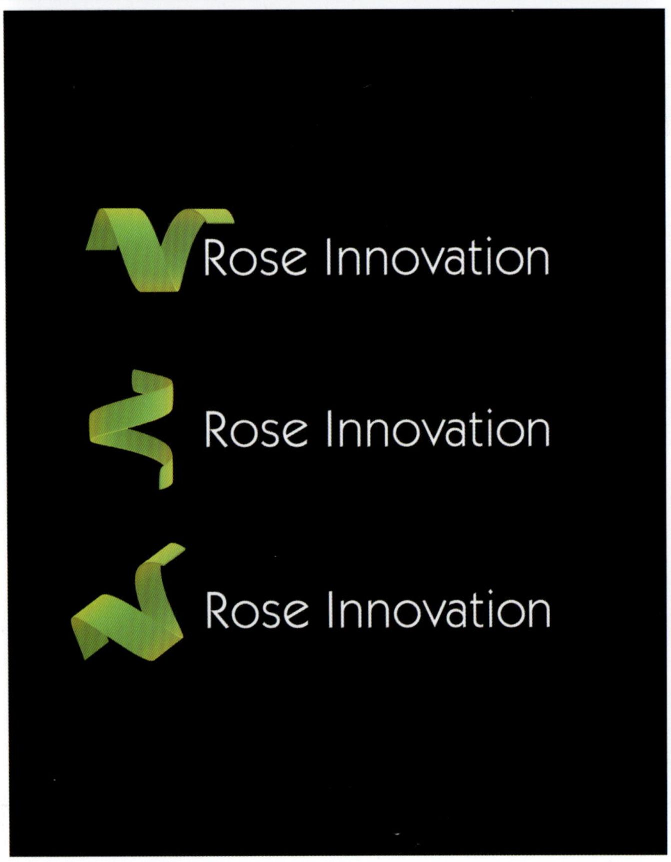

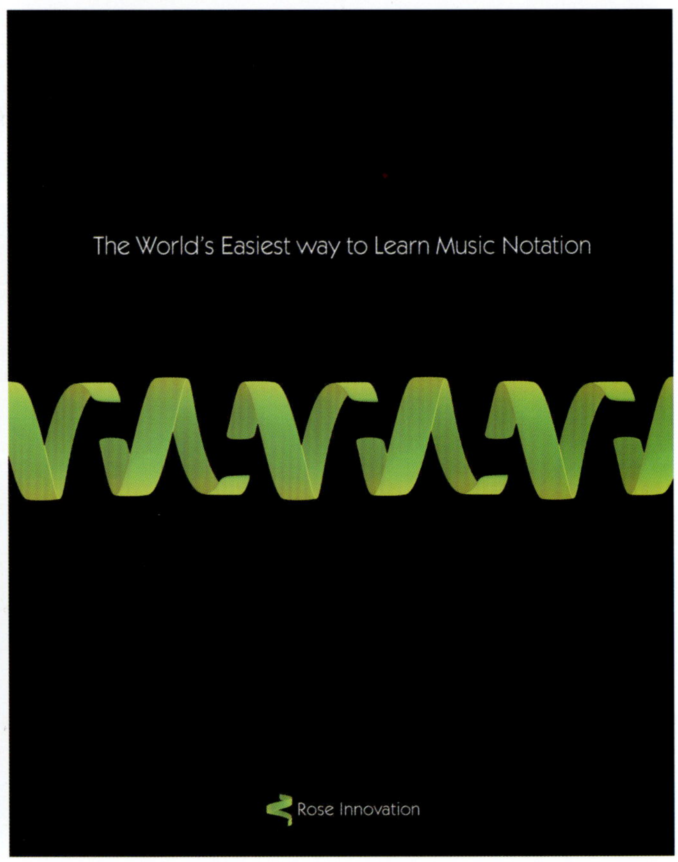

Rose Innovation™
The World's Easiest way to Learn
Music Notation
Rose Innovation™

Rose Innovation™

Rose Innovations™
Anita S. Rose
CEO, Rose Innovations
360-440-5899
ineedaninvention@gmail.com
www.roseinnovations.com

Rose Innovation
The World's Easiest way
to Learn Music Notation

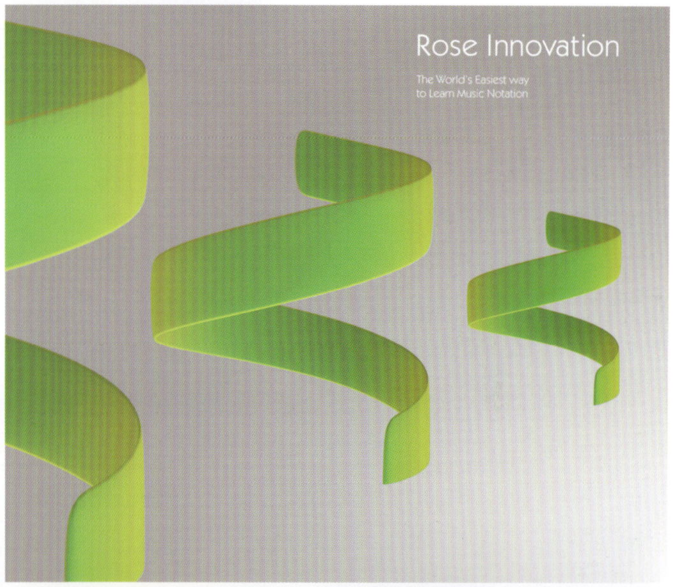
Rose Innovation
The World's Easiest way
to Learn Music Notation

Rose Innovation
The World's Easiest way
to Learn Music Notation

Rose Innovation
The World's Easiest way
to Learn Music Notation

KRAKOWSKIE SZKOŁY ARTYSTYCZNE

Client_ Krakowskie Szkoły Artystyczne
Creative Director_ Nina Gregier
Designer_ Nina Gregier
Country_ Poland

The aim of this project was to refresh the logotype and to design a coherent visual identity system for Krakowskie Szkoły Artystyczne (Cracow School of Art and Fashion Design). The system includes new logotypes (for KSA and its five subsidiary schools), printed materials, gadgets, posters and the website. The project is fully implemented.

Krakowskie Szkoły Artystyczne

KRAKOWSKIE
SZKOŁY ARTYSTYCZNE
www.ksa.edu.pl

Krakowskie Szkoły
Artystyczne

Szkoła Artystycznego
Projektowania Ubioru

Szkoła Wnętrz
i Przestrzeni

Szkoła Kreatywnej
Fotografii

Szkoła
Aktorska SPOT

Szkoła Visual
Merchandisingu

Krakowskie Szkoły
Artystyczne

C 0 / M 90 / Y 25 / K 0	R 232 / G 50 / B 115	Pantone 213 C
C 85 / M 0 / Y 65 / K 0	R 0 / G 164 / B 122	Pantone 3405 C
C 85 / M 70 / Y 0 / K 0	R 64 / G 84 / B 161	Pantone 2726 C
C 60 / M 90 / Y 20 / K 0	R 130 / G 56 / B 123	Pantone 259 C
C 0 / M 85 / Y 75 / K 0	R 233 / G 74 / B 66	Pantone 032 C
C 0 / M 0 / Y 0 / K 100	R 29 / G 29 / B 27	Pantone Process Black C

AaBbCc123

AĄBCĆDEĘFGHIJKLŁMNŃOÓPQRSŚTUVWXYZŹŻ
aąbcćdeęfghijklłmnńoópqrsśtuvwxyzźż

Signika Light
Signika Regular
Signika Semibold
Signika Bold

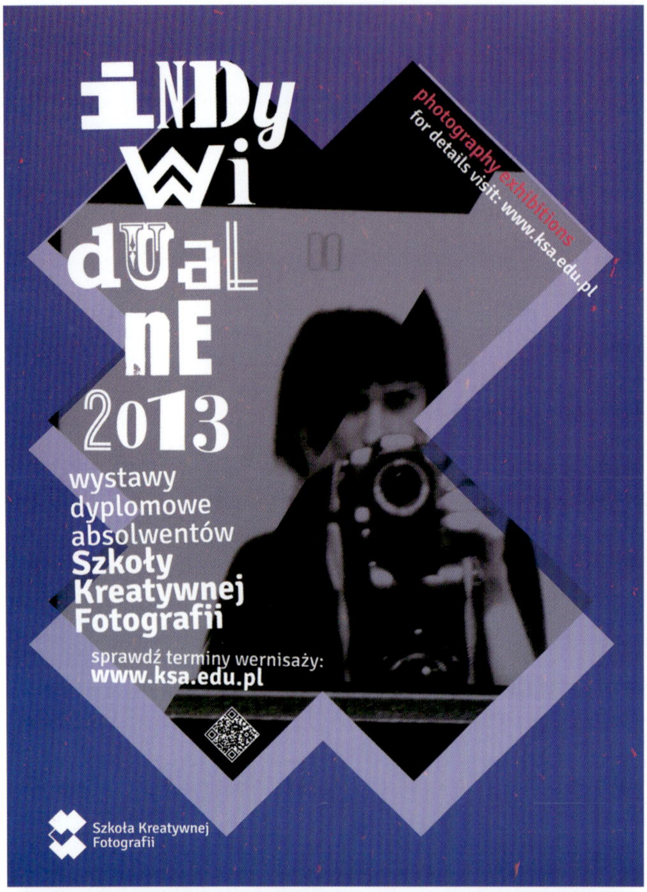
iNDy
Wi
dUaL
nE
2013
photography exhibitions
for details visit: www.ksa.edu.pl
wystawy
dyplomowe
absolwentów
Szkoły
Kreatywnej
Fotografii
sprawdź terminy wernisaży:
www.ksa.edu.pl
Szkoła Kreatywnej
Fotografii

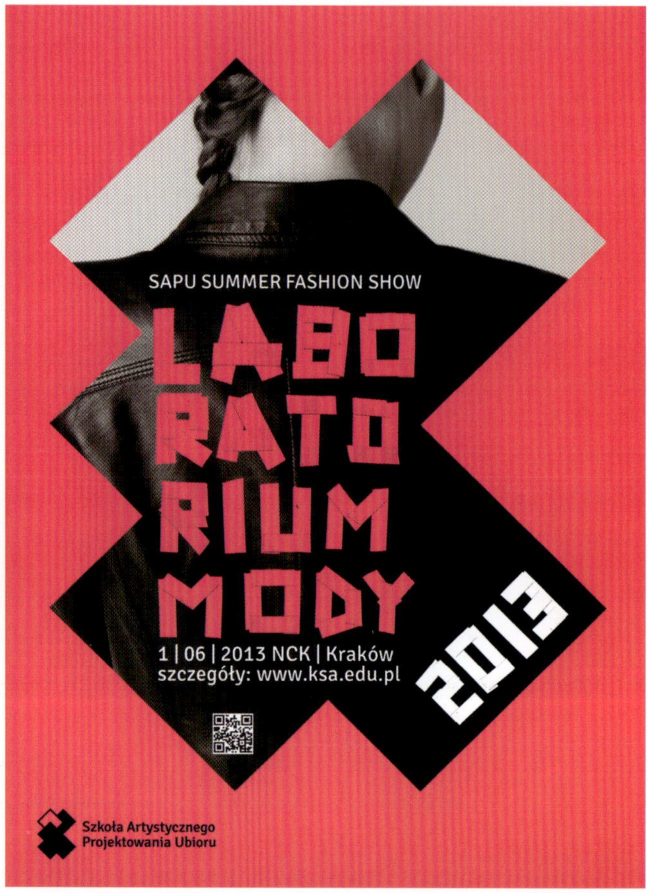
SAPU SUMMER FASHION SHOW
LABO
RATO
RIUM
MODY
2013
1 | 06 | 2013 NCK | Kraków
szczegóły: www.ksa.edu.pl
Szkoła Artystycznego
Projektowania Ubioru

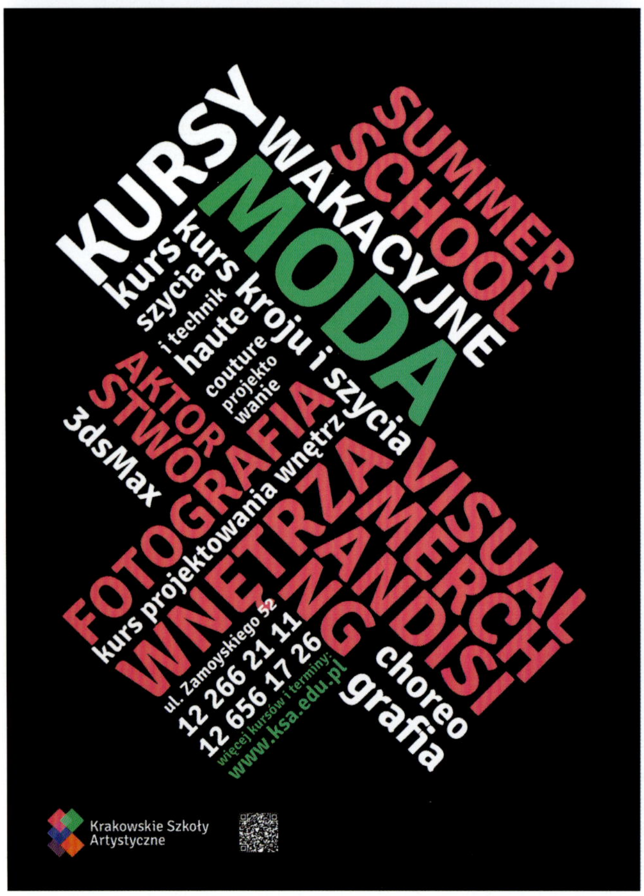
KURSY
WAKACYJNE
SUMMER
SCHOOL
MODA
kurs
kurs
szycia
kurs
i technik
haute
couture
projekto
wanie
kroju i szycia
AKTOR
STWO
3dsMax
FOTOGRAFIA
kurs projektowania wnętrz
WNĘTRZA
VISUAL
MERCH
ANDISI
NG
choreo
grafia
ul. Zamoyskiego 52
12 266 21 11
12 656 17 26
więcej kursów i terminy:
www.ksa.edu.pl
Krakowskie Szkoły
Artystyczne

END OF YEAR
EXHIBITION
Wystawa
Końcoworoczna
FOTOGRAFIA | PHOTOGRAPHY
VISUAL MERCHANDISING
WNĘTRZA | INTERIOR
MODA | FASHION
wernisaż: 20 | 06 | 2013
godz. 18.00 siedziba KSA
ul. Zamoyskiego 52, Kraków
wystawa do 15 września
info: www.ksa.edu.pl
Krakowskie Szkoły
Artystyczne

Krakowskie Szkoły
Artystyczne

SPIS TREŚCI
Logo Krakowskich Szkół Artystycznych
Wersje logo na jasnym i ciemnym tle
Budowa logo
Pole ochronne logo
Minimalne wielkości logo
Kolorystyka logo
Typografia logo
Stosowanie logo
Stosowanie logo na jednobarwnych tłach
Stosowanie logo na wielobarwnych tłach
Niedopuszczalne modyfikacje logo
Logotypy poszczególnych szkół

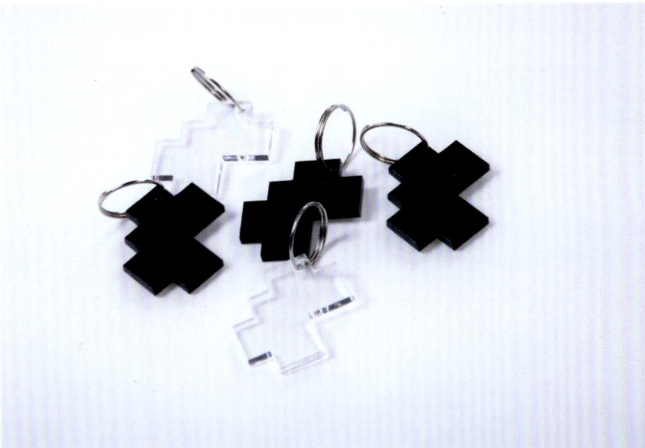

Krakowskie Szkoły
Artystyczne

www.ksa.edu.pl
Szkoła Visual
Merchandisingu
Krakowskie Szkoły
Artystyczne

DUMBAR DESIGN COLLEGE (DDC)

Client_ Dumbar Design College
Design Firm_ Studio Dumbar
Designer_ Rejane Dal Bello
Country_ Netherlands

Dumbar Design College is an initiative by Michel de Boer at Studio Dumbar to establish a school in China to emcourage exchanges of knowledge between the west and the east. The typography represents the exchange between the two countries.

DDC

DUMBAR DESIGN COLLEGE

POWERED BY: Willem De Koning

EX=
CHANGE
M. T. CICERO'S
CATO MAJOR
OR HIS
DISCOURSE
OF
DDC
DUMBAR DESIGN COLLEGE
POWERED BY: Willem de Kooning Academy
Double VISION.
SHANGHAI:
Printed and Sold by B. FRANKLIN,
MDCCXLIV.

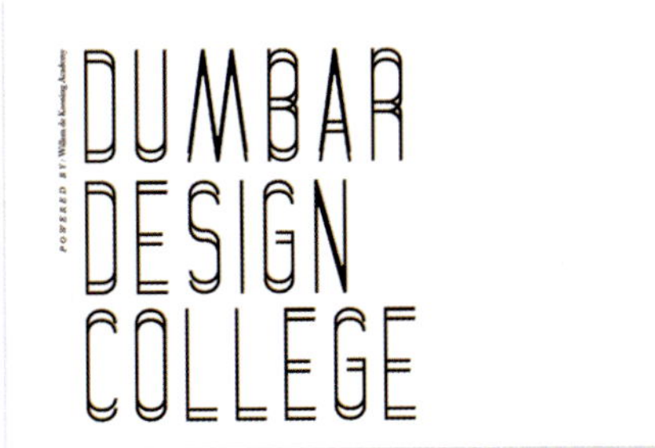
DUMBAR
DESIGN
COLLEGE
POWERED BY: Willem de Kooning Academy

DDC
DUMBAR DESIGN COLLEGE
POWERED BY: Willem de Kooning Academy
MICHEL DE BOER
LLOYSTRAAT 21
3024 EA Rotterdam
The Nederlands
T +31 (0)10 448 2222
F +31 (0)10 448 2222
www.studiodumbar.com
michel@studiodumbar.com

DDC
DUMBAR DESIGN COLLEGE
BREAK
THE
PATTERN
AND
CREATE
A NEW
ONE
With Explanatory NOTES.
-2010-
SHANGHAI:
Printed and Sold by B. FRANKLIN,
MDCCXLIV.

DUMBAR DESIGN COLLEGE
POWERED BY: Willem De Kooning
MOVIE
NIGHT
SHANGHAI:
Street / Time by St. FRANKLIN 28,
20:00 hrs - 21:00
DDC
OF
MY
OLD AGE
With Explanatory NOTES.

DDC
DUMBAR DESIGN COLLEGE
OPEN DAY
DDC
OPEN

DDC
WORKSHOP
DDC
LECTURES

DDC
DUMBAR DESIGN COLLEGE
POWERED BY: Willem de Kooning Academy

Client_ Make
Design Firm_b2s6
Creative Director_ Alexander Pomidor
Designer_ Alexander Pomidor
Country_ Russia

Make is a fund that creates and promotes innovative technologies in the sphere of art. The studio developed a brand identity that is not just creative but also really provocative. Weightless substances have composed the graphic language of the brand; they create the feeling of dynamic motion. This allows the designer to form the unique communications by creating bright, recognizable images.

make
JAPANESE
ARTS FESTIVAL
Performances
by Eric Brown
and the group
Great Axe
in the exhib
make
19:30AM
new
in
contemporary
video
art
young
make
make
THE
ARCHITECTURAL
STYLE OF MOSCOW
GROUP EXHIBITION PSTUDIO
AND ROMAN SHIROKO
16-26April
FELIPE GONZALEZ:
PAINTINGS SCULPTURE
make
5-12 NOVEMBER
18-29 July
JOHN BENSON:
PEOPLE AND THECITY
make
Imaginary Museum
make
Frans Hals
Imaginary Museum
make
Anthony van Dyck

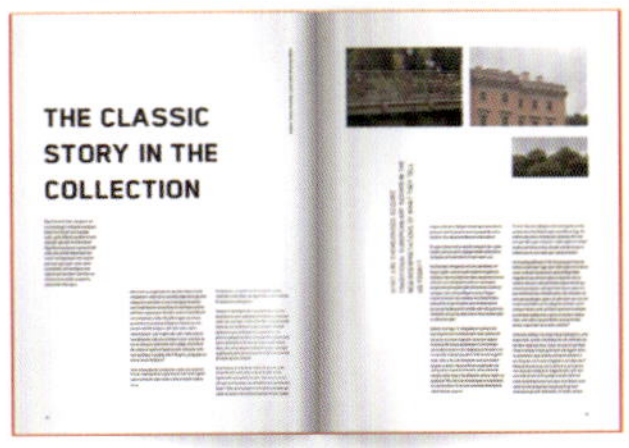
THE CLASSIC
STORY IN THE
COLLECTION

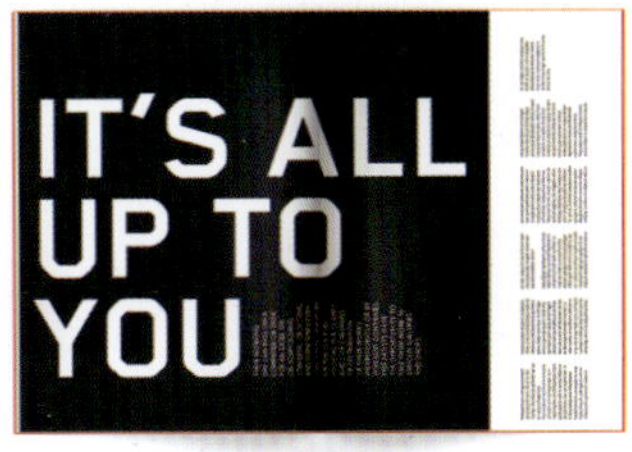
IT'S ALL
UP TO
YOU

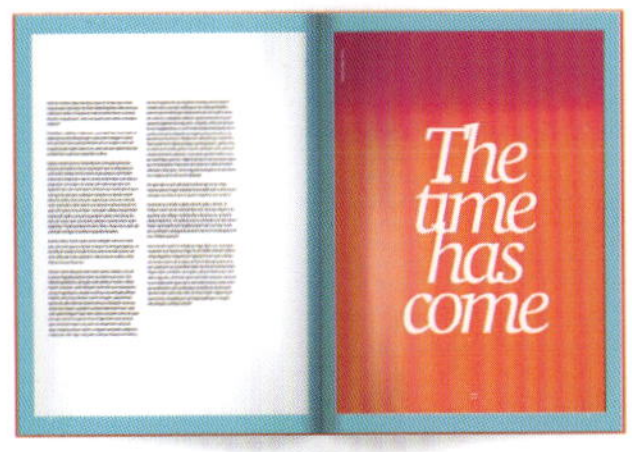
The
time
has
come

MAKE

make

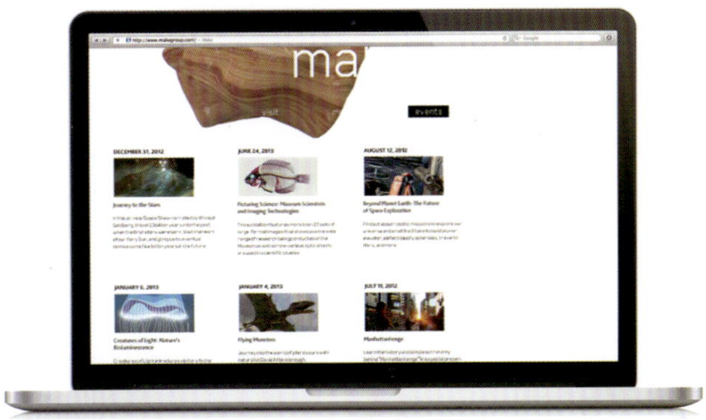
ma

make

make
OPEN DAILY

JHERONIMUS BOSCH'S 500 YEARS' ANNIVERSARY

Client_ City of Den Bosch
Design Firm_ Studio Dumbar
Designer_ Rejane Dal Bello
Country_ Netherlands

This visual identity proposal is for the City of Den Bosch, in combination with the celebration for the painter Jheronimus Bosch's 500-year anniversary (2016). The city name and the painter's name are intertwined.

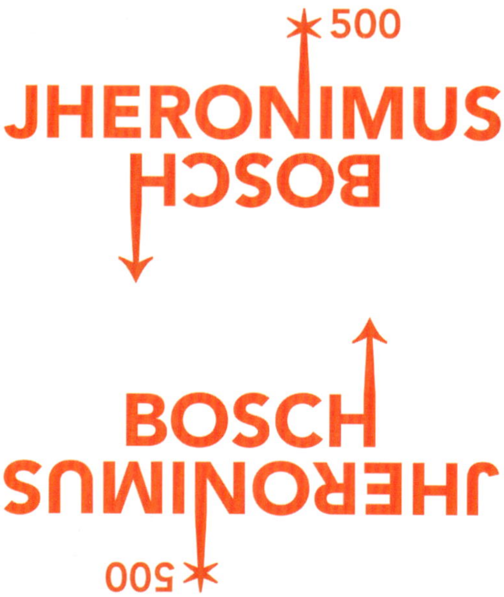

VISMARKT
HALLO

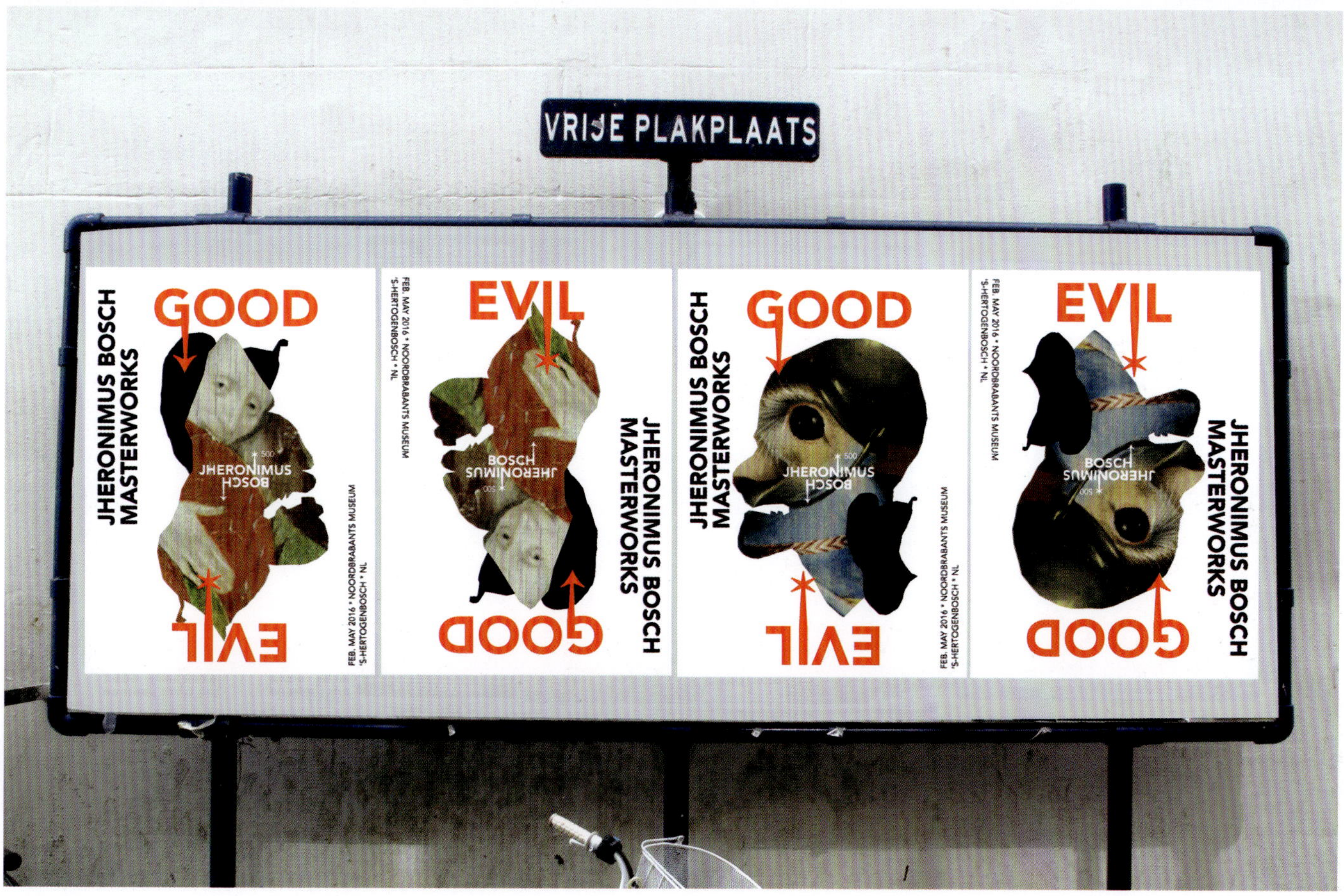
VRIJE PLAKPLAATS
GOOD
EVIL
JHERONIMUS BOSCH MASTERWORKS
JHERONIMUS
BOSCH
500
FEB. MAY 2016 • NOORDBRABANTS MUSEUM
'S-HERTOGENBOSCH • NL

SOFIA 2019 — EUROPEAN CAPITAL OF CULTURE

Client_ Municipality of Sofia
Designer_ Boris Bonev
Country_ Bulgaria

The concept of this project is based on the definition of culture as the integrated pattern of human knowledge, belief, and behavior. The designer took the shield from the crest of Sofia with its contrasting colors. Then, inspired by the definition of culture, he created three different patterns of the shield to represent the three elements. Combined with color, these patterns became tiny display-like structures. The system becomes richer in every following step and thus the logos open up numerous possibilities for communicating the diverse events surrounding the initiative.

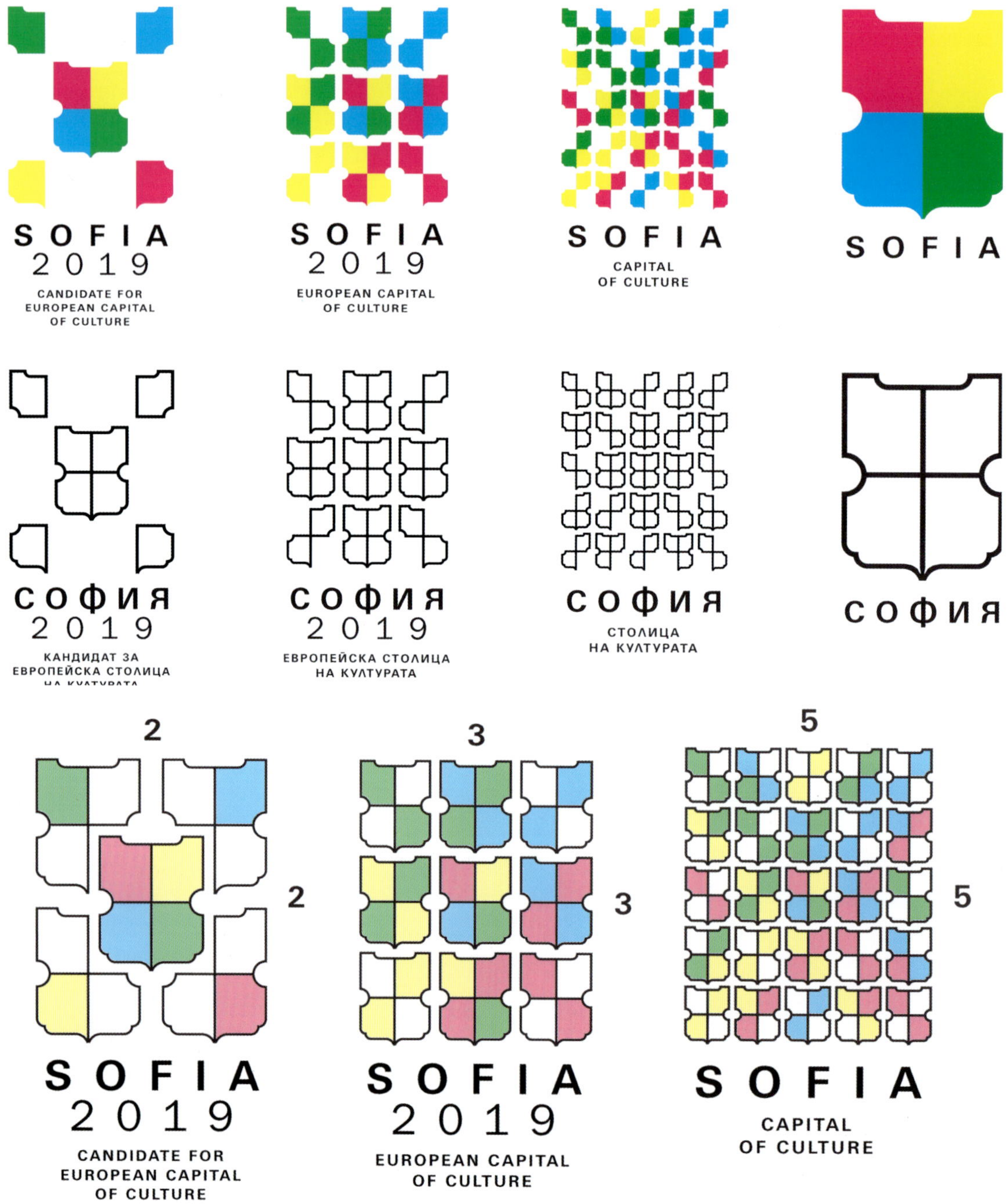

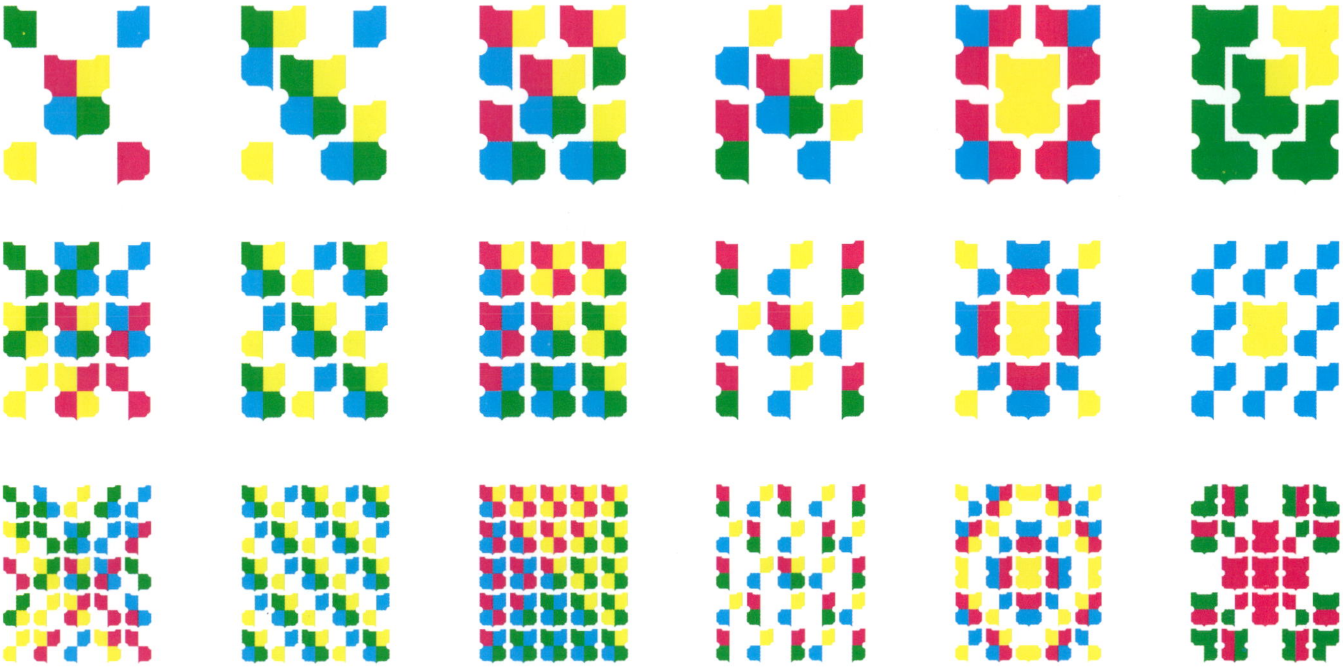

BASIC
STRUCTURE 2/2
BASIC
STRUCTURE 3/3
BASIC
STRUCTURE 5/5

PRESENT
CITY
PRESENT
CITY
PRESENT
CITY

DIVERSE
CITY
DIVERSE
CITY
DIVERSE
CITY

CREATIVE
CITY
CREATIVE
CITY
CREATIVE
CITY

YOUTH
CITY
YOUTH
CITY
YOUTH
CITY

ALTERNATIVE
CITY
KNOWLEDGE
CITY
TRADITION
CITY

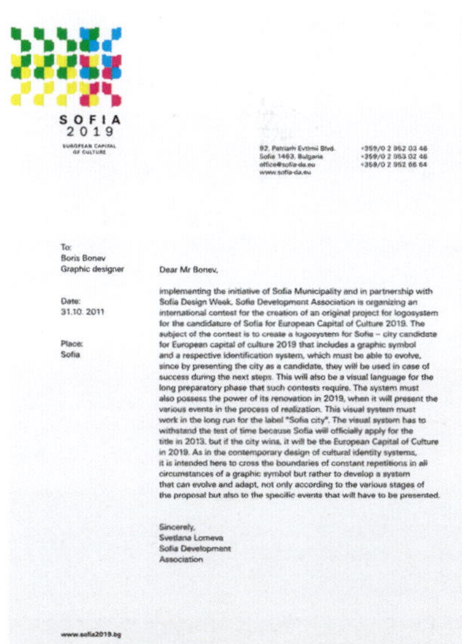

SOFIA
2019
EUROPEAN CAPITAL
OF CULTURE

92, Patriarh Evtimii Blvd.
Sofia 1463, Bulgaria
office@sofia-da.eu
www.sofia-da.eu

+359/0 2 952 03 46
+359/0 2 953 02 46
+359/0 2 952 66 64

To:
Boris Bonev
Graphic designer

Date:
31.10. 2011

Place:
Sofia

Dear Mr Bonev,

implementing the initiative of Sofia Municipality and in partnership with Sofia Design Week, Sofia Development Association is organizing an international contest for the creation of an original project for logosystem for the candidature of Sofia for European Capital of Culture 2019. The subject of the contest is to create a logosystem for Sofia – city candidate for European capital of culture 2019 that includes a graphic symbol and a respective identification system, which must be able to evolve, since by presenting the city as a candidate, they will be used in case of success during the next steps. This will also be a visual language for the long preparatory phase that such contests require. The system must also possess the power of its renovation in 2019, when it will present the various events in the process of realization. This visual system must work in the long run for the label "Sofia city". The visual system has to withstand the test of time because Sofia will officially apply for the title in 2013, but if the city wins, it will be the European Capital of Culture in 2019. As in the contemporary design of cultural identity systems, it is intended here to cross the boundaries of constant repetitions in all circumstances of a graphic symbol but rather to develop a system that can evolve and adapt, not only according to the various stages of the proposal but also to the specific events that will have to be presented.

Sincerely,
Svetlana Lomeva
Sofia Development
Association

www.sofia2019.bg

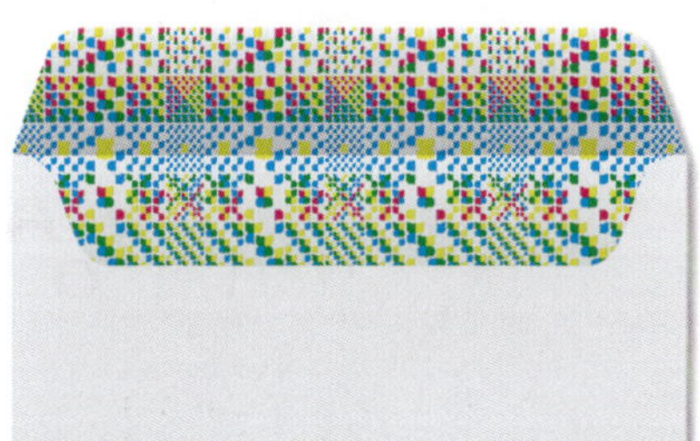

CITY OF DELFT

Client_ City Marketing of Delft
Design Firm_ Studio Dumbar
Designer_ Rejane Dal Bello
Country_ Netherlands

The studio was challenged with creating an identify package for the city of Delft that shows its well-known historical image as well as its innovative character, and that can be used for city marketing activities. The logo unites traditional typographic elements with newly designed characters; icons show silhouettes of both historical and modern Delft and its products; typography combines a sans serif with a refined serif font. The slashes under the "D" historically indicate an abbreviation. This "D" now stands for Delft.

Delft

CREATING HISTORY

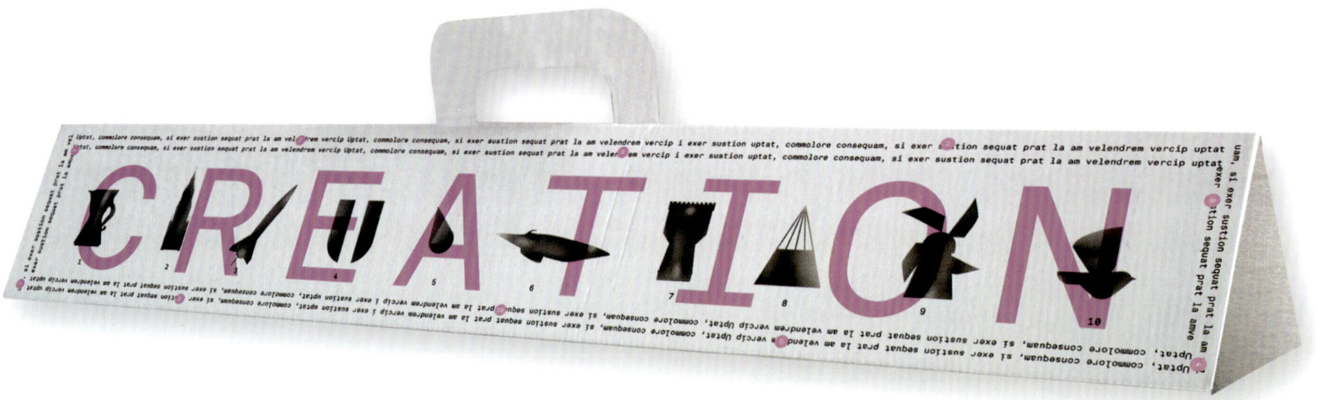

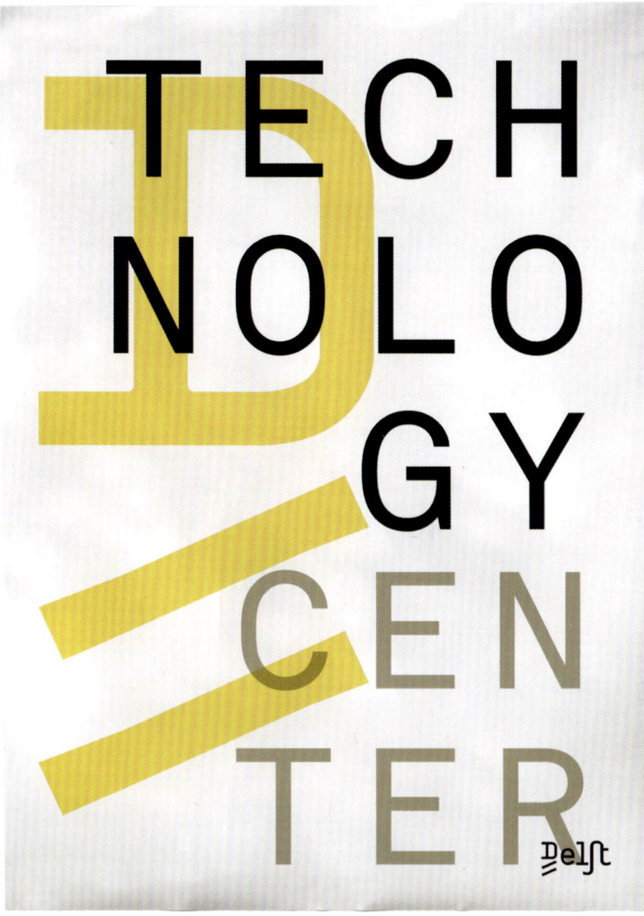
TECH
NOLO
GY
CEN
TER
Delft

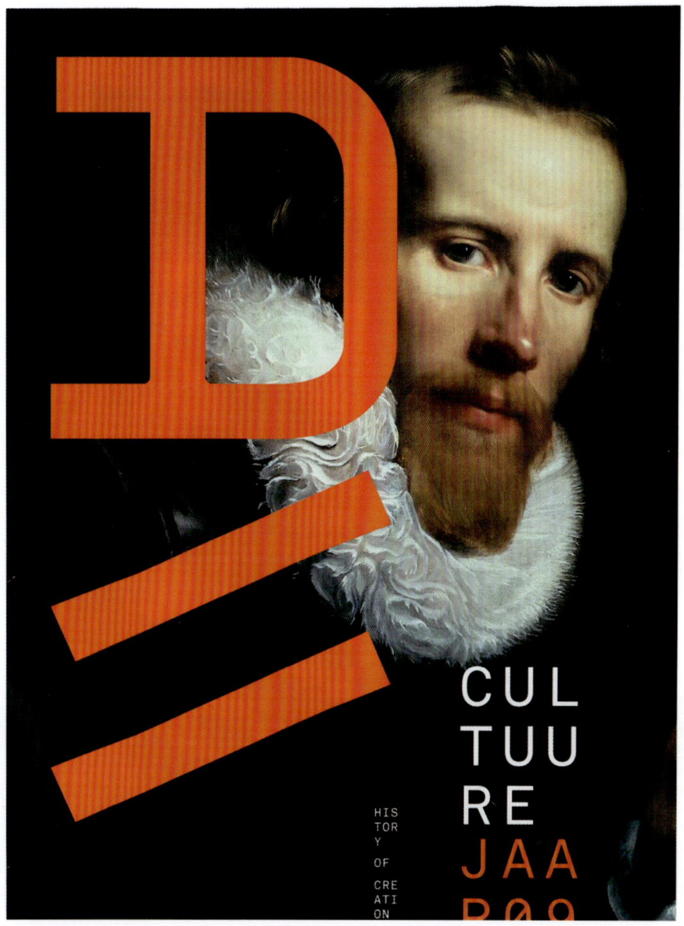
CUL
TUU
RE
JAA
HIS
TOR
Y
OF
CRE
ATI
ON

Delft
DELFT
SHOPP
ING
2009
Delft
HISTO
RICAL
CITY
WALK
Delft
DE
KONINK
LIJKE
PORCE
LEYNE
FLES

CITY OF AVILA

Client_ Avila City Council
Design Firm_ Entre Líneas
Creative Directors_ Monica Villoslada, Oscar Luis
Designers_ Monica Villoslada, Oscar Luis
Country_ Spain

The Spanish city of Avila is a UNESCO World Heritage Site. Its most representative monument is its medieval wall, which encloses the old city. The city brand combines, in a single stroke, the silhouette of the footprint of this wall with what resembles a thought bubble. This isotype carries the claim, "Think of Avila." The corporate identity is completed by a set of sub-brands that are used to identify the multiple faces of the city.

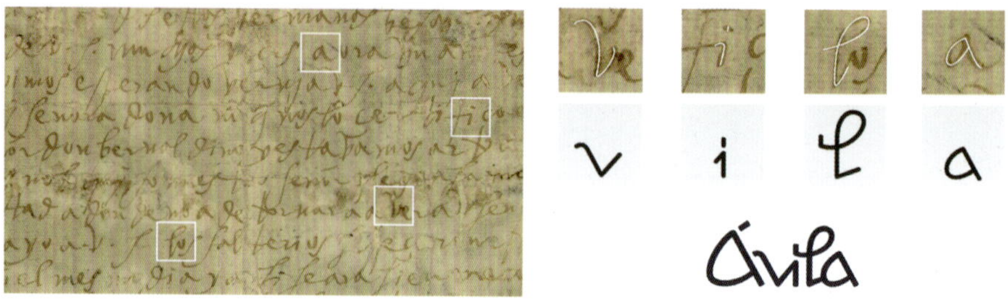

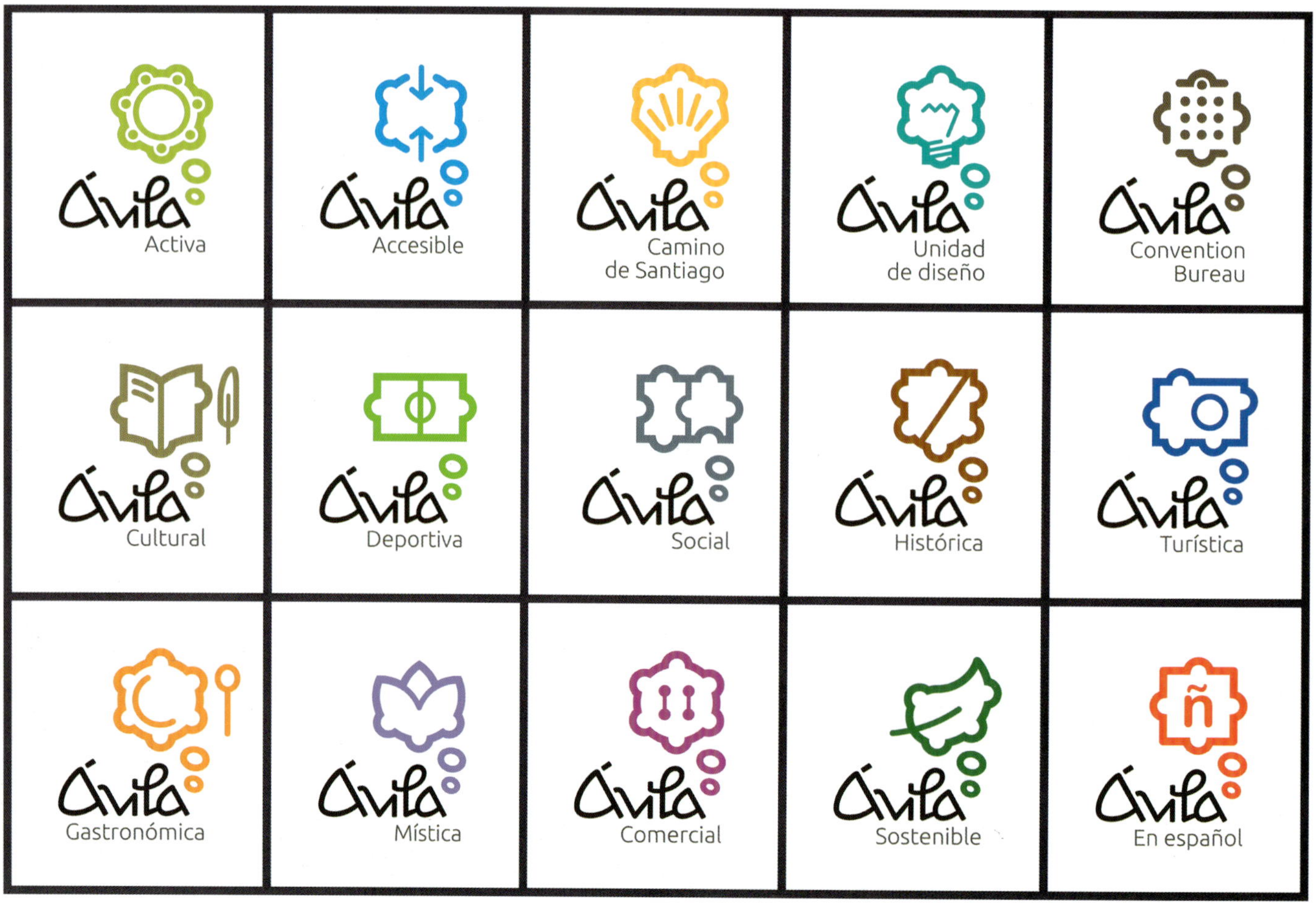

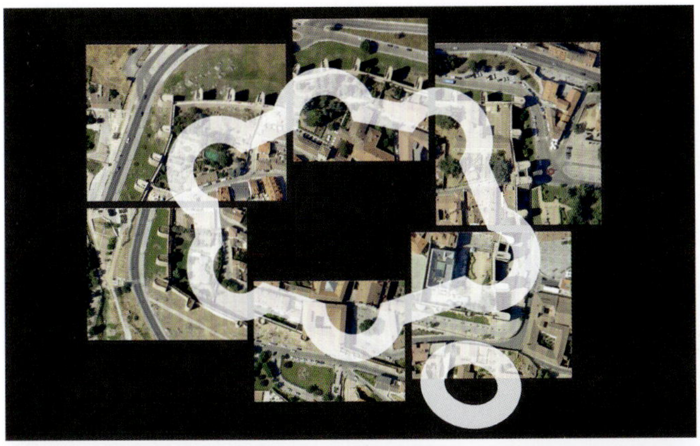

Patrimonial
Loren ipsum sit amet consectetuer
adipiscing elit sed diam nonummy nibh
"EUISMOD TINCIDUNT" ut laoreet dolore
magna aliquam erat volutpat
ut wisi enim ad minim
Tradicional
Loren ipsum sit amet consectetuer
adipiscing elit sed diam nonummy nibh
"EUISMOD TINCIDUNT" ut laoreet dolore
magna aliquam erat volutpat
ut wisi enim ad minim
Cultural
Loren ipsum sit amet consectetuer
adipiscing elit sed diam nonummy nibh
"EUISMOD TINCIDUNT" ut laoreet dolore
magna aliquam erat volutpat
ut wisi enim ad minim
Participativa
Loren ipsum sit amet consectetuer
adipiscing elit sed diam nonummy nibh
"EUISMOD TINCIDUNT" ut laoreet dolore
magna aliquam erat volutpat
ut wisi enim ad minim

Innovadora
Las redes sociales

CITY OF MELBOURNE

Client_ City of Melbourne
Design Firm_ Landor Associates
Creative Director_ Jason Little
Strategy Directors_ James Cockerille, Cable Daniel-Dreyfus
Designers_ Jefton Sungkar, Jason Little, Sam Pemberton
Country_ Australia

Melbourne is a dynamic and progressive city, internationally recognized for its diversity, innovation, sustainability and livability. Its new identity should reflect Melbourne's cool sophistication, capture the passion of the council and the people, and enable a unified and future focus for the city. Centered on a geometric framework, the identity is as iconic and multi-faceted as the city itself. This framework allows for creative interpretation. At its heart, the "M" provides an iconic surface for endless visual executions to take place, adapting to suit the full range of audiences.

Total Watermark
City as a catchment
CITY OF MELBOURNE

Activation, Infrastructure, Regulation, Partnership
POLICY FOR THE 24 HOUR CITY
A framework for action
CITY OF MELBOURNE

Summer in the City
Event Guide
CITY OF MELBOURNE

A focus on safety
2010
OUT & ABOUT
CITY OF MELBOURNE

City of Melbourne
2010
Cultural Diversity
CITY OF MELBOURNE

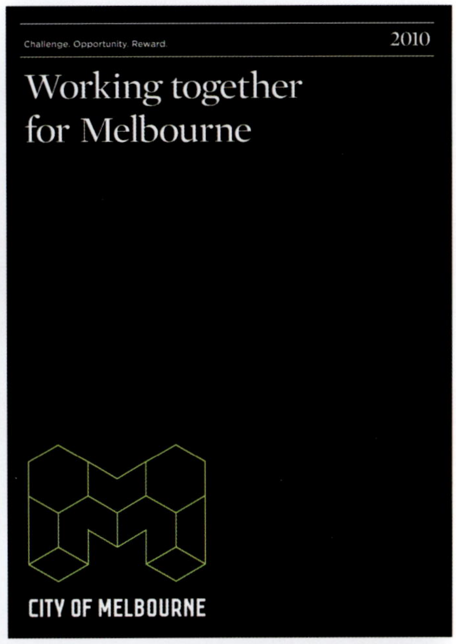
Challenge. Opportunity. Reward.
2010
Working together for Melbourne
CITY OF MELBOURNE

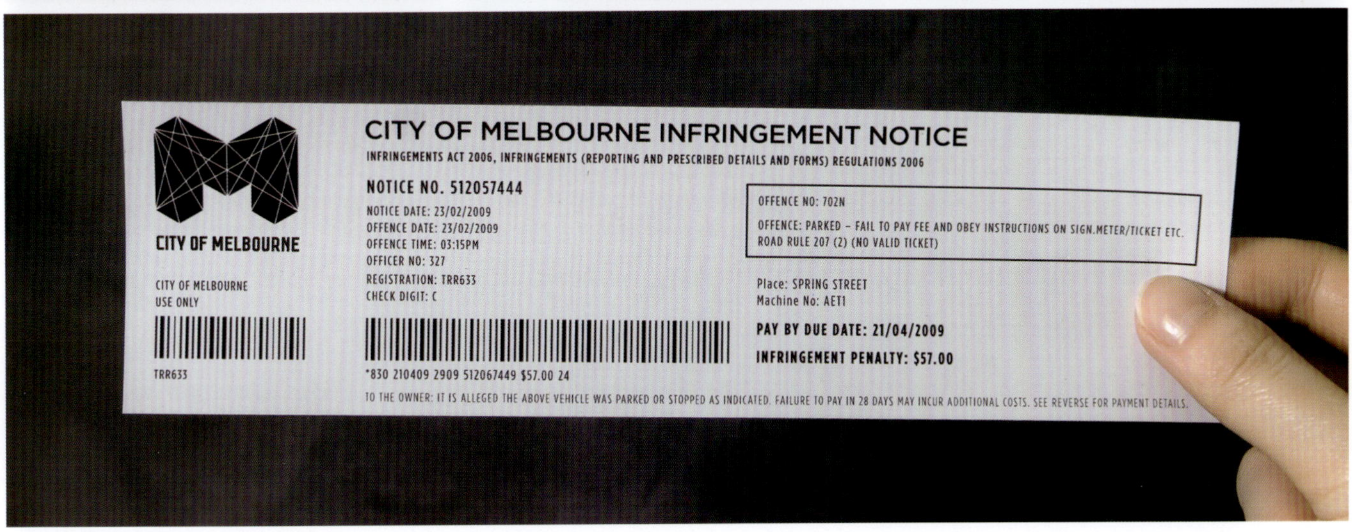
CITY OF MELBOURNE
CITY OF MELBOURNE USE ONLY
TRR633
CITY OF MELBOURNE INFRINGEMENT NOTICE
INFRINGEMENTS ACT 2006, INFRINGEMENTS (REPORTING AND PRESCRIBED DETAILS AND FORMS) REGULATIONS 2006
NOTICE NO. 512057444
NOTICE DATE: 23/02/2009
OFFENCE DATE: 23/02/2009
OFFENCE TIME: 03:15PM
OFFICER NO: 327
REGISTRATION: TRR633
CHECK DIGIT: C
*830 210409 2909 512067449 $57.00 24
OFFENCE NO: 702N
OFFENCE: PARKED - FAIL TO PAY FEE AND OBEY INSTRUCTIONS ON SIGN.METER/TICKET ETC.
ROAD RULE 207 (2) (NO VALID TICKET)
Place: SPRING STREET
Machine No: AET1
PAY BY DUE DATE: 21/04/2009
INFRINGEMENT PENALTY: $57.00
TO THE OWNER: IT IS ALLEGED THE ABOVE VEHICLE WAS PARKED OR STOPPED AS INDICATED. FAILURE TO PAY IN 28 DAYS MAY INCUR ADDITIONAL COSTS. SEE REVERSE FOR PAYMENT DETAILS.

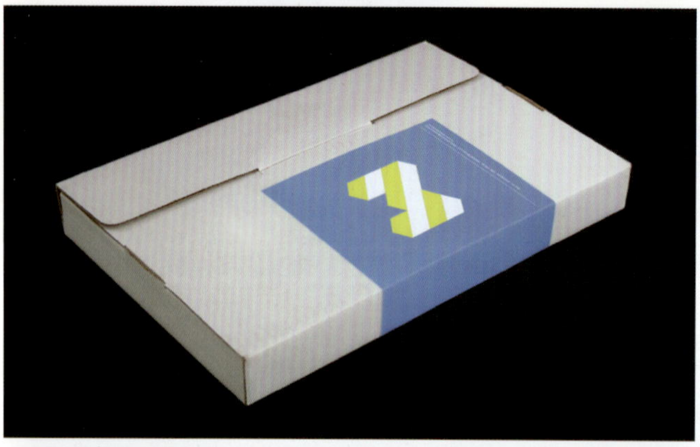

CITY OF MELBOURNE
ARCADE-ART
LANEWAY-ART
STREET-ART
MELBOURNE 15-25 MARCH 2010

Melbourne's February Waterfest
MOOMBA
WaterFest
CITY OF MELBOURNE

CITY
RHYTHMS

EVENTS
MANAGEMENT

YOUR MELBOURNE
CITY OF MELBOURNE

quare
Swanston Street - Flinders Street Station - Federation Square
MELBOURNE PERSON OF THE YEAR
Vote for your Melbourne person of the year by visting:
MELBOURNEPERSONOFTHEYEAR.COM.AU
CITY OF MELBOURNE

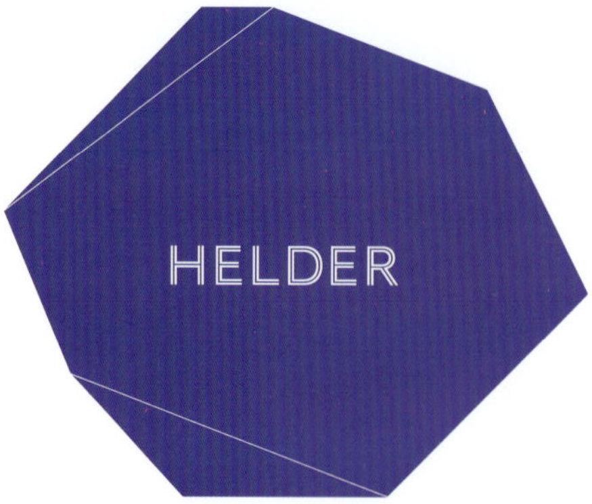

Client_ Helder
Design Firm_COOEE
Designer_ Leon Dijkstra
Country_ Netherlands

Helder is a centre for mental health, self-realization and meditation. In Dutch the word "helder" means "clear." The starting point for this identity was the idea of reflection and symmetry. This resulted in a base grid that is built on a simplified mandala symbol, which often exhibits radial balance. This principle results in a variety of logos built up from triangles, which can be rotated independently of each other. Each constructed logo represents an individual and personal character, but remains recognizable. The logotype consists of a geometric moonscape typeface by making use of the same grid.

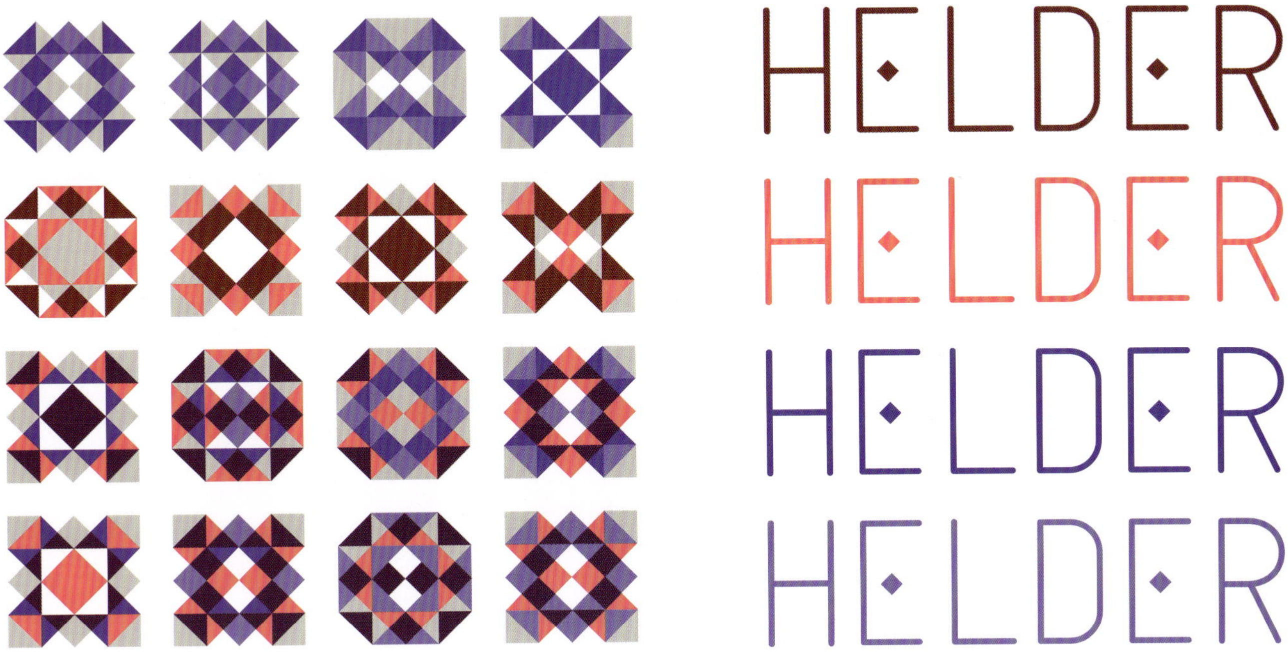
HELDER
HELDER
HELDER
HELDER

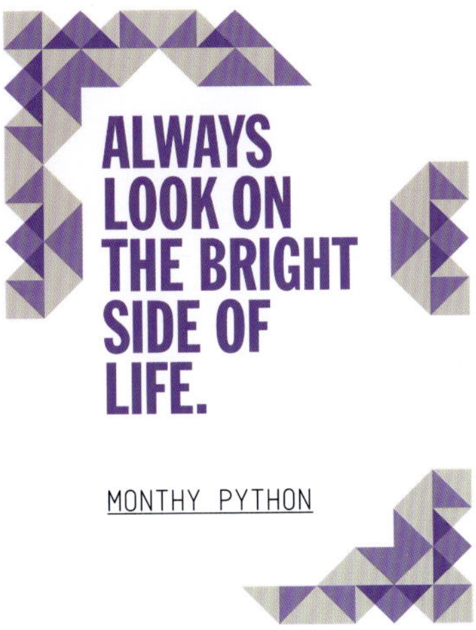
ALWAYS LOOK ON THE BRIGHT SIDE OF LIFE.
MONTHY PYTHON

IK BEN NIET LABIEL, IK BEN EMOTIONEEL FLEXIBEL.
THEO MAASSEN

MENSEN, DE ZIN VAN HET LEVEN IS ZIN IN HET LEVEN.
WIM DE BIE

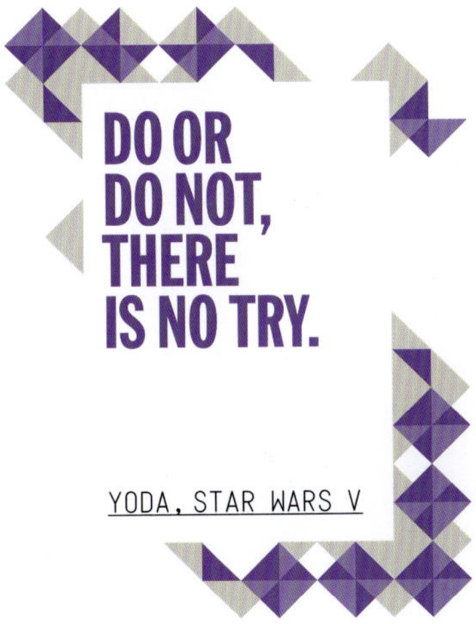
DO OR DO NOT, THERE IS NO TRY.
YODA, STAR WARS V

WEES WAT JE BENT. KOPIEER NIET. VOLG NIEMAND.
MAITREYA

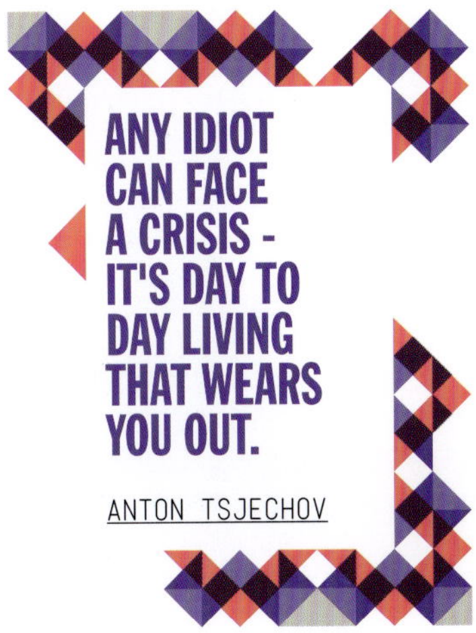
ANY IDIOT CAN FACE A CRISIS - IT'S DAY TO DAY LIVING THAT WEARS YOU OUT.
ANTON TSJECHOV

WOW

Client_WOW. Karaoke School Moscow
Designer_Vlad Likh
Country_Russia

WOW. Karaoke School is the place where anyone can learn how to perform with confidence on stage, and gain applause. The designer decided to use the characters of famous singers as an implication that when people hold the microphone — they can easily become their favorite singers.

WOW

KARAOKE SCHOOL

MAY 20
7 PM
WORKSHOP
BY A. MERCH
MAY 25
2 PM
WORKSHOP
MAY 24
9 PM
WOW
KARAOKE SCHOOL

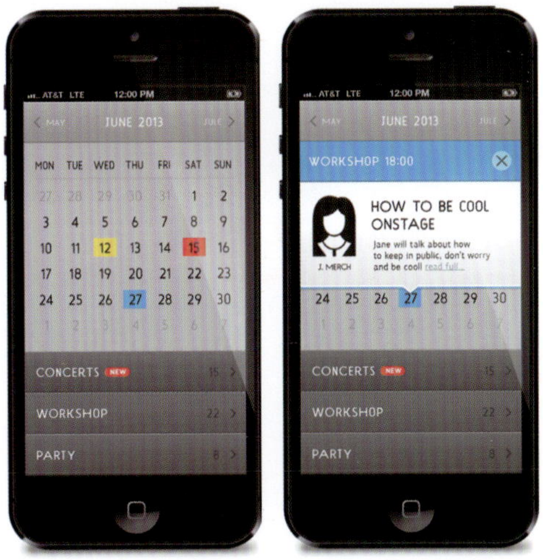
JUNE 2013
WORKSHOP 18:00
HOW TO BE COOL
ONSTAGE
CONCERTS
WORKSHOP
PARTY

WOW
KARAOKE SCHOOL
SING LIKE AMY
TVERSKAYA, 4 / WOW.RU

ARCHITECTURE DESIGN

Client_Personal Work
Design Firm_Michele Mazzucco
Creative Director_Michele Mazzucco
Designer_Michele Mazzucco
Country_Italy

Woodou is an architecture studio focused on sustainable technologies. Inspired by Antoni Gaudi's sketches for the "Sagrada Familia" building structure, the designer came up with a matrix which has been used as the basis for the dynamic identity. The logo is a continuous rotating solid, showing different views of itself in different situations, like a floating architectural block. The color palette recreates a virtual environment, where the green becomes an ever-present natural element in the grey scale. A pattern for the identity system comes from the same matrix, like a fragmented version of the logo.

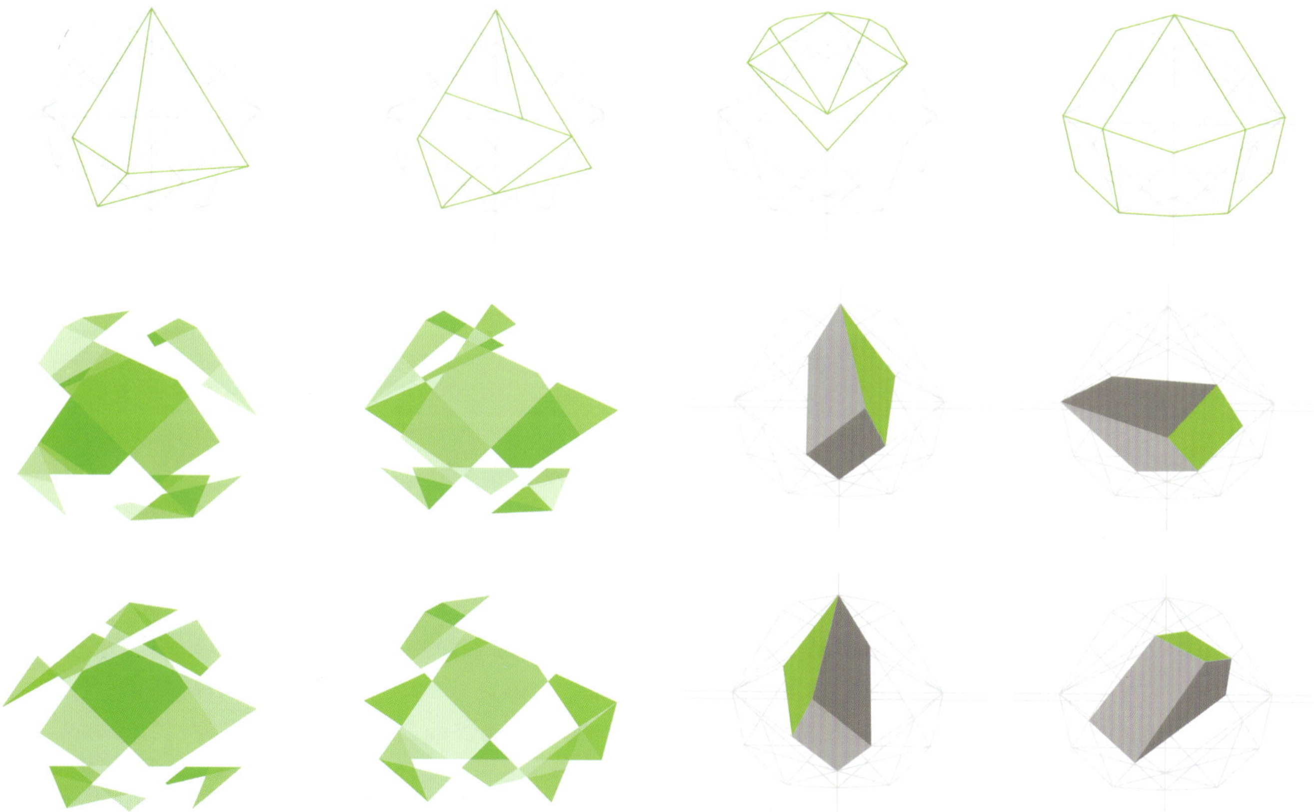

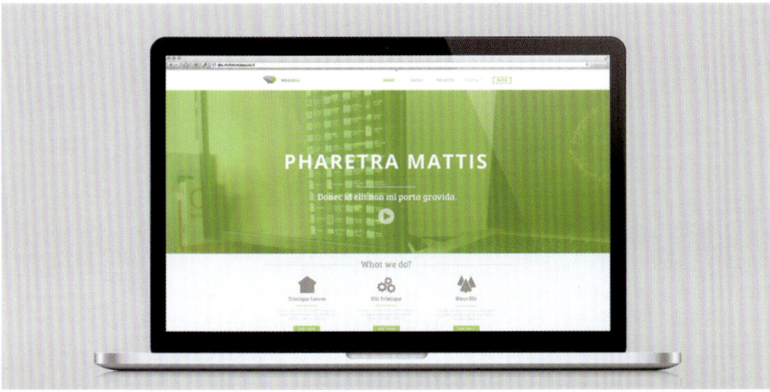
PHARETRA MATTIS
What we do?

Woodou

Woodou
Woodou

Woodou
WOODOU
20, Friar John Way
PERON WA · 6168
(08) 9424 5600
www.woodou.co
hsmythe@woodou.co

Woodou
Woodou
Woodou
TOBY WATERHOUSE
WOODOU
WOODOU
HUNTER SMYTHE
Woodou
HUNTER SMYTHE
Co-Founder

KOUNKUEY DESIGN INITIATIVE

Client_Kounkuey Design Initiative
Design Firm_Oui Oui Danni Sinisi
Art Director_Danni Sinisi
Designer_Danni Sinisi
Country_Kenya

This is a logo and identity system created for the Kounkuey Design Initiative (KDI), a landscape architecture firm dedicated to the thoughtful design of buildings, parks and infrastructure, as well as the social and economic programs to support them. The typographic logo was created with the intention of distinguishing the studio as a leader in the field, while referencing their African roots. A supporting icon, created by the stamp and rotation of the "D" character, was created to communicate the firm's dynamic approach.

KDI

KOUNKUEY DESIGN INITIATIVE

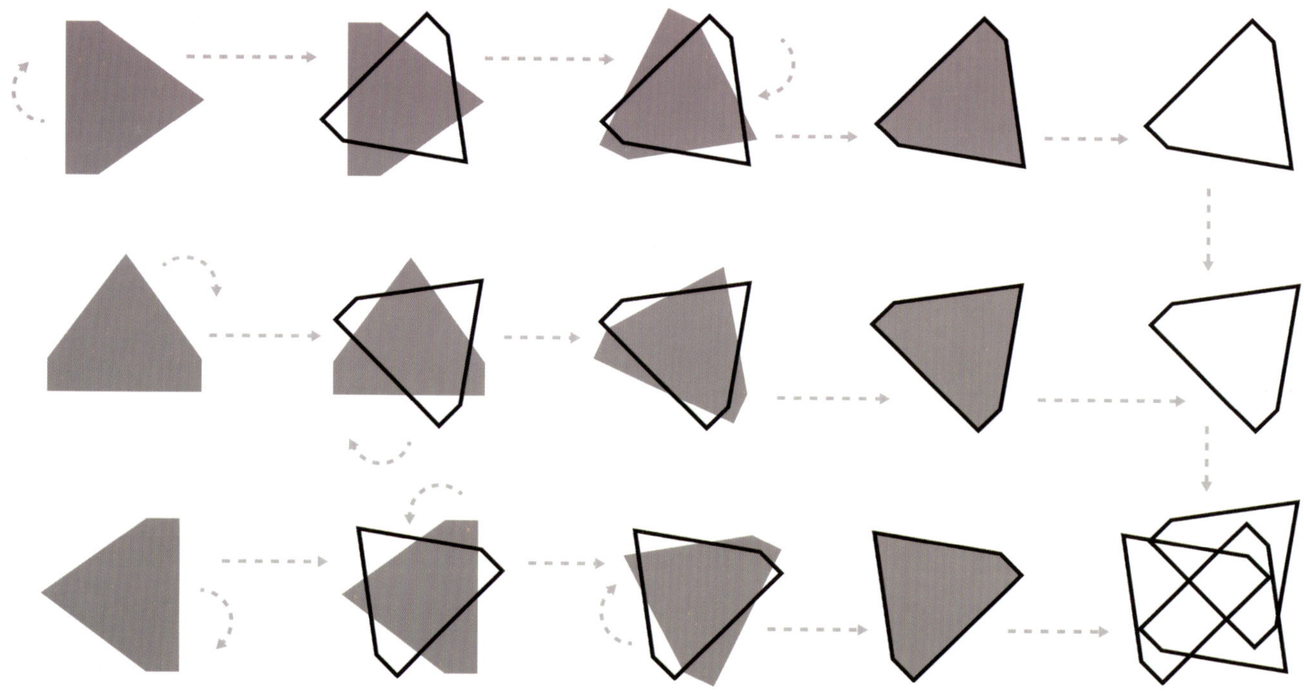

Stone Black
C 0
M 0
Y 0
K 100

Cloud White
C 0
M 0
Y 0
K 0

Pantone 583
C 23
M 0
Y 100
K 17

Pantone 3272
C 100
M 0
Y 44
K 0

Pantone 180
C 0
M 79
Y 100
K 11

Pantone 287
C 100
M 68
Y 0
K 12

Pantone Cool Gray 10
C 0
M 2
Y 0
K 60

Pantone Cool Gray 4
C 0
M 0
Y 0
K 24

Color Pairing
There are three dominant colors within the KDI system:

Pantone 583
Pantone 3272
Pantone 180

They must be paired with the proper accent colors as shown

Pantone 583
C 23
M 0
Y 100
K 17

Pantone 3272
C 100
M 0
Y 44
K 0

Pantone 180
C 0
M 79
Y 100
K 11

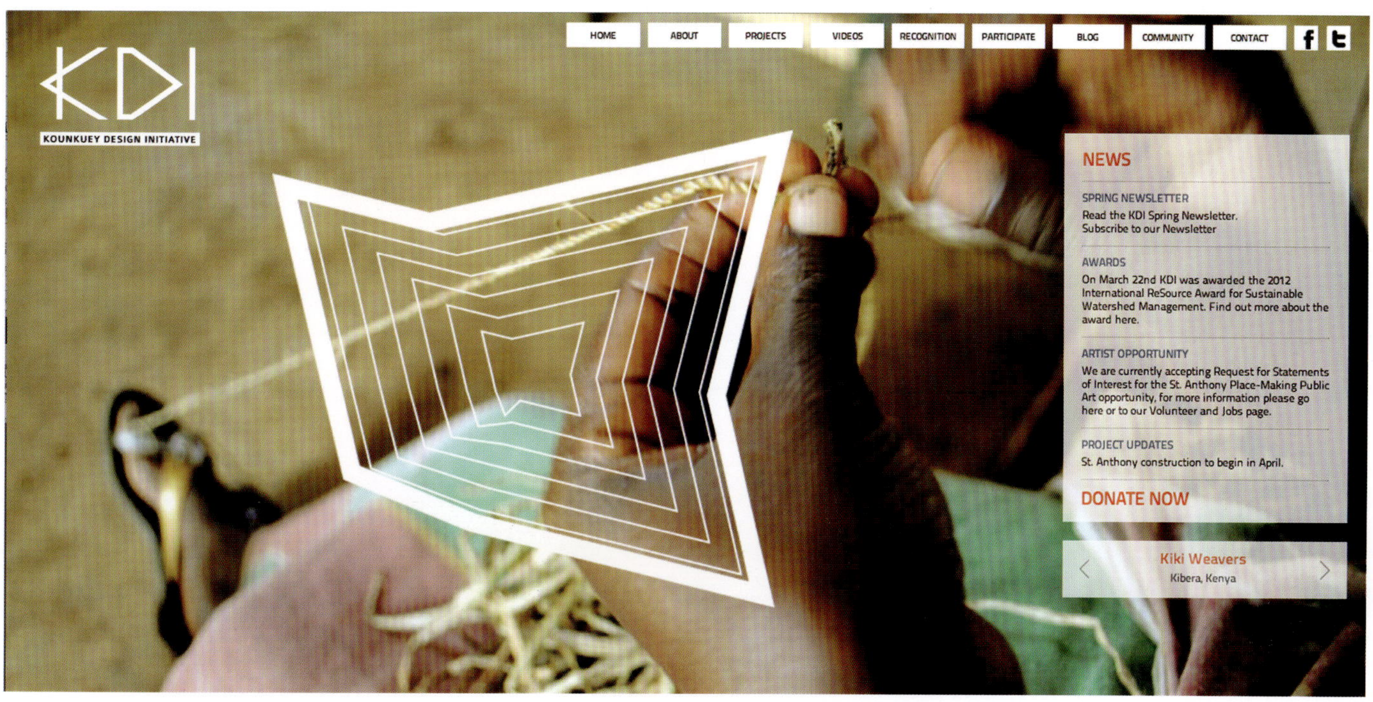

Client_ISIS
Design Firm_Landor Associates
Creative Director_Jason Little
Designers_Ivana Martinovic, Jason Little, Joao Peres
Country_Australia

Expressive branding and design does not normally feature highly with organizations that work within construction, project management and environmental organizations, but ISIS approved an identity that could express itself with the same degree of diversity as the projects the firm takes on and completes. The concept of the window or lens to the future proves ISIS with the opportunity to tailor prospectuses, communicate their plans onsite, and show the transformation at work, which is at the very heart of the brand strategy.

Hello
G'day
Cheers
Thanks
Mick

Unfortunately one

2008
Review

Client_ Flux Consultants
Design Firm_ RE
Creative Director_ Jason Little
Designers_ Ellie See, Erin Hoffman, Jason Little
Country_ Australia

Flux is a specialist environmental design and engineering consultancy, dedicated to transformative sustainability in the built environment. Their approach is about stripping out much of the over-engineering to help buildings thrive with better living and working conditions through innovative natural systems, cleaner materials, ventilation, etc. It can almost be described as anti-engineering. The flexible identity emphasizes this process of simplification and elimination. The strike-through device is used to distil lengthy information to its core message, and act as a recognizable visual language for the organization.

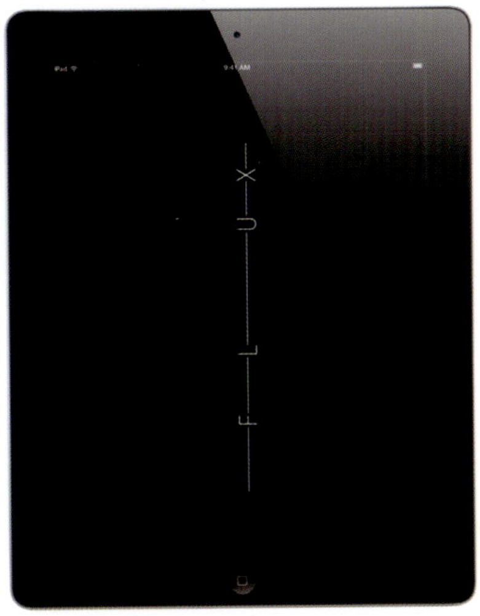

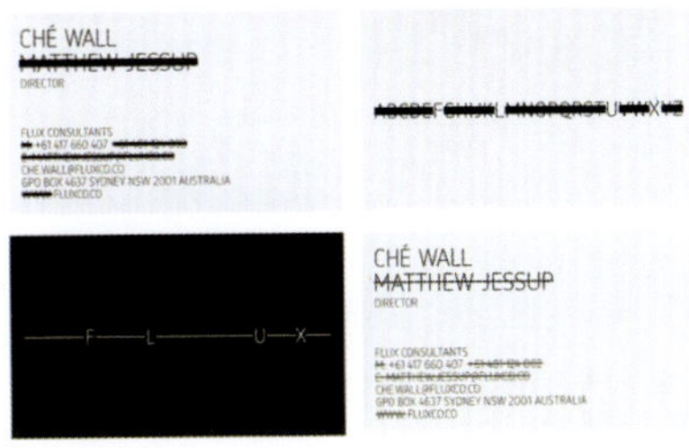

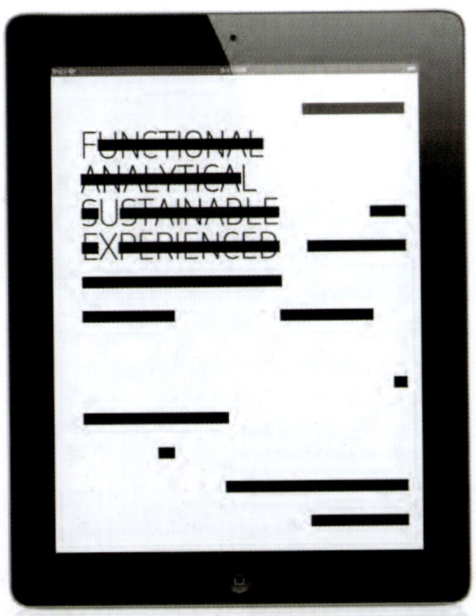

Client_ Eshes
Design Firm_ Pianofuzz Design Studio
Country_ Brazil

The studio was hired to develop the visual identity project for Eshes, a new product design studio. Giving a meaning and a different approach to the design performance, producing without harming the environment and life, approaching consumerism healthily without natural damage and waste are some essential points that define the philosophy of Eshes. The design studio and the client worked together, collaboratively, in distinct stages to develop the identity.

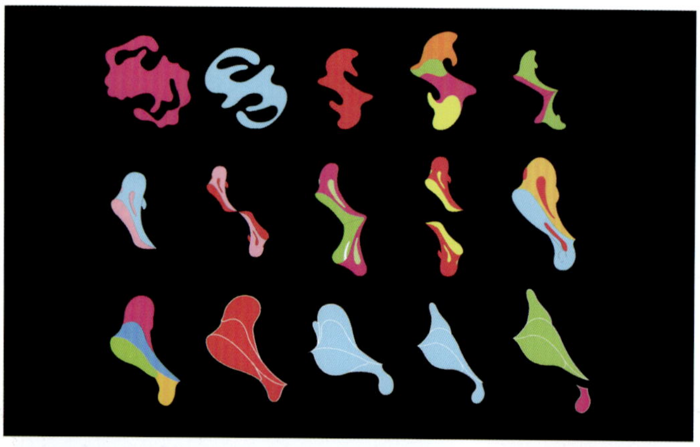

eshes
SIMBIOSE
SIMBIOSE
COMBINAÇÕES
&
MUTAÇÕES
AGUA
AR
FOGO
TERRA
eshes
INDUSTRIAL
DESIGN
eshes
eshes

BOOLAB

Client_ Boolab
Design Firm_ Mucho
Country_ Spain

Boolab is a simple word that conceals a graphic gift: It can be formed from just four lines and five circles. This allowed designers to develop a graphic game related to the client's activity as an animation production company. Because of the client's involvement in the project, animated versions of the logo were created in addition to the graphic stationery and promotional items. Beyond designing a fixed corporate image, this project saw the creation of a game.

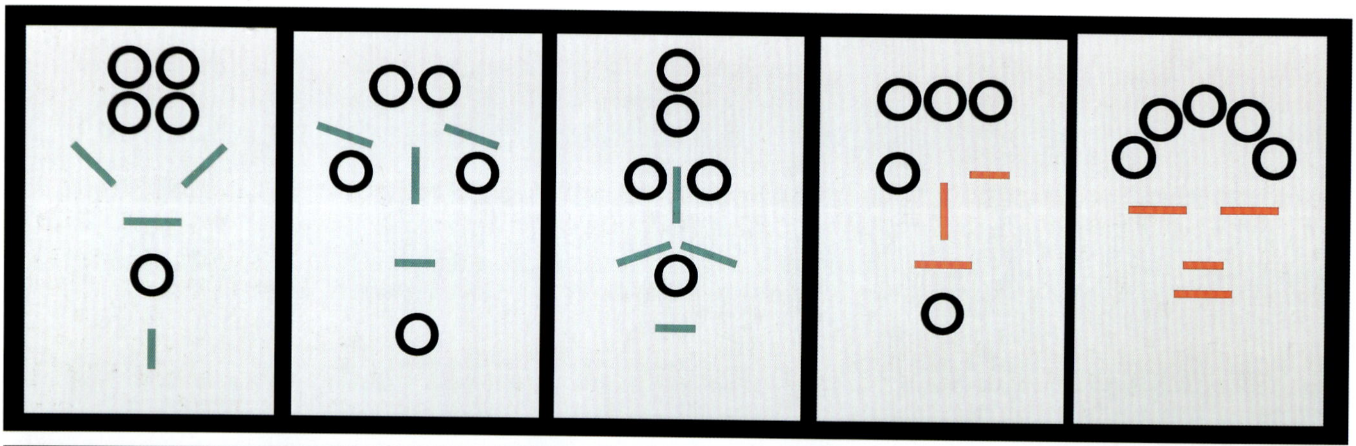

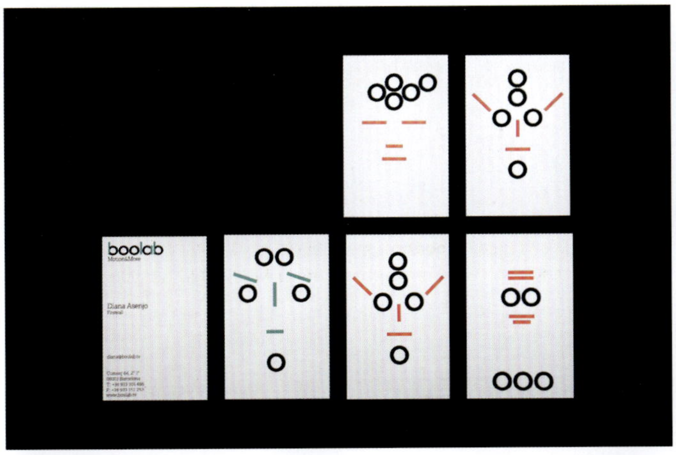
boolab
Motion&More

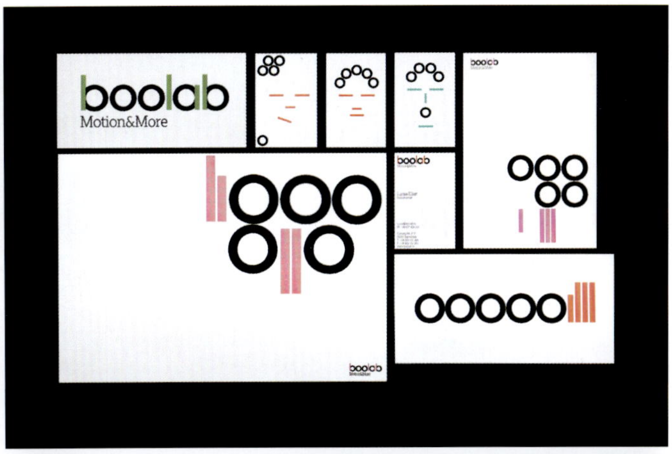
boolab
Motion&More

boolab
Motion&More

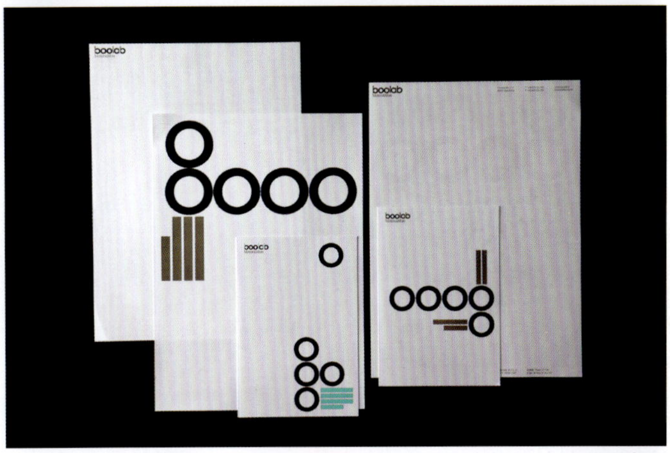

boolab
Motion&More

ELEMENTS — 4D MOTION PICTURES

Client_ Personal Work
Designer_ Jhade Villa Dean
Country_UK

Elements is a 4D production studio. They're responsible for imagining and implanting physical, environmental effects into 4D feature films. Such effects include: scents, winds, rain, bubbles, additional lighting, snow, special motion seats, among others. The concept brings to life the idea of "adding the elements," not only just to motion pictures but to the brand as an experience. By referring to the effects as "elements," it presents the opportunity for the effects to be portrayed in a simpler, graphic form.

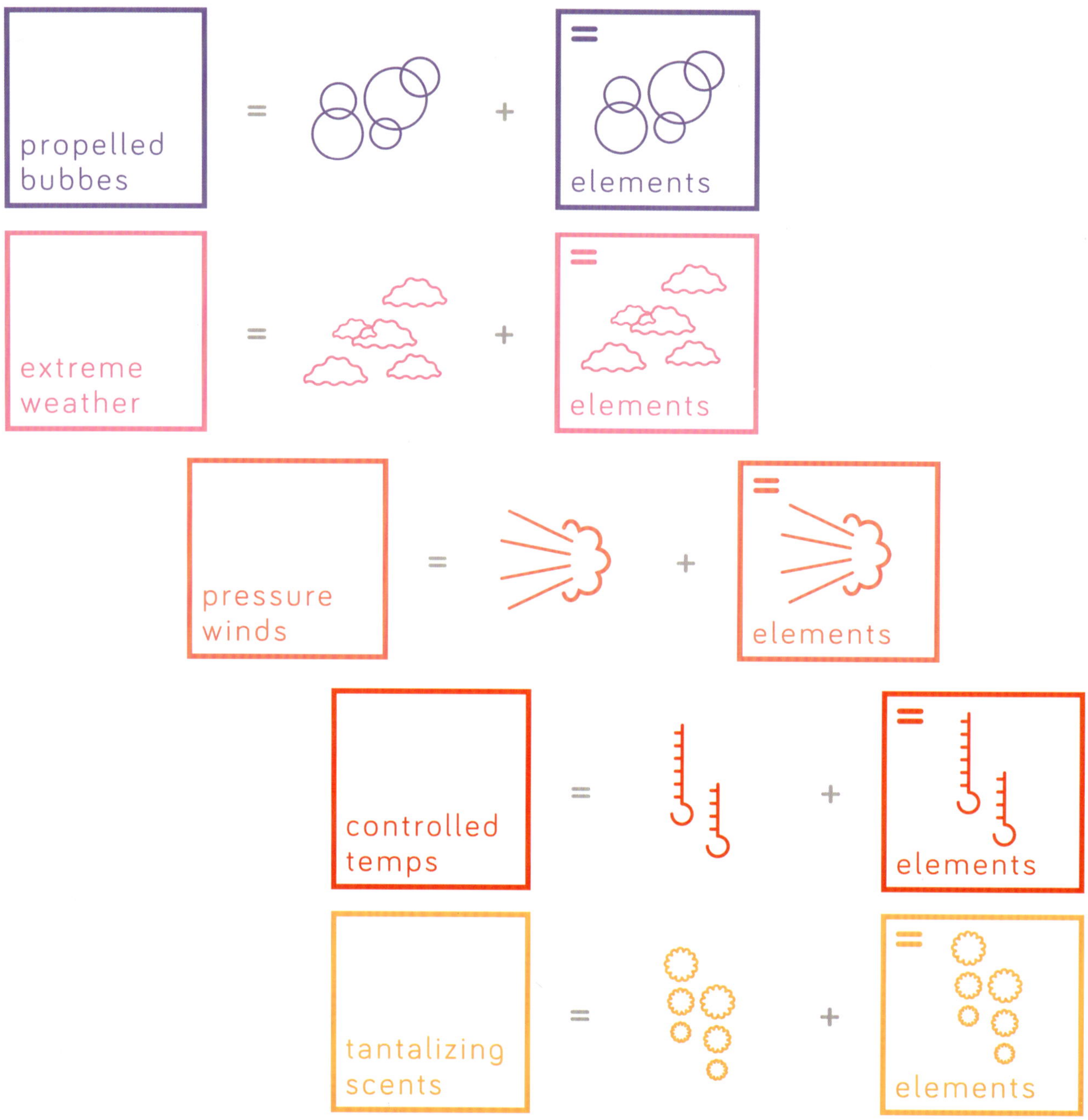

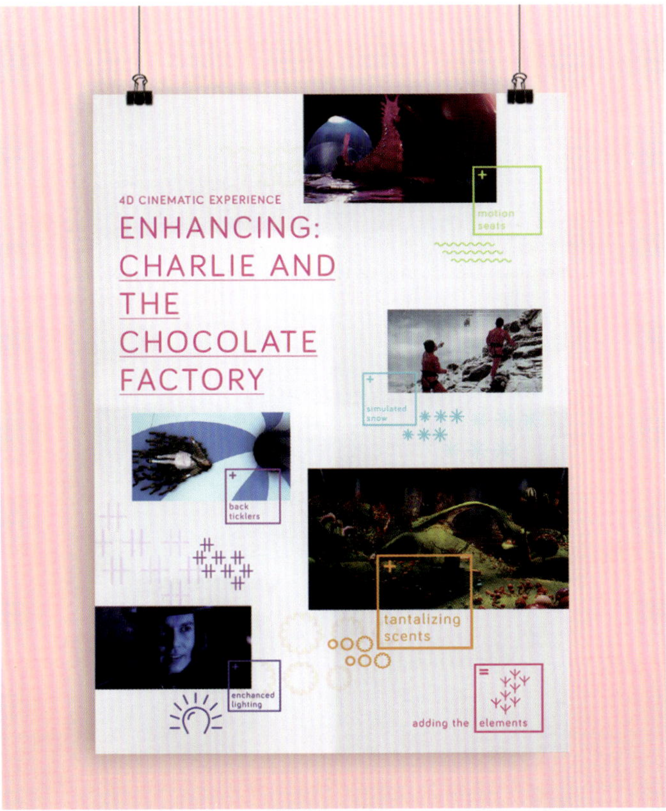
4D CINEMATIC EXPERIENCE
ENHANCING: CHARLIE AND THE CHOCOLATE FACTORY
motion seats
simulated snow
back ticklers
tantalizing scents
enchanced lighting
adding the elements

4D CINEMATIC EXPERIENCE
ENHANCING: AVENGERS ASSEMBLE
rumble seats
simulated smoke
pressure winds
controlled temps
adding the elements

adding the elements
CREATING 4D CINEMATIC EXPERIENCES
ENHANCING FUTURE FILMS
With Compliments
elements

PLANT YOUR DREAMS AND LET THEM GROW

Client_ Personal Work
Design Firm_ Sophia Georgopoulou | Design
Creative Director_ Sophia Georgopoulou
Designer_ Sophia Georgopoulou
Country_ Greece

"Plant Your Dreams and Let Them Grow" is the title of Sophia's self-initiative project and her wish for the New Year. The actual tulip flowers and their "unique" names (e.g. "Pink Diamond," "Sweetheart" etc.) inspired the designer to create a series of ecological packages containing tulip bulbs. The packages were sent as gifts to friends and clients; these packages offered them a unique experience by telling them to "Plant Their Dreams," take care of them, and see if they will grow (and come true) the following year.

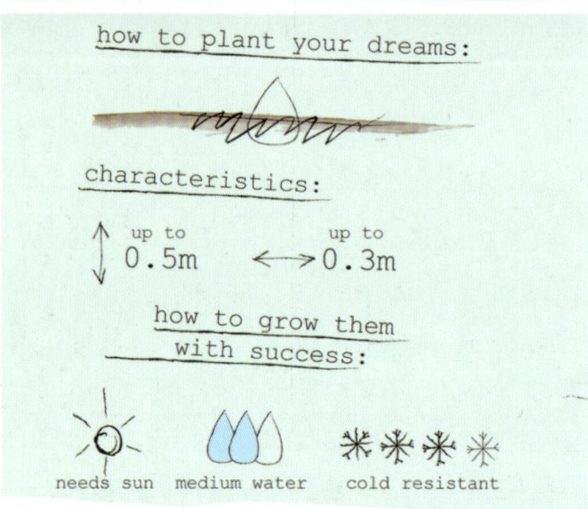

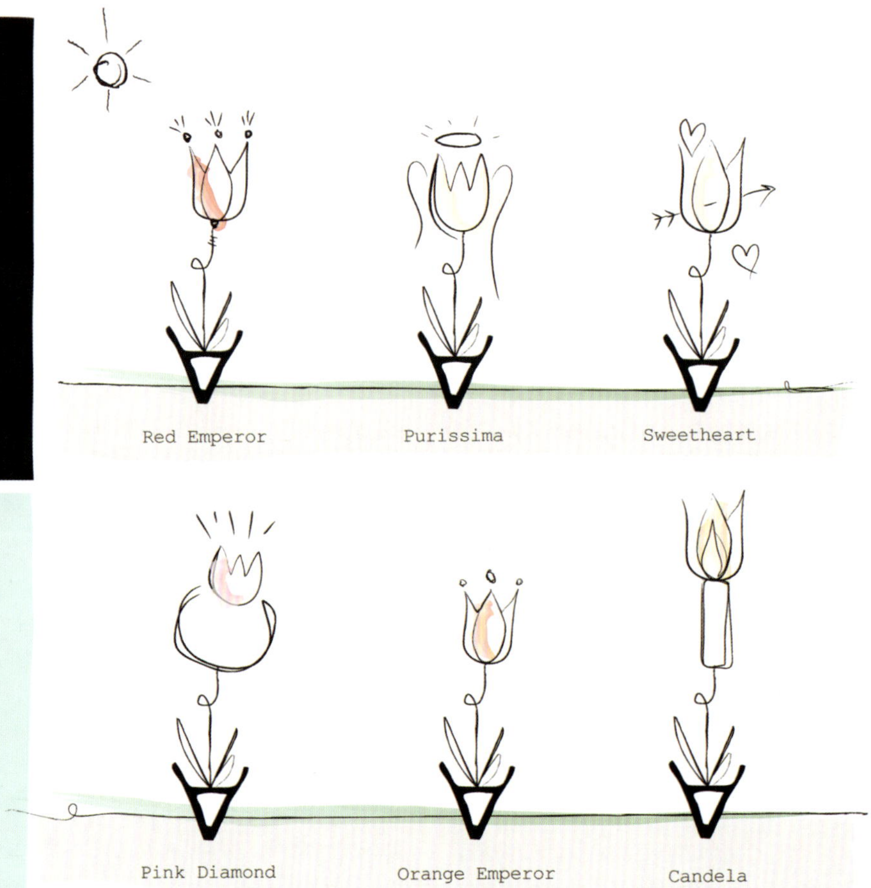

PLANT
YOUR DREAMS
AND LET THEM
GROW!

PLANT
YOUR DREAMS
AND LET THEM

PLANT
YOUR DREAMS
AND LET THEM
GROW!
2011 2 x Red Emperor
Tulip bulb
Red Emperor

PLANT
YOUR DREAMS
AND LET THEM
GROW!
2011 2 x Pink Diamond
Tulip bulb

NTH ROOT

Client_ Personal Work
Creative Director_ Harris Aidonopoulos
Designer_ Harris Aidonopoulos
Country_UK/Greece

This is a self-promotional project based on an earlier, original logo design. To best describe himself through his favorite items, habits and personality, the designer transformed the logo accordingly. Twenty-five different faces were laid out in an A3 poster that can be folded down to the size of a business card. Recipients may enjoy a game of unfolding it and folding it back differently, matching the front and back sides of each of the business cards.

HARRIS AIDONOPOULOS
Graphic Designer/Illustrator
www.harrisaidonopoulos.com
xarabalos@gmail.com
Harris Aidonopoulos
Graphic Designer/Illustrator
www.harrisaidonopoulos.com
xarabalos@gmail.com
HARRIS AIDONOPOULOS
Graphic Designer/Illustrator
www.harrisaidonopoulos.com
xarabalos@gmail.com
HARRIS AIDONOPOULOS
Graphic Designer/Illustrator
www.harrisaidonopoulos.com
xarabalos@gmail.com
HARRIS AIDONOPOULOS
Graphic Designer/Illustrator
www.harrisaidonopoulos.com
xarabalos@gmail.com
HARRIS AIDONOPOULOS
Graphic Designer/Illustrator
www.harrisaidonopoulos.com
xarabalos@gmail.com
HARRIS AIDONOPOULOS
Graphic Designer/Illustrator
www.harrisaidonopoulos.com
xarabalos@gmail.com
HARRiS AiDONOPOULOS
Graphic Designer/Illustrator
www.harrisaidonopoulos.com
xarabalos@gmail.com
Graphic Designer/Illustrator
www.harrisaidonopoulos.com
xarabalos@gmail.com
Harris Aidonopoulos
Graphic Designer/Illustrator
www.harrisaidonopoulos.com
xarabalos@gmail.com
harris aidonopoulos
Graphic Designer/Illustrator
www.harrisaidonopoulos.com
xarabalos@gmail.com
HARRIS AIDONOPOULOS
Graphic Designer/Illustrator
www.harrisaidonopoulos.com
xarabalos@gmail.com
HARRIS AIDONOPOULOS
Graphic Designer/Illustrator
www.harrisaidonopoulos.com
xarabalos@gmail.com
HARRIS AIDONOPOULOS
Graphic Designer/Illustrator
www.harrisaidonopoulos.com
xarabalos@gmail.com
HARRIS AIDONOPOULOS
Graphic Designer/Illustrator
www.harrisaidonopoulos.com
xarabalos@gmail.com

harris
aidonopoulos
HARRIS
AIDONOPOULOS
Graphic Designer/Illustrator
www.harrisaidonopoulos.com
xarabalos@gmail.com
HARRIS
AIDONOPOULOS
Graphic Designer/Illustrator
www.harrisaidonopoulos.com
xarabalos@gmail.com

Harris
Aidonopoulos
HARRIS
AIDONOPOULOS
Graphic Designer/Illustrator

HARRIS
AIDONOPOULOS
Harris
Aidonopoulos
harris
aidonopoulos

HARRIS
AIDONOPOULOS
Graphic Designer/Illustrator
www.harrisaidonopoulos.com
xarabalos@gmail.com

Harris
Aidonopoulos
HARRIS
AIDONOPOULOS
harris
aidonopoulos

PAULA CRUZ

Client_Personal Project
Creative Director_Paula Cruz
Designer_Paula Cruz
Country_Brazil

This is Paula Cruz's visual identity and its main concept is plurality. She does seek a mixed career that involves design, writing, and illustration; so she decided to demonstrate variety in a dynamic logo and to incorporate her last name to its signal. "Cruz" means "cross" in Portuguese and Spanish. In order to not relate it with any religion or ideology, Paula Cruz has chosen the mathematical cross, the plus sign. It incorporates also the meaning of quality and addition, which are characteristics Paula Cruz explores in her work.

paula cruz

paula cruz

paula cruz

paula cruz

paula
cruz

paula
cruz

paula
cruz
as melhores
ideias começam
num rabisco!

Aprender
nunca
desgasta
a mente.
Leonardo da Vinci

paula
cruz

1984
george orwell
ESCHER

paula
cruz
@ paula.oacruz@gmail.com
Bē behance.net/paulacruz

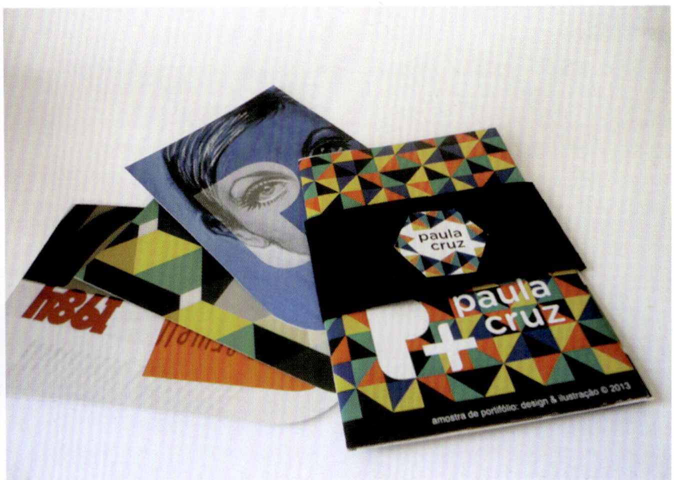
paula
cruz
amostra de portfólio: design & ilustração © 2013

BENCHMARK
DESIGN

Client_ Benchmark Design
Design Firm_ Benchmark Design
Designer_ Pascal Gabriel
Country_ Germany

This is a dynamic identity for Benchmark Design. Every member is able to design his own color scheme for his individual Benchmark logo by selecting an image and feeding a processing program with it. The program will automatically extract the colors and put them in order from dark (top) to light (bottom) to keep the arrow dynamic. Afterwards the member can save and use his personal vector logo.

BENCHMARK
DESIGN

Brand Identity
is too often limited
to personal style.
DAVID S. STUEBE

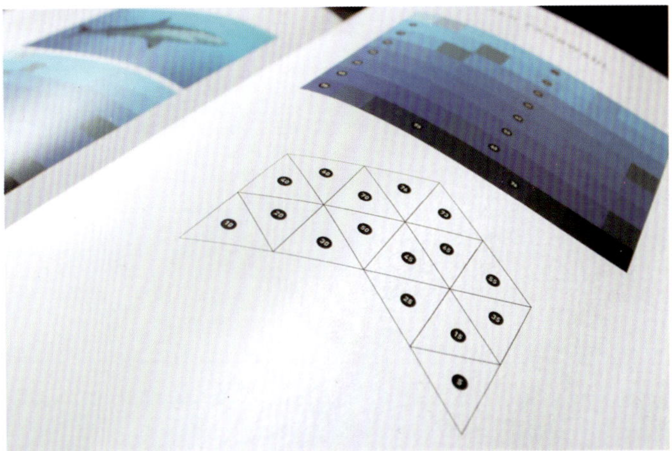

Client_ Paramount
Design Firm_ Mind Design
Country_ London, UK

This is an identity project for Paramount, a members' club and event space situated on the top three floors of the 33-story Centre Point building. The concept for the identity is simple and based on two main aspects: the architecture of the building and the notion of height. Another strong influence was the 1960s' Op Art, especially the work of Victor Vasarely.

The Paramount identity consists of a set of four graduation patterns, which expresses an upward movement. Each pattern is made from one of the four simple shapes (hexagon, triangle, circle and stripe) that can be found in the building or the interior, repeated 33 times (for 33 floors). Different sections of the pattern have been used for different applications. The difficulty was to produce a design that is elegant and appealing to the members of this rather prestigious club but at the same time staying true to the raw aesthetics of the building. The work was done in collaboration with Design Research Studio.

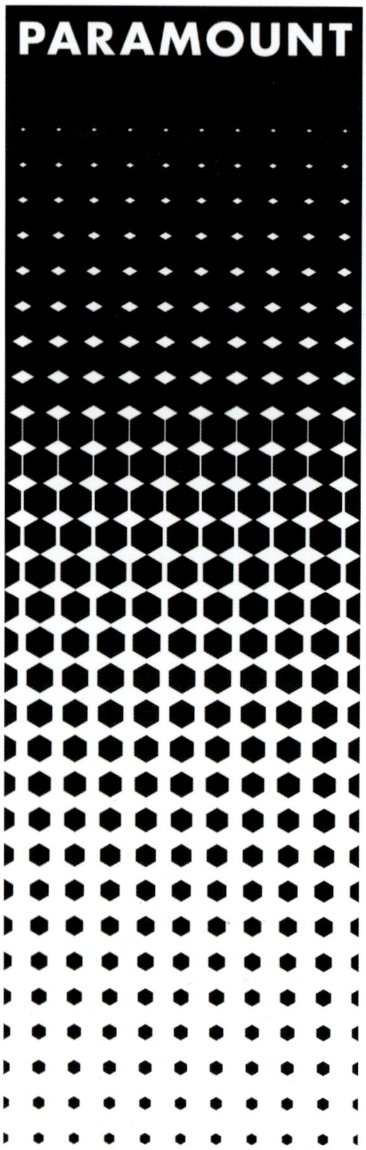

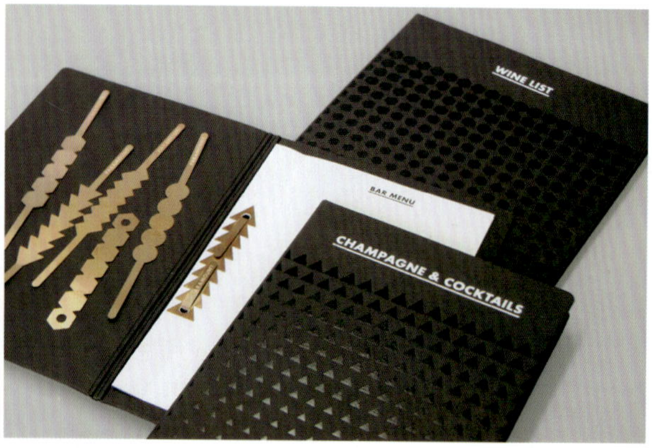

31
PARAMOUNT

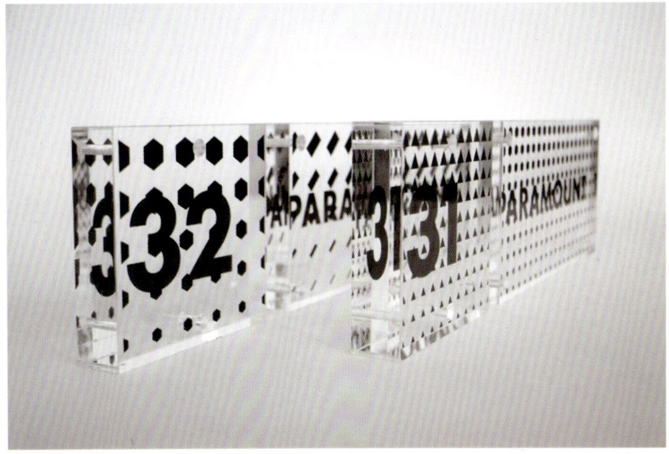
32
31
PARAMOUNT

PARAMOUNT

PARAMOUNT

FOOD

CATERING

TOURISM

LODO ICE CREAM STORE

Client_ Fictional Brief for Masters Project
Creative Director_ Dagny Janowska
Designer_ Dagny Janowska
Country_UK

The brand offers premium ice cream, fully natural with locally sourced ingredients. The store allows customers to create their own flavors by combining the available ingredients. The aim is to communicate this customer influence on the product through the visuals and has them (in a controlled way) adjust the identity. The result is a base logotype and a set of graphic elements (flavors), all based on the same primary grid, designed to resemble the structure of ice. As the user chooses his flavor combination, the corresponding icons are applied to the main logo, creating a new and unique result.

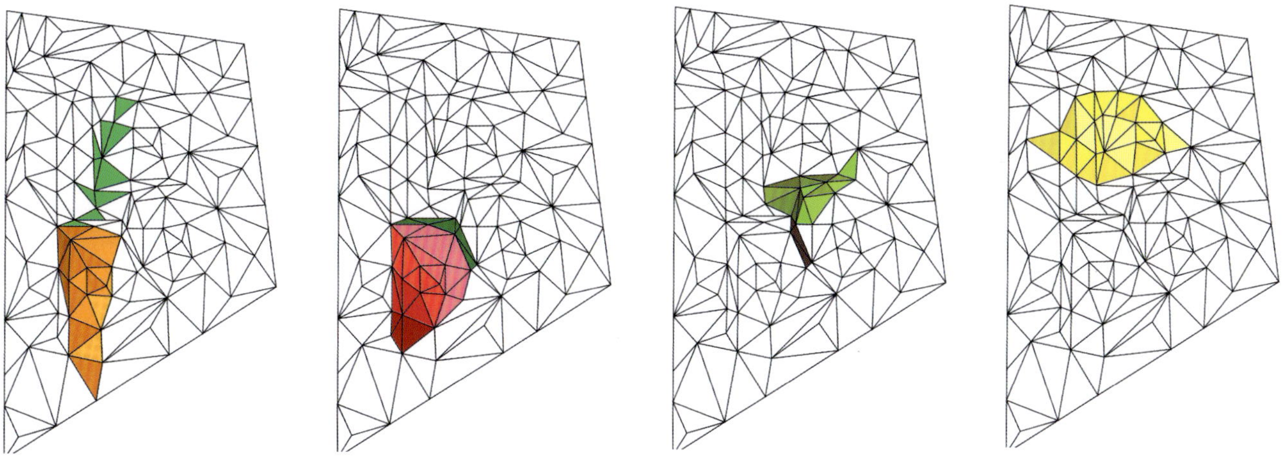

carrot
plum
mint
avocado
watermelon
vanilla
pistacio
pear
coconut
orange
chocolate
apple
strawberry
melon
cherry

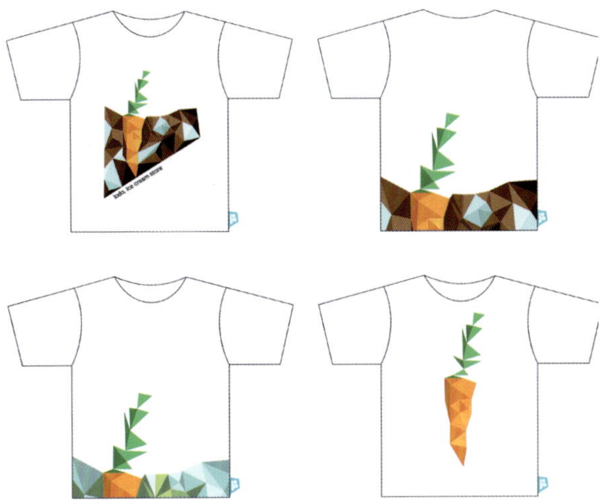

LITTLE
DONKEY

Client_ Fictional Brief for Masters Project
Creative Director_ Dagny Janowska
Designer_ Dagny Janowska
Country_UK

Little Donkey is a new chain of Mexican restaurants. The brand focus is on being inviting, natural, fresh, and playful. Even though it's a Mexican restaurant, the brief specifically demands avoiding Mexican themes, instead it asked for a design which is very playful, modern, not overly clever but easy to implement. The final solution is a smooth typographic logo, with a play on letters (where a donkey is based on the typography) in order to create an element of positive surprise, while maintaining a simple form. The main logo is supported by a series of basic graphic shapes representing each of the food categories in the restaurant, which are also used as a base to create various illustrations for the signage and packaging. Three logo concepts were presented as solutions to the brief.

little donkey

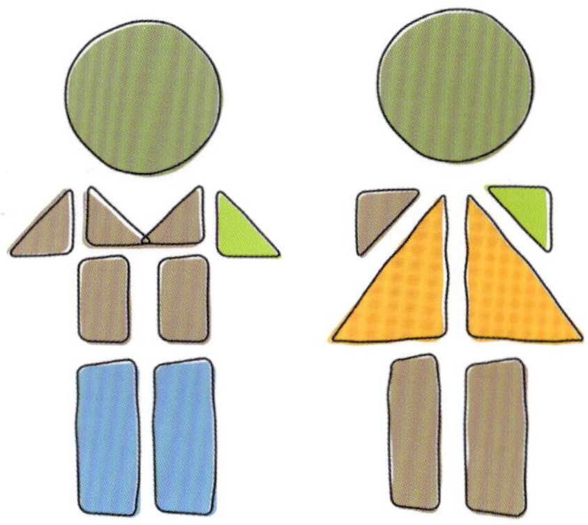

little donkey

little donkey

little donkey

HOTEL DANIEL VIENNA

Client_ Weitzer Hotels Betriebsges.m.b.H
Creative Firm_ Moodley Brand Identity
Designer_ Sabine Kernbichler
Country_ Austria

Simplicity instead of flamboyant excess and fresh ideas instead of awkward hospitality, the hotel's owner, Florian Weitzer, calls it "Smart Luxury" — perfectly tailored to the needs of the modern traveler. "Smart Luxury" doesn't force anything on you; instead it offers possibilities and inspiration. This also applies to the identity design of the entire hotel, which is the polar opposite of being heavy and sedate. And this is what is called stylish reduction in corporate design. There's no "just pretend" but rather "be yourself," in simple black and white with a personal touch.

KEINE SCHLECHTE LAUNE
NO BAD TEMPER

KRAWATTE? PROBIER'S MAL OHNE
TIE? WHY NOT TRY WITHOUT

KEINE BETRIEBSSPIONAGE
NO SPIES

flotte BIENEN
DIE WELT BRAUCHT MEHR
BIENEN
BIENEN-STOCK-DUNKEL.
URBAN STAY
DANIEL
SMART LUXURY
HI HONEY!
Süß! MARZIPAN-HONIG IM GLAS.
UND DAS BRAUCHST DU DAFÜR:
JETZT GEHT'S LOS.
STÜCK FÜR STÜCK.
FAST GESCHAFFT!
DAS SÜSSE FINALE.
OPTIMISTIC FOR THE WORLD
Bikes & Vespas
15,- 5,-
Einfach machen
Von Blumen und Bienen
Bee Station
BUY IN OUR SHOP!
1886

HOTEL DANIEL GOES VIENNA.
AB HERBST 2011
BAKERY
115 ZIMMER
AB 92€
FAHRRÄDER
HOTEL EST. 1886
ALOIS DANIEL
DANIEL
HOTEL EST. 1886

777
PRIVATE ROOM
DO NOT DISTURB
Wanna have a look inside?
Please visit our website.

DANIEL

DANIEL

SORRY, WE'RE CLOSED.
EINLADUNG
OPENING HOTEL DANIEL VIENNA
DANIEL
WELCOME
FLORIAN WEITZER
DANIEL
BODY & HAIR WASH

AYERS ROCK RESORT

Client_ Voyages Indigenous Tourism Australia
Design Firm_ RE
Creative Directors_ Graeme Smith, Jason Little
Designer_ Samuel Byrnes
Country_ Australia

Uluru, also known as Ayers Rock, is one of the largest monoliths in the world, situated in the southern part of the Northern Territory, central Australia. The designer's task was to reinvent the Ayers Rock Resort brand to drive the commercial and community imperatives, and create a true Uluru-Kata Tjuta experience. The essence of the brand, "respectfully indigenous," runs through everything. Designers worked closely with local indigenous artists and finally got a brand with a new lease on life.

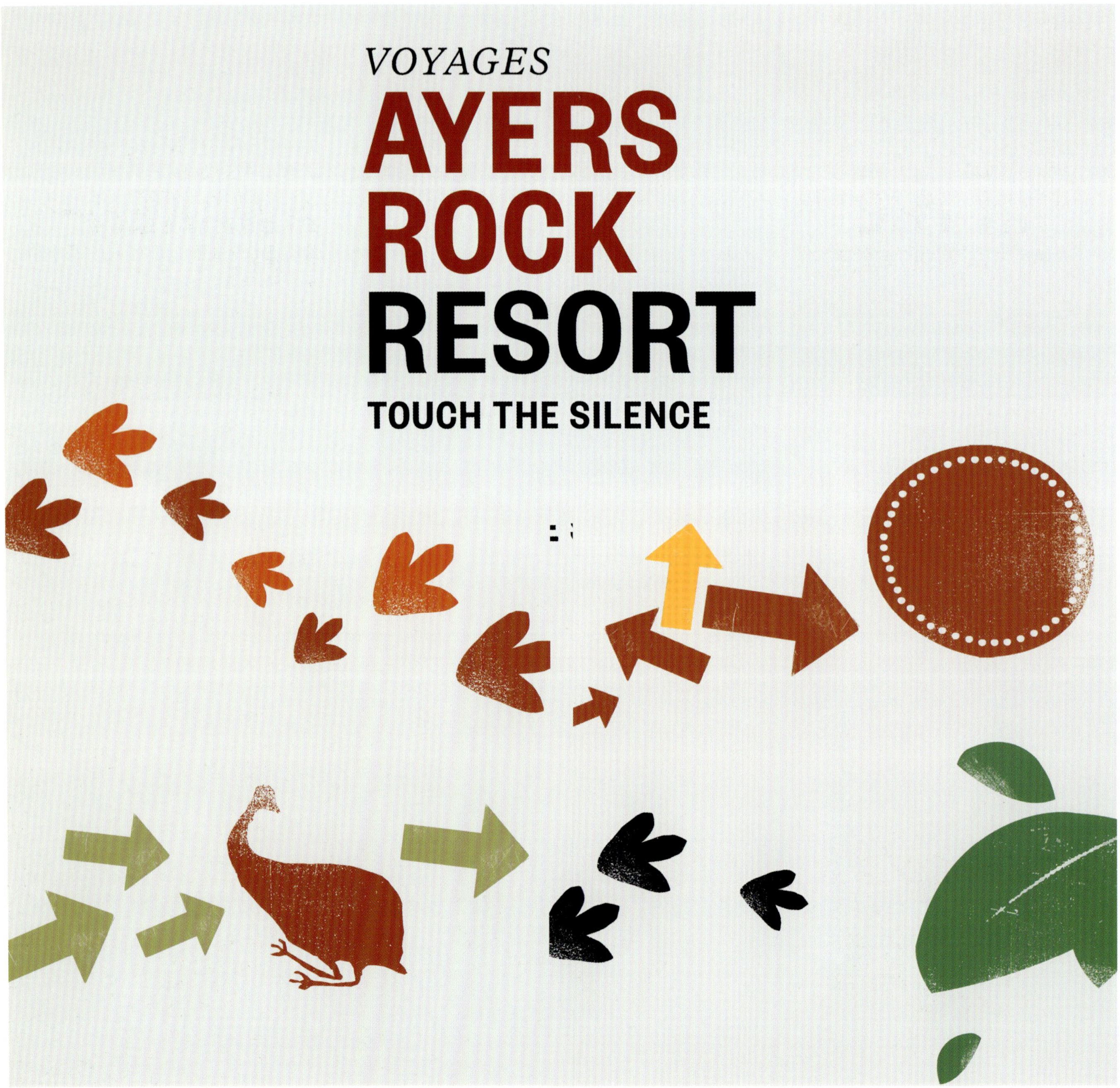

Logotype for Ayers Rock Resort

VOYAGES
AYERS
ROCK
RESORT
TOUCH THE SILENCE

Voyages publication title

VOYAGES
AYERS ROCK
RESORT
EMPLOYEE
GUIDELINES

Property portfolio extension

VOYAGES
HOME
VALLEY
STATION
EAST KIMBERLEY
WESTERN AUSTRALIA

VOYAGES
SAILS
IN THE
DESERT

Voyages property logotype

SAILS IN
THE DESERT
RED
OCHRE
SPA

Facility or service within a property

VOYAGES
DESERT
AWAKEN–
INGS

General Ayers Rock Resort product

VOYAGES
AYERS
ROCK
RESORT
TOUCH THE SILENCE

VOYAGES
SAILS
IN THE
DESERT

VOYAGES
DESERT
GARDENS
HOTEL

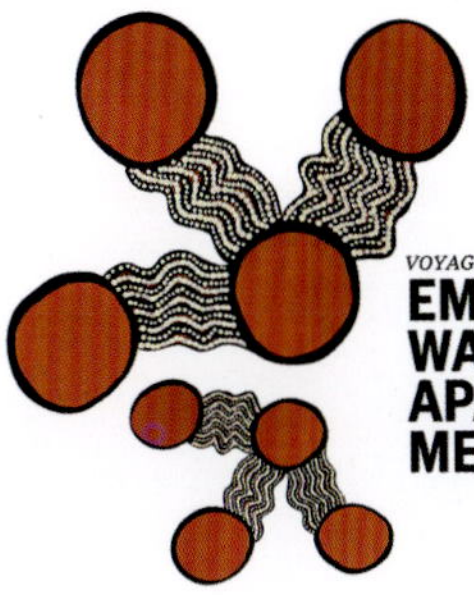

VOYAGES
EMU
WALK
APART–
MENTS

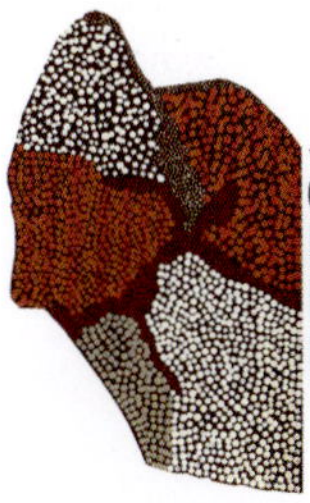

VOYAGES
OUTBACK
PIONEER
HOTEL &
LODGE

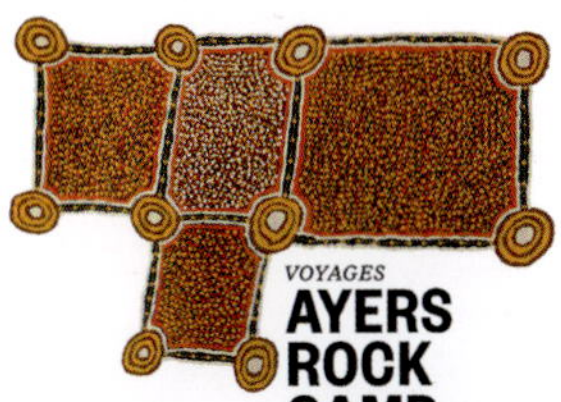

VOYAGES
AYERS
ROCK
CAMP–
GROUND

SAILS IN THE DESERT
DESERT GARDENS HOTEL

AYERS ROCK RESORT
AYERS ROCK CAMP-GROUND
DESERT GARDENS HOTEL
OUTBACK PIONEER HOTEL & LODGE
EMU WALK APART-MENTS

SEPTEMBER AT ULURU
21
7
23
9
30

THE INDIG-ENOUS CHEF
Cook your own kangaroo steak

AYERS ROCK CAMP-GROUND

GONE WALK-ABOUT. PLEASE CLEAN.
DO NOT DISTURB

AYERS ROCK RESORT
HOME VALLEY STATION
LONGITUDE 131°
TOUCH THE SILENCE

PALYA WEL-COME
AYERS ROCK RESORT

VOYAGES
AYERS ROCK RESORT
TOUCH THE SILENCE
AYERS ROCK CAMP-GROUND
AYERS ROCK RESORT
OUTBACK PIONEER HOTEL & LODGE
EMU WALK APART-MENTS
SAILS IN THE DESERT
DESERT GARDENS HOTEL

JCDecaux
VOYAGES
TOUCH THE SILENCE
MUST DO EXPERIENCES AT
AYERSROCKRESORT.COM.AU
AYERS ROCK RESORT

BETLEM GASTRO BAR

Client_ Betlem
Design Firm_ Toormix
Creative Directors_ Oriol Armengou, Ferran Mitjansr
Designer_ Gerard Marin
Country_ Spain

This project was created for Betlem, an old deli grocery store in Barcelona, converted now into a gastro-bar specializing in quality tapas and sandwiches. The logo is a contemporary interpretation of the modernist style of the 20th century that decorated this type of groceries in this zone of Barcelona. The ornaments are now made with the food icons; additionally, the corporate type used is an ornamental font, but is one that's less floral, and more readable and clean.

BETLEM
MISCEL·LÀNIA GASTRONÒMICA
— DES DE 1892 —

BEU BON VI,
MENJA BON PA
I VIURÀS SEMPRE SA

BOOM BURGER

Client_ Boom Burger
Design Firm_ Yawn Creative
Designers_ Harry Fowler, Joe George
Country_UK

Boom Burger is a Jamaican-style Burger Company that can be found in the heart of Notting Hill, London. Designers wanted the identity to reflect the unique, vibrant colors and flavors that are indigenous to Jamaica and the Reggae culture. Boom pushes the boundaries of the traditional burger. This originality called for a creative and playful response.

BOOM TASTE BOOM TUNES
BOOM BURGER
WWW.BOOMBURGER.CO.UK

BOOM BURGER
BOOM TASTE BOOM TUNES
BOOM FOOD WITH LOUD JAMAICAN FLAVOURS
WWW.BOOMBURGER.CO.UK
BOOM BURGERS
JERK BOOM
VEGGIE BOOM
BRUNCH B:OOM
BURGERS
SIDES
BOOM WINGS
PLANTAIN FRIES
FRENCH FRIES
THE SMALLS
PLEASE CHECK BOARD FOR SPECIALS & DESSERTS

BOOM TASTE
BOOM TUNES
BOOM BURGER
THE EARL OF PORTOBELLO, W10 5PR

SWEEZ — SWEET & FREEZING

Client_ Sweez
Design Firm_ Epic! Aventuras Criativas
Creative Director_ Maurício Cardoso
Designers_ Maurício Cardoso, Marina Procházka
Country_ Brazil

The idea behind Sweez was to open a modern business that allied gastronomy and redemption of weakened values. From decor to uniforms, everything alludes to the nostalgic 1950s in Sweez which originated from the junction of two words: sweet and freezing. Inspired by the concept behind the establishment, designers tried to portrait this graphically, so they created a character that symbolizes the values and the good humor that the project wanted to convey.

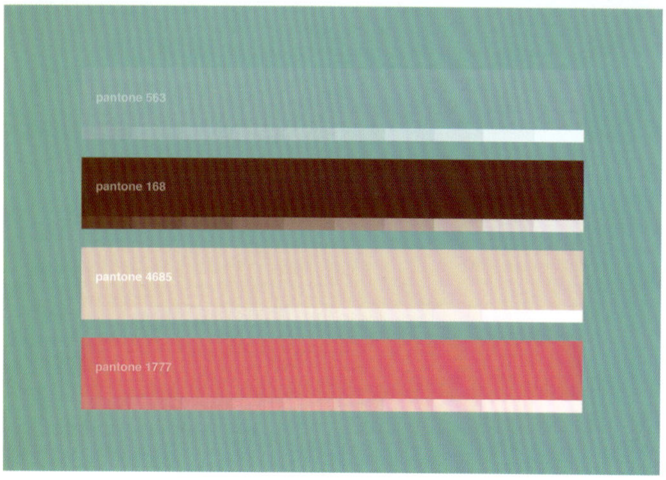

sweez.com.br

Sweez
sweet & freezing

Sweez

Sweez
sweet & freezing

CATALAN
WINES

Design Firm_ Toormix
Creative Directors_ Oriol Armengou, Ferran Mitjans
Designer_ Gerard Marin
Country_ Spain

This project aims to promote Catalan wines to the domestic and international audience. The branding consists of 12 different variations (as many as the wine designations of origin in Catalonia). The synthetic graphical design that combines land, territory and climate of different regions through graphic codes is different from the typical wine code. Designers worked on the brand extension for communication, including the point of sale, ads with opinion leaders' quotes about Catalan wines, and a variety of support and merchandising materials.

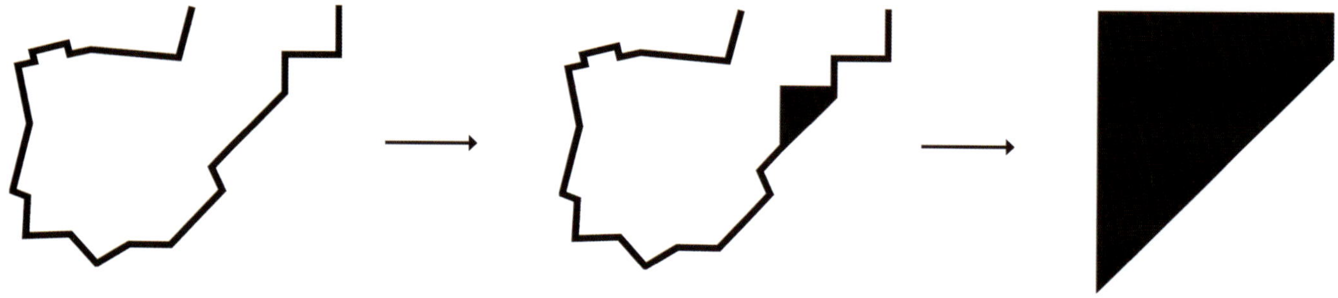

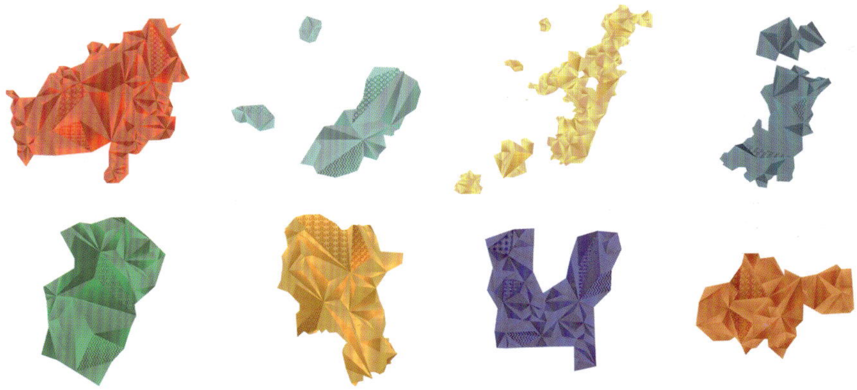

CATALAN
WINES.
CAT
GREAT WINES
WITH DESIGNATION OF ORIGIN
PRIO-
RAT
ALE-
LLA
CON-
CA DE
BAR-
BERÀ
COS-
TERS
DEL
SEGRE
EM-
PORDÀ
PE-
NE-
DÈS
CATA-
LUNYA
PLA
DE
BAGES
MO-
NT-
SANT
TARRA
GONA
TERRA
ALTA
CA-
VA

VINS
CATA-
LANS
DO
PE-
NE-
DÈS
GRANS VINS
AMB DENOMINACIÓ D'ORIGEN
BLANCS
LLEUGERS
COS
ALEGRES
FRAGANTS
MACABEU
AROMÀTICS

VINS
CATA-
LANS
DO
TERRA
ALTA
GRANS VINS
AMB DENOMINACIÓ D'ORIGEN
ROBUSTOS
MACABEU
AMPLIS
BLANCS
CORPULENTS
TERRASSES
MEDITERRANI
POTENTS

VINS
CATA-
LANS
DO
TARRA
GONA
GRANS VINS
AMB DENOMINACIÓ D'ORIGEN
LLUMINOSITAT
LLEUGERS
SUMOLL
ROSATS
AFRUITATS
XAREL·LO
AROMÀTICS
BLANCS

VINS
CATA-
LANS
DO
COS-
TERS
DEL
SEGRE
GRANS VINS
AMB DENOMINACIÓ D'ORIGEN
ESTRUCTURA
MUNTANYES
INNOVACIÓ
ESTRUCTURATS
SOL
POTENTS
CONTINENTAL

VINS
CATA-
LANS
DO
ALE-
LLA
GRANS VINS
AMB DENOMINACIÓ D'ORIGEN
MICROCLIMA
BRISA
FRESCOS
LLEUGERS
BLANCS
FRUITATS
PANSA BLANCA

TERRA
ALTA

TARRA
GONA

VINS
CATA-
LANS
UN
VI
CATA-
LÀ
AMB FUSTA
FLORAL
SEDOS
CARNÓS
MONOVARIETAL

PLA
DE
BAGES

CATALAN
WINES.
CAT

CATALAN
WINES.
CAT
CATALAN
WINES.
CAT
CATALAN
WINES.
CAT
CATALAN
WINES.
CAT

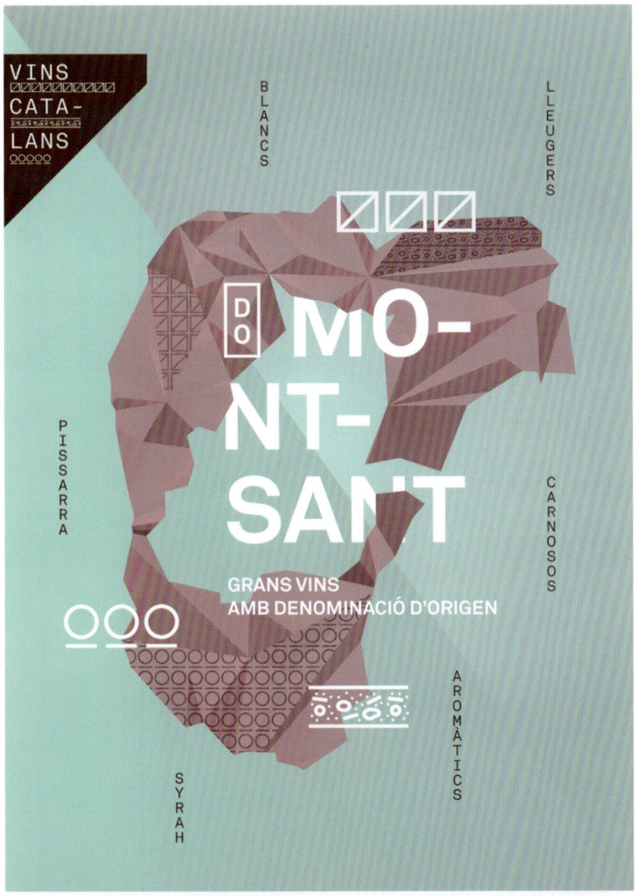
VINS
CATA-
LANS
BLANCS
LLEUGERS
DO
MO-
NT-
SANT
GRANS VINS
AMB DENOMINACIÓ D'ORIGEN
PISSARRA
CARNOSOS
AROMÀTICS
SYRAH

VINS
CATA-
LANS
TRADICIÓ
FRANCOLÍ
TREPAT
DO
CON-
CA DE
BAR-
BERÀ
GRANS VINS
AMB DENOMINACIÓ D'ORIGEN
FRESCOR
CHARDONNAY
TANINS

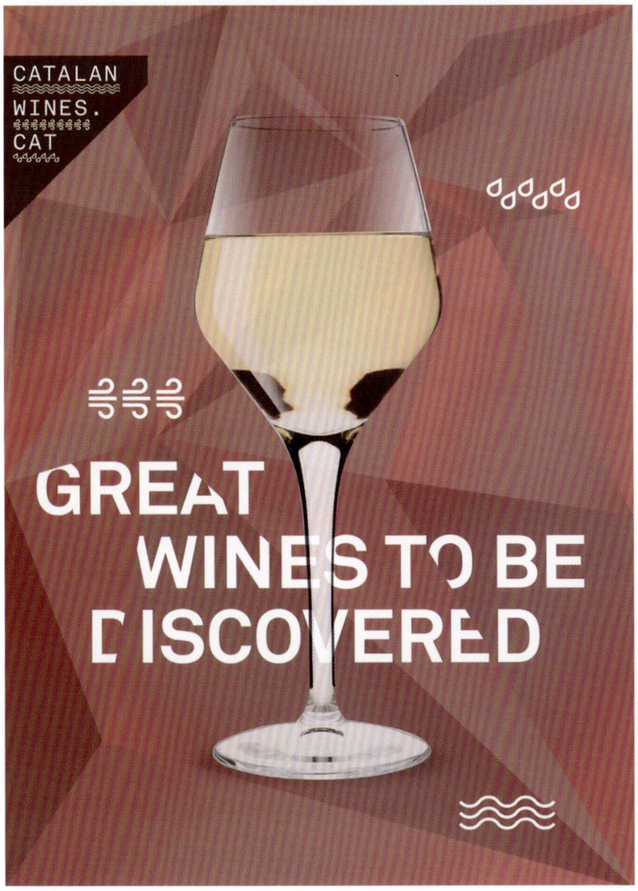
CATALAN
WINES.
CAT
GREAT
WINES TO BE
DISCOVERED

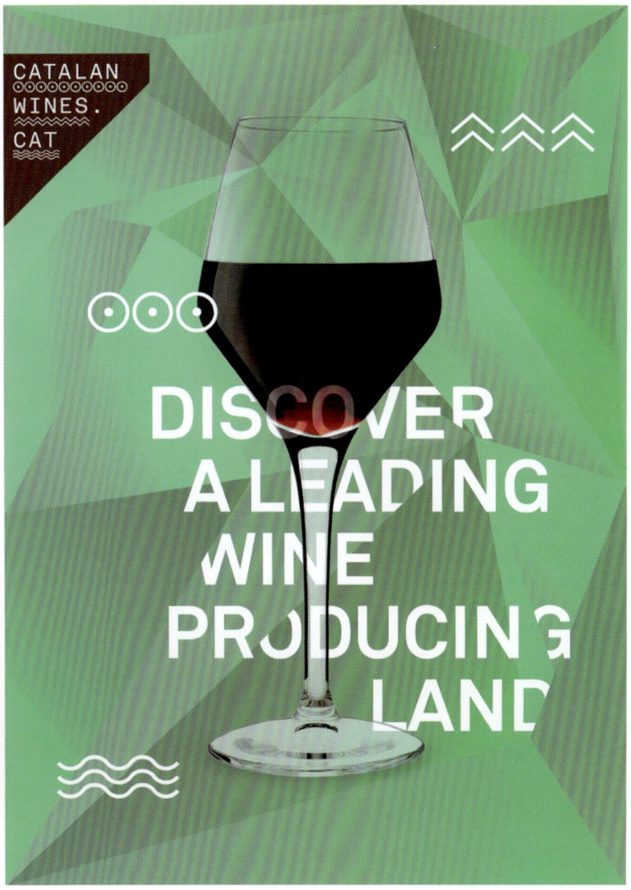
CATALAN
WINES.
CAT
DISCOVER
A LEADING
WINE
PRODUCING
LAND

PRIMA VINA STIRIAE SLOVENAE

Client_ Prima Vina Stiriae Slovenae Group of Wineries
Design Firm_ IlovarStritar
Creative Directors_ Robert Ilovar, Jernej Stritar
Designers_ Robert Ilovar, Jernej Stritar, Ranko Novak
Country_ Slovenia

This is the visual identity for Prima Vina Stiriae Slovenae, a group of wineries and wine cellars from the Styria region. Wine tasting events of the group offer a chance to get a taste of the broader cultural experience, as the wine tasting is often accompanied by painting and sculpture exhibitions, musical, dance or theatrical performances. Because of this cultural and art context, designers used different techniques when creating portraits of the 10 winemakers and representatives of wine cellars, showing them in different ballet positions.

P&F Jeruzalem Ormož

Kogl

Ptujska Klet

Steyer

V
I
N
A
P
R
I
M
A

P
R
I
M
A
V
I
N
A

Client_ Poble Espanyol Barcelona
Design Firm_ Atipus
Country_ Spain

This is a proposal for the redesign of the corporate identity of Poble Espanyol Barcelona. Poble Espanyol, an open-air architectural museum in the city of Barcelona, shows Spain's cultural diversity through several representative buildings, streets, and squares. In short, it shows a global and abstract image of the Spanish territory. Here designers transferred this feature into its identity.

CLUB
Welcome to the cruel world
CLUB

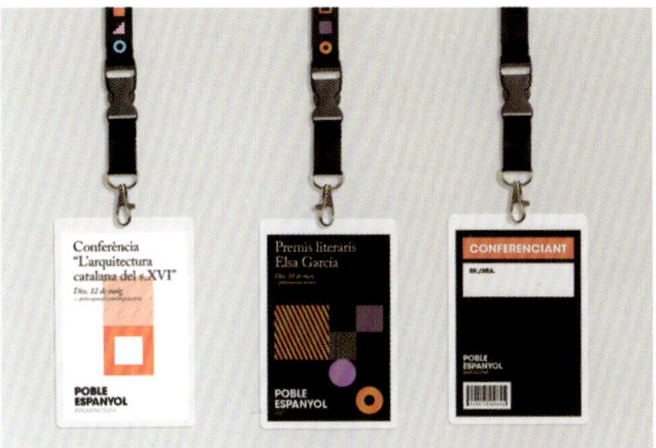
Conferència
"L'arquitectura catalana del s.XVI"
POBLE ESPANYOL
Premis literaris
Elsa García
POBLE ESPANYOL
CONFERENCIANT
POBLE ESPANYOL

Toute l'Espagne en une seule visite...
Et bien plus!
POBLE ESPANYOL
Agenda d'activitats familiars 2012
POBLE ESPANYOL
POBLE ESPANYOL
BARCELONA

POBLE ESPANYOL
XI Premis literaris Xavier Ortega
Retrospectiva "Nous territoris"
POBLE ESPANYOL

Presentació del llibre
Jornada de portes obertes
XI Premis literaris Xavier Ortega

Activitats familiars tot l'any!
POBLE ESPANYOL

Benvinguts
Bienvenidos
Benvido
Ongi Etorri
POBLE ESPANYOL
BARCELONA

VAPORETTO DELL'ARTE

Client_Vela
Design Firm_Cappelli Identity Design
Designers_Emanuele Cappelli, Francesco Di Muro, Emiliano Gatti
Country_Italy

Vaporetto dell'Arte (ADV) is a service that takes tourists to discover the art in Venice along its main waterway. The designers created this identity system by starting from the combination of a few drops of water connected to each other, forming the sinuous and elegant shape of the art on water. This system becomes dynamic when adapted to different works of art in Venice, and results in a flexible format applied to corporate material and ADV's needs of the service. The colors used are blue and gold, colors that recall the landscape and art of Venice.

VAPORETTO™
DELL'ARTE
Canal Grande

THE

EGATIVO SU SCALA DI GRIGIO
VAPORETTO® DELL'ARTE Canal Grande

Canal Grande

HEART
E 1
VE 8424

Client_ Circus
Design Firm_ Mind Design
Country_ London, UK

The designers were challenged with creating an identity for a new club and restaurant with a burlesque theme and changing performances. Since the club interior features many mirrored surfaces, the design of the logo is based on the shape of a kaleidoscope. The outline shape and basic construction of the logo always remains the same while the inside changes depending on its application. Other influences came from Surrealism, Art Deco and *Alice in Wonderland*. A main feature of the interior is a three-dimensional version of the logo built from different layers of Perspex, set into a wall and illuminated from the back in changing colors. The work was created in collaboration with Design Research Studio.

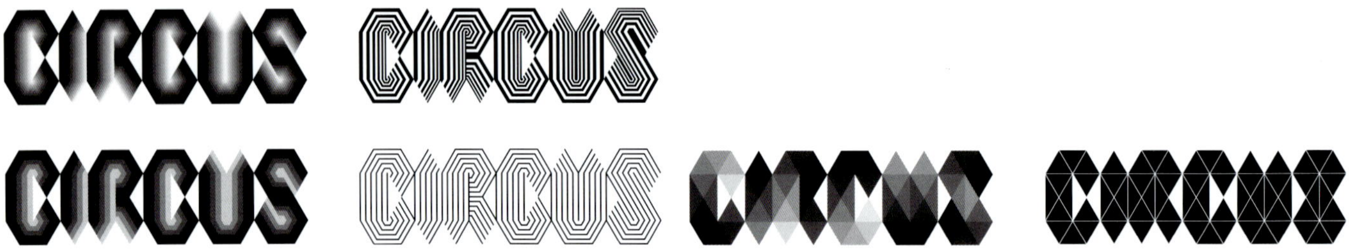

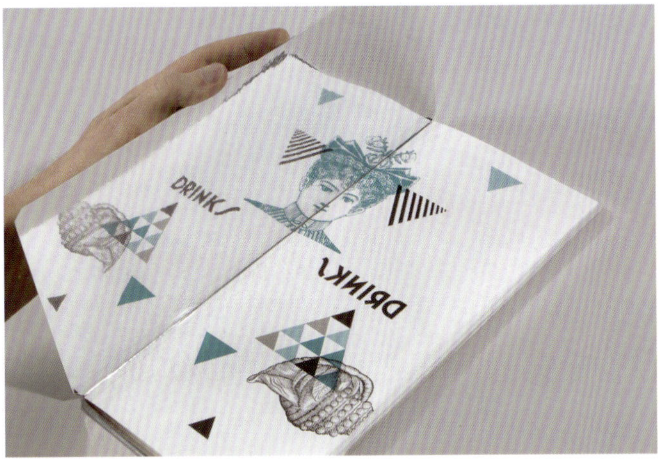
DRINKS
DRINKS

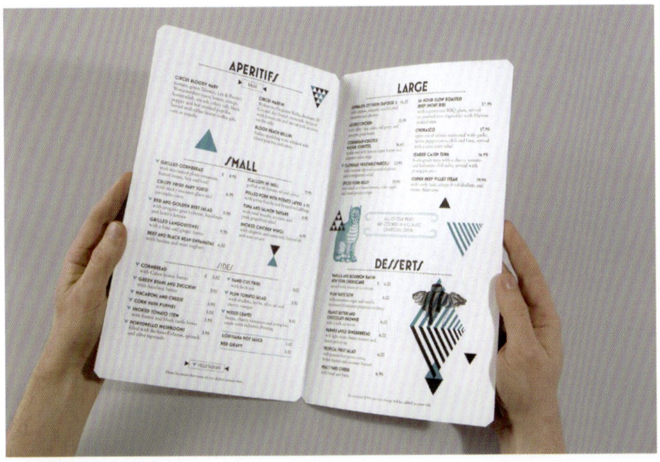
APERITIFS
LARGE
SMALL
DESSERTS

DESSERTS
£ 6.00
TROPICAL FRUIT SALAD
with passion fruit panna cotta, lychee liqueur and coconut biscuit
CHOCOLATE ESPRESSO CAKE 6.00
served with vanilla cream and bourbon raisins
PLUM TARTE TATIN 6.00
with cinnamon sugar and vanilla ice-cream
PEANUT BUTTER BROWNIE 6.00
with dark chocolate sauce and 3 milk ice-cream
WARMED APPLE GINGERBREAD 6.00
with light cream cheese mousse and lemon peel syrup
NEAL'S YARD MARKET CHEESE 6.95
with bread and fruits
DESSERT WINE
Bottle
£ 40.00
CHATEAU COUTET
Sauternes, 1998 (50cl)
COFFEES
£ 2.50
3.00
2.50
3.00
3.25
3.25
3.25
TEAS
£ 3.00
DAMMANN FRERES TEAS
English Breakfast
Earl Grey
Green Tea
Chamomile
Peppermint
CALVADOS
V.S.O.P CHAUFFE CO
HENNESSY X.O
MARTELL V.S.O.P
MARTELL X.O
MARTELL CORD
TAYLOR'S
DESSERTS
CIRCUS

2x4

Location: New York, USA
Tel: +212 647 1170
Fax: 647 0454
Web: www.2x4.org

Founded in 1994 by Michael Rock, Susan Sellers and Georgianna Stout, 2x4 is a global design consultancy headquartered in New York City with satellite studios in Beijing and Madrid. The focus of their work is brand strategy for cultural and commercial clients who value the power of design.

Aero

Location: Moscow, Russia
Tel: +7 906 781 45 93; +7 499 263 05 91
Web: www.aeroidea.ru

Aero is an advertising and digital production agency, founded in 2005. Their clients include well-known local and international brands like JTI, BAT, Autodesk, Conde Nast, Forex and others. Historically strong in graphic design and branding, they are now also focusing on complex web projects.

Aleksey Popovtsev

Location: Lisichansk, Ukraine
Tel: +38 063 799 26 05
Web: www.composition.in.ua

Aleksey Popovtsev is an artist and designer. He has been working professionally since 2002. He graduated from Kharkiv Academy of Design and Arts ahead of schedule. Aleksey is one of the founders of the "Nachala" ("Elements") composition school, where he lectures on modular grids, fonts and typography. Aleksey also leads a color studies workshop.

Another Day

Location: Nijmegen, Netherlands
Tel: +31 06 835 614 67
Web: www.studioanotherday.nl

Another Day is the graphic design studio of Yorick de Vries. Yorick was born in 1985 in Lelystad, the Netherlands. Now he lives and works in Nijmegen. In 2012, Yorick de Vries started the studio. Another Day's main focus lies in the field of art and culture with a specialization on typography and printed matter.

Art & Science

Location: Toronto, Canada
Tel: +416 366 2266 x222
Web: www.artscience.ca

Art & Science Digital Experience Design is a team of creative technologists who don't see art and science as two separate things. Based in Toronto, they have a 10-year history of creating digital projects for some of the biggest brands in Canada, launching new brands designed from the ground up, and helping new businesses get off the ground with proven customer-centric strategies.

Atipus

Location: Barcelona, Spain
Tel: +34 93 485 13 95
Web: www.atipus.com

Atipus is a graphic communication studio, created in Barcelona in 1998. They are a team of expert professionals, trained in various disciplines, including corporate identity, art direction, packaging design and web services. Its aim is to communicate through outstanding graphic design, conceptually and simply.

b2s6

Location: St. Petersburg, Russia
Tel: +7 981 829 86 06
Web: www.b2s6.com

b2s6 is a design studio that focuses on visual concept. It was established in 2009. The members are young and ready for experiments. They like to mix art and creativity, concept and design, always looking for innovative visual solutions in order to get a fresh new image.

Benchmark Design

Location: Munich, Germany
Tel: +49 179 925 94 84
Web: www.benchmark-design.de

Benchmark Design was set up by Pascal Gabriel, who is a multidisciplinary designer and thinker from Munich, Germany. Benchmark Design, a thinking and design collective, specializes in the fields of brand identity and design. Together with top creatives and skilled designers, the collective solves the problems of their clients through creativity and emotional design with an innovative approach.

Boris Bonev

Location: Berlin, Germany
Email: boris1bonev@gmail.com
Web: www.borisbo.com

Boris Bonev is a Bulgarian graphic designer currently located in Berlin. As of this printing, he practices as a freelancer. A main focus of his work is the development of visual identities and communication campaigns for commercial and cultural institutions. He uses a conceptual approach combining creative use of various media with a strong emphasis on graphic design.

BTS

Location: Moscow, Russia
Tel: +7 495 710 86 80
Web: www.brand-ts.ru

BTS is an international team of branding experts with competency covering the whole range of branding disciplines. The consultancy has maintained a presence on the corporate identity market for more than 10 years, implementing complex projects for Russian and foreign companies in different industries such as telecommunications, heavy industries, mass media, transportation, education, healthcare, professional services, NGO, entertainment, tourism and recreation. BTS has also a unique experience of development and implementation of political and regional brands.

Cappelli Identity Design

Location: Roma, Italy
Tel: +39 06 71546354
Fax: +39 06 64780254
Web: www.cappellidesign.com

Cappelli Identity Design is a design and strategic communication agency specialized in dynamic branding. Cappelli's key to success is partnering with its customers, which aims at making them achieve significant business results through the definition of a high-level identity and corporate image, and through the management of their communication activities.

Charsky Studio

Location: Moscow, Russia
Tel: +7 499 951 05 30; +7 499 951 05 31
Email: info@charsky.ru
Web: www.charsky.ru

The advertising agency Charsky Studio was founded in 2011 by art-director Eugene Charsky. During the last two years, the studio created many smart ideas and memorable images for a variety of brands. Its main clients include Unilever, Takeda, Johnson & Johnson, and Moscow City Department of Culture.

COOEE

Location: Amsterdam, Netherlands
Tel: +31 618397297
Web: www.cooee.nl

COOEE is an Amsterdam-based studio founded in 2010 and run by Leon Dijkstra. He specializes in visual communication with a strong focus on publication design and visual identities. In this way, he provides organizations and brands with a print platform from which to define and visualize their story and image.

Dagny Janowska

Location: London, UK
Tel: +44 7835 764494;
Email: d.janowska@gmail.com
Web: www.dagnyjanowska.com

Dagny Janowska is a print and digital graphic designer who is based, as of this printing in London, UK. She holds a Master Degree in Branding and Identity Design with a special distinction awarded by Birmingham Institute of Art and Design. Dynamic branding remains her main area of interest. She curates Brands Alive — an online blog devoted to the area (www.brandsalive.net).

Danni Sinisi

Location: Philadelphia, USA
Tel: +484 883 8363
Web: www.dannisinisi.com

Danni Sinisi is a Philly-based designer interested in exploring the relationships between humans, objects, and space as they apply to sustainability, popular culture, and the urban realm. She received a Bachelor Degree of Science in Graphic Design from Drexel University where she also studied printmaking and film. She currently works at Grid, a monthly print publication dedicated to demystifying the complexities of sustainability.

David Mcmenemy

Location: Belfast, UK
Tel: +44 7513469112
Web: www.davidmcmenemy.com

David Mcmenemy is a creative designer from the United Kingdom. He uses strategic creative thinking to conceptualize the most appropriate solutions to communication problems across disciplines, which include digital design, graphic design, and branding.

Dawid Cmok

Location: Zabrze, Poland
Tel: +48517403458
Web: www.behance.net/dawidcmok

Dawid Cmok is a graphic designer and graffiti writer from Zabrze, Poland. Currently he holds a BFA Degree in Graphic Design at the Academy of Fine Arts in Katowice, and continues his education with MFA studies. He has been doing graffiti since 2007. Dawid Cmok keeps his style evolving, and is always looking for new challenges, skills, experience and ideas.

Denis Ulyanov

Location: Tula, Russia
Tel: +7 903 659 53 04
Web: www.caspa.ru

Denis Ulyanov is professional designer and corporate style creator, developing brand books and new brands as well as re-branding and re-styling the existing trademarks.

Elvire Delanote

Location: Ghent, Belgium
Tel: +32 485 86 86 49
Web: www.cargocollective.com/elviredelanote

Elvire Delanote is a freelance graphic designer based in Ghent. She studied Communication and Graphic Design in Antwerp and Ghent. She loves minimal, functional and typographic design that also has warmth, personality and solidity. She believes in the importance of an honest and concept-driven approach to assure intriguing and effective communication.

Emiliano Gatti

Location: Rome, Italy
Tel: +39 06 71546354
Web: www.cappellidesign.com

Emiliano Gatti, born in 1975, is the lead designer at Cappelli Identity Design. After graduating from Industrial Design, he worked as a designer with some architects, working on tasks from taking care of construction to renovation of spaces. Subsequently he worked at MC Group in marketing area. Since 2008, he has been working at Cappelli Identity Design. He currently takes care of exhibition, way-finding signage, and industrial and graphic design.

Entre Líneas

Location: Logroño, Spain.
Tel: +34 636 840 575
Web: www.entre-lineas.es

Entre Líneas is a design studio specialized in corporative identity and interior architecture, composed of designers Mónica Villoslada and Óscar Luis. From its beginnings in 2004, they seek originality in each new project, making the observers ponder on the meaning of their designs.

Epic! Aventuras Criativas

Location: Caxias do Sul, Brazil
Tel: +55 54 3419 1561
Email: contato@weareepic.com.br
Web: www.weareepic.com.br

Epic! Aventuras Criativas ("Creative Adventures" in English) is an illustration and design studio set up by Marina Procházka and Mauricio Cardoso. Both of them studied at the University of Caxias do Sul in Brazil and have, combined, nine years of experience in design. The union of their powers results in an epic adventure in search of salvation of design and its values.

Erre Gálvez

Location: Alicante, Spain
Tel: +34 625 809 920
Web: www.erregalvez.com

Erre Gálvez is a graphic designer born in 1988 in Elda, Spain. He studied at Alicante College of Art. His work is based in typographic experimentation and creation of images with a new concept. He is very much interested in new techniques and new materials. His work has been published in graphic design books of different languages, a variety of magazines and online culture webs.

Evan Dorlot

Location: Prague, Czech Republic
Tel: +420 777 116 039
Web: www.evandorlot.com

Evan Dorlot came to Prague from Paris in 2012 and has been practicing graphic design for five years. He graduated with an International Bachelor Degree in Graphic Design from the Paris design school la Fonderie de l'image, where he wrote a thesis on the importance of graphic design for young fashion designers. He also holds an Associate Degree in Graphic Design with a Print Speciality.

Flëve Design Consultancy

Location: Moscow, Russia
Tel: + 7 903 132 32 25
Web: www.fleve.co

Flëve is an award-winning interaction and communication design consultancy.

Gabriele D'Asaro

Location: Palermo, Italy
Tel: +39 340 5306133
Web: www.dasaro.it

Gabriele D'Asaro is a graphic designer born in 1988 in Palermo, Italy. He has a secondary school diploma focusing on humanities and he holds a degree with highest honors in Industrial Design from the University of Palermo. His thesis, entitled "Dynamic Brand Identity," has also been published. Gabriele's works consist mainly of branding, editorial design, and interaction design projects.

Gaston Yagmourian

Location: San Francisco, USA
Email: gastony@gmail.com
Web: www.yagmourian.com/gaston

With more than a decade of experience in graphic design and branding, Gaston Yagmourian has been involved in the creation or direction of corporate identity systems, print collateral, environments, packaging, online communications and presentations. He has been an independent design director since 2010. Gaston designs or directs projects around the US and abroad.

Gen Design Studio

Location: Braga, Portugal
Tel: +351 253 217 900; +351 938 633 690
Web: www.gen.pt; www.gendesignstudio.blogspot.pt; www.be.net/gen-design

Gen Design Studio is a company dedicated to the development of graphic, product, environment and web design and illustration. Placing great emphasis on project methodologies, they see design as a corporative emancipation discipline. With this strategic design perspective in mind, they're constantly aware of the world around them, predicting future scenarios and programming lines of sustainable action.

Harris Aidonopoulos

Location: London, UK
Tel: +44 7453 288685
Web: www.harrisaidonopoulos.com; www.behance.net/harrisaidonopoulos

Harris Aidonopoulos is a London-based designer and illustrator with a restless passion for every aspect of design. Having a degree in Graphic Design, as well as an MA in Illustration & Animation, he believes that curiosity is the fuel of the contemporary world.

IlovarStritar

Location: Ljubljana, Slovenia
Tel: +386 41 389 714
Web: www.ilovarstritar.com

IlovarStritar design studio was founded in 2008 by Robert Ilovar and Jernej Stritar, established designers with rich professional backgrounds and experience from the fields of corporate identity and newspaper design. Today the studio consists of five people who are skilled and well experienced in the fields of brand design, visual communications, and illustration.

Jhade Villa Dean

Location: Oxford, UK
Tel: +44 0 7503 157 493
Web: www.villa-dean.com

Jhade Villa Dean previously practiced graphic design from his hometown in rural Oxfordshire. He moved to Cornwall, UK in 2010 to further his design skills by partaking in a degree course in Graphic Design at the renowned Falmouth University. Further collaborative works from Jhade Villa Dean have won the Red Dot Award: Best of the Best 2013, shortlisted for the Best Editorial Design Award at the 2013 Design Week Awards, and has received many other recognitions.

Landor Associates

Location: Sydney, Australia
Tel: +61 2 8908 8700
Web: www.landor.com

With 24 offices in 18 countries, Landor Associates is one of the world's leading strategic brand consulting and design firms. Partnering with clients, Landor drives business transformation and performance by creating brands that are more innovative, progressive, and dynamic than their competitors. Landor's holistic approach to branding is a balance of rigorous, business-driven thinking and exceptional creativity.

Luis Francisco

Location: São Paulo, Brazil
Tel: +55 11 988 066 029
Web: www.lu.isfrancis.co

Luis Francisco is a young graphic designer from São Paulo, with a degree in Graphic Design from Fundação Armando Alvares Penteado, which, commonly referred to as FAAP, is a higher education institution in Higienópolis, São Paulo, Brazil. He also got a diploma from the Digital Design program at Vancouver Film School. He is currently working in a digital design company in São Paulo, but is also a freelance graphic designer for many board game companies in the USA.

Lumen Bigott

Location: Milan, Italy
Email: mail@lumenbigott.com
Web: lumenbigott.com

Lumen Bigott is a young designer from Venezuela. She studied Graphic Design at the Instituto de Diseño de Valencia, Venezuela. A year after graduation, Lumen got a Master Degree in Marketing and Communication at the Istituto Europeo di Design in Italy. Lumen is currently living in Milan and working as Digital Art Director at BBDO, which creates digital platforms and mobile applications.

Make®

Location: Copenhagen, Denmark
Tel: +45 35 25 35 80
Web: www.make.dk

Make® is a creatively led, multidisciplinary design agency based in Copenhagen, Denmark. The world is their playground and the team is passionate about creating compelling visual strategies and communicating brand stories that captivate their audiences. Their focus is always on the clients' business and the customer needs.

Maxim Pavlov

Location: Moscow, Russia
Tel: +7 925 081 01 13; +7 495 995 15 21
Web: www.notamedia.ru; www.behance.net/MaximPavlov/; www.revision.ru/a/noiz/

Maxim Pavlov was born in 1980 in the city of Zaporizhia. He drew much as a child, and visited fine art studios for five years. He graduated from Bauman Moscow State Technical University in 2003 and started his career as a graphic and web designer in 2000. In 2004 Maxim Pavlov accepted a proposal from Notamedia Company and has worked as its art director since.

Marco Moccia

Location: Hamburg, Germany
Email: mail@marcomoccia.com
Web: www.marcomoccia.com

Marco Moccia is a designer from Schweinfurt, Germany. He studied communication designs in Würzburg, and got his diploma in 2009. He is currently working for a design agency in Hamburg.

Meike Adler

Location: Hamburg, Germany
Email: post@meikeadler.de
Web: www.meikeadler.de

Meike Adler is a designer from Bielefeld, Germany. She graduated in the year of 2011, and currently lives and works in Hamburg.

Michael Schmitz

Location: Cologne, Germany
Tel: +49 221 16866991
Web: www.interaktivegestaltung.net

Michael Schmitz is a generative designer and teacher based in Cologne, Germany. He studied visual communication at the Berlin University of the Arts and graduated in 2006 focusing on digital media. Since then he has worked freely and collaboratively for design agencies and clients alike. He combines design and programming with a conceptual way of thinking — creating generative, moving and highly interactive experiences.

Michele Mazzucco

Location: Brescia, Italy
Tel: +39 3471032982
Web: www.michelemazzucco.it

Michele Mazzucco is a graphic designer from Belluno. He received his diploma in 2011 in Graphic Design with the highest marks. He then moved to Brescia, where he began his university studies in Graphic Design and Multimedia at LABA. Here his interest in the graphic design world has grown and matured, together with his knowledge of the field. He works in brand and web design, experimenting and developing various kinds of projects.

Mind Design

Location: London, UK
Tel: +44 (0)20 7254 2114
Web: www.minddesign.co.uk

Established in 1999, Mind Design is an accomplished design consultancy that specializes in the development of visual identities. It is run by Holger Jacobs and Romilly Winter. Combined, they have more than 20 years' experience and have worked for a wide range of clients. Depending on the demands of a project, they take advantage of their large network of creative professionals to maximize its potential.

Moodley Brand Identity

Location: Graz, Austria
Tel: +43 316 822922 0
Fax: +43 316 822922 22
Web: www.moodley.at

Moodley Brand Identity is an owner-led, award-winning strategic design agency with offices in Vienna and Graz. Since 1999 Moodley has worked together with customers to develop corporate and product brands which live, breathe and grow. Moodley believes that its key contribution is to analyze complex requirements and develop simple, smart solutions with emotional appeal — whether corporate start-up, product launch or brand positioning.

Mucho

Location: Barcelona, Spain; Berlin, Germany; Newark/San Francisco, USA; London, UK
Email: info@wearemucho.com
Web: wearemucho.com

Mucho is a global boutique design studio. With offices in Europe and the U.S., their principals represent multiple cultures yet are dedicated to a singular mission: To define how companies are perceived in the world, so they can stand out and succeed. In short, they are "mucho" committed to creating the best design in the world.

Neha Tulsian

Location: Gurgaon, India
Tel: +91 9910057520
Web: www.nh1design.com

Neha Tulsian, founder of NH1 Design, has over 10 years of experience and expertise in branding and corporate communication. She is an alumna of the London College of Communication and a member of the International Society of Typographic Designers. She has been involved in various projects from developing the design strategy to creating a "brand" new world for clients.

Nina Georgieva

Location: Skopje, Macedonia
Email: geometrieva@gmail.com
Web: www.ninageorgieva.com

Nina Georgieva has created visual identity for quite a short time, but she's had plenty of opportunities to work with companies and agencies all over the world. Her interests revolve mostly around building brand identities, but she is always in an exploration mode, looking for new ways to make the hours of the day disappear in seconds.

Nina Gregier

Location: Cracow, Poland
Tel: +48 798 827 118
Web: www.ninagregier.com

Nina Gregier is an art director and graphic designer focused on typography, branding and print design. Based in Cracow, Poland, she works internationally. She graduated from the Academy of Fine Arts in Katowice, Poland.

North

Location: London, UK
Tel: +44 20 7357 0071
Web: www.northdesign.co.uk

North is an independent London-based agency, established in 1995. Past and current clients include HSBC, Coca-Cola, Nokia, V&A, Barbican, and The Royal Mint. North builds identities and brands that achieve business success and have transformational effects on organizations.

Ola Krupa

Location: Myslowice, Poland
Tel: +48 504 701 096
Web: www.olakrupa.com

Ola Krupa has a Master Degree in Graphic Design from the Academy of Fine Arts in Katowice, Poland. She is interested in corporate identity, information architecture, posters, and advertising design. Ola is also interested in documentary photography. She is working as a freelance graphic designer currently. Don't be afraid to give her an interesting job to do!

Paula Cruz

Location: Rio de Janeiro, Brazil
Tel: +55 8604 1859
Web: www.behance.net/paulacruz

Paula Cruz is a native of Rio de Janeiro, Brazil. She is

currently studying design at the Federal University of Rio de Janeiro. While doing her studies, she develops personal projects that unite design, text and research, such as books, posters and illustrated stories. Her work intends to ennoble content using aesthetic and, to achieve it, she manages tools and references that encompass both traditional and contemporary techniques.

Pianofuzz Design Studio

Location: Londrina, Brazil
Tel: +55 043 3024 5066
Web: www.pianofuzz.com

Pianofuzz is a design studio formed by people who share the value of learning and the desire to improve. In this context, Pianofozz performs projects immersed in a process of dialogue, research, perception, and creation. The studio owns the unusual and clever visual representation, realizing concepts and expanding possibilities, regardless of its surface, printed or virtual.

Plus X

Location: Seoul, South Korea
Tel: +82 2 518 7717
Fax: +82 2 518 7714
Web: www.plus-ex.com

Plus X sends the message that "We Add Experience for Your Brand." Brand experience design means providing consumers with valuable brand experience through consolidated online and offline designs based on the consistent brand strategy. They believe that key brand messages or service functions can be effectively delivered when various media channels meet strategic marketing.

Pompei A.D.

Location: New York, USA
Tel: +1 212 431 1262
Web: www.pompeiad.com

Pompei A.D. is a full-service creative agency with branding, experience design and website design expertise for retail and real estate clients. Founded more than 20 years ago by visionary artist and designer Ron Pompei, the New York City-based firm has created transformative environments for some of the world's most iconic brands.

Rafael Bessa

Location: Curitiba, Brazil
Tel: +55 41 9705 2284
Web: www.rafaelbessa.com

Rafael Bessa is a visual designer from Brazil, currently living in Curitiba. After running his own graphic design studio with friends back in 2010, he joined R/GA São Paulo and spent two years helping great people create disruptive interactive platforms for major brands. Now he is directing new models of design consultancy and collaboration as an independent designer.

RE

Location: Sydney, Australia
Tel: +61 478794899
Web: www.re-sydney.co

RE is a strategic branding and design consultancy based in Sydney. The agency is made up of a number of strong-minded idealists who aim to change the world through design. Working with ambitious clients, they strive to build outstanding brands, delivered through remarkable ideas and executed with brilliance.

Rejane Dal Bello

Location: London, UK
Tel: +44 7872827645
Web: www.rejanedalbello.com

Senior Graphic Designer & Illustrator from Brazil, Rejane Dal Bello has been based in London since 2012. Rejane is currently a senior designer at Wolff Olins, a well-known established brand consultancy that specializes in developing brand experiences, creatively-led business strategies, and visual identities.

Rudd Studio

Location: London, UK
Tel: +44 7966 285 024
Web: www.ruddstudio.com

Matt Rudd studied graphic design in London at the Central Saint Martins College of Art and Design and the Royal College of Art. He set up Rudd Studio in 2002. Matt brings design, creative direction, musicianship and strategic thinking to projects. Accompanying him in the studio are a team of specialists. Throughout its 10 years, the studio has enjoyed working in the commercial arena with an artistic sensibility.

Silvia Acerbi, Matilde Arduini, Paola Berardelli, Mikele Corradini

Location: Milan, Italy
Tel: +393347783491; +393468337260; +393400857652; +39 3496866619
Web: www.silviaacerbi.com; www.behance.net/Secondary_Action;www.paolaberardelli.com; www.mikelecorradini.tk

Silvia Acerbi, Matilde Arduini, Paola Berardelli and Michele Corradini are four young graphic designers who studied together in Communication Design in Politecnico di Milano, Milan. Their work competences include corporate identity, editorial, packaging and advertising projects.

Sophia Georgopoulou | Design

Location: Athens, Greece
Tel: +30 6974015018
Web: www.sophiag.com

Sophia Georgopoulou is a graphic designer from Athens, Greece, who studied in London and is experienced in the fields of branding, logo design, visual communication, corporate identity, packaging, and print. Her personal interests also involve illustration, photography, painting and handcrafting clothes and accessories. In her work, she favors the combination of creativity and aesthetic simplicity that does the job without unnecessary noise.

Studio Dumbar

Location: Rotterdam, Netherlands
Tel: +31 10 448 22 22
Web: studiodumbar.com

Studio Dumbar is an international agency with a Dutch heritage. The studio attracts talented individuals from around the world and this has led to an endless run of remarkable personalities and projects. The studio is led by Liza Enebeis (Creative Director), Karmen Kekic (Client Service Director) and Tom Dorresteijn (CEO and Strategy).

Studio Fnt

Location: Seoul, South Korea
Tel: +82 2 337 0151;
Fax: +82 2 337 5374
Web: www.studiofnt.com

Studio Fnt is a design studio that works in print, identities, interactive or digital media, typeface design, media art collaborations, and more. Founded in 2006 and based in Seoul, Southe Korea, Studio Fnt launched in 2010 Fnt Press, a publisher of books and other material regarding design, art and anything inventive.

Toormix

Location: Barcelona, Spain
Tel: +34 93 486 90 90
Web: www.toormix.com

Toormix is a creative studio born in Barcelona in 2000 and directed by Oriol Armengou and Ferran Mitjans. They specialize in design and brand identity. They face their projects with a clear strategic and conceptual vision, always looking for innovative visual approaches. They also work within their atelier, a parallel space oriented towards research, thinking, and their own projects.

Vlad Likh

Location: Moscow, Russia
Tel: +7 916 447 71 48
Web: www.be.net/Likh_v; www.likhvlad.tumblr.com

Vlad Likh is a Moscow-based designer and art director. He graduated from the British Higher School of Art and Design in Moscow. Vlad has worked in famous Russian design studios and currently is available for freelance work.

Yawn Creative

Location: London, UK
Tel: +44 20 8932 0276
Web: www.yawncreative.com

The Yawn designers believe that modern brands should take risks, daring to be different. Say boring or repetitive things and you run the risk of being ignored or even excluded. They aim to help brands start original, relevant and engaging conversations with consumers. Whether it's through beautiful visual identity or a crafted social voice, Yawn's designers want to banish the boredom from brands!

Zebra

Location: Singapore, Singapore; Perth, Australia
Email: martin@madebyzebra.com; michelle@madebyzebra.com
Web: www.madebyzebra.com

Zebra is an independent brand agency with offices in Singapore and Perth, Australia. It specializes in the creation of brand identity and visual language. Its designers believe in strong, simple ideas which connect with the target audience and stand out by being innovative, compelling and unique. Their strategic ideas come to life through full brand identity programs, print, digital and environmental design.